BEST
INTENTIONS

BEST INTENTIONS

THE EDUCATION AND KILLING OF EDMUND PERRY

Robert Sam Anson

RANDOM HOUSE   NEW YORK

Copyright © 1987 by Robert Sam Anson

All rights reserved under International
and Pan-American Copyright Conventions.
Published in the United States
by Random House, Inc., New York, and
simultaneously in Canada by
Random House of Canada Limited, Toronto.

Library of Congress Cataloging-in-Publication Data
Anson, Robert Sam, 1945–
Best intentions.
1. Perry, Edmund, d. 1985. 2. Crime and criminals—
New York (N.Y.)—Biography. 3. Afro-Americans—New
York (N.Y.)—Biography. 4. Afro-American youth—New
York (N.Y.) 5. Police shootings—New York (N.Y.)
I. Title.
HV6248.P416A57   1987   305.2'350899607307471   86-10150
ISBN 0-394-55274-1

Manufactured in the United States of America
24689753
First Edition

TYPOGRAPHY AND BINDING DESIGN
BY BARBARA M. BACHMAN

FOR MY MOTHER

If a soul is left in darkness, sins will be
committed. The guilty one is not he who
commits the sin, but he who
causes the darkness.

MARTIN LUTHER KING, JR.
quoting Victor Hugo

When we reflect upon the grand design of the
Great Parent of the Universe in the creation of
mankind, and the improvements of which the
mind is capable, both in knowledge and virtue,
as well as upon the prevalence of ignorance and
vice, disorder and wickedness, and upon the
direct tendency and certain issue of such a
course of things, such reflections must
occasion in thoughtful minds an earnest
solicitude to find the source of those evils and
their remedy; and a small acquaintance with
the qualities of young minds, how susceptible
and tenacious they are of impressions,
evidences that the time of youth is the
important period, on the improvement or
neglect of which depend the most weighty
consequences, to individuals themselves
and to the community.

JOHN PHILLIPS, founder
The Phillips Exeter Academy
May 17, 1781

ACKNOWLEDGMENTS

An extraordinary number of people helped in the making of this book, and I would like to thank at least some of them, however inadequately.

My principal appreciation goes to Karen Emmons, whose research and reporting were invaluable; Erroll McDonald, who brought insight far beyond his nominal role as editor, and Peter Shepherd, my agent, tutor, guide, and friend. I would also like to thank the editors of *Life*, who provided the initial resources that made my reporting possible; Jason Epstein of Random House, who saw this as a book when I didn't; and Amanda Kyser, Alice Mayhew, Cheryl Merser, and Robert Loomis, all of whom read the manuscript with a welcome critical eye. My gratitude goes as well to several of my colleagues, who graciously shared of their time and notebooks. They include: Len Levitt of *Newsday*; Marcia Guager of *Time*; Juan Williams of the *Washington Post*; Peter Noel of the *Amsterdam News*; James Simon Kunen of *People*, and Sarah Rimer and Myron Farber of the *New York Times*.

I also owe an enormous debt to the scores of people, in Harlem, at Phillips Exeter, and elsewhere, whose recollections made my reporting possible. In particular, I would like to thank Veronica Perry, "Carolyn Jones," Lamont O'Neil, Edouard Plummer, Doris Brunson, Anja Greer, Kennet Marshall, David Weber, Jamie Snead, Joel Motley, Billy Carreras, Jay Stein, Jack Herney, David McIlhiney, and Stephen Kurtz.

Finally, there is my son, Sam.

A NOTE ABOUT METHODS

This book is a product of—and to a large extent, a story of—reporting.

The reporting in question occurred during a fourteen-month period between July 1985 and September 1986. During that time, a total of 115 sources were interviewed, a number of them on several occasions. The length of the interviews varied from a few minutes to many hours. Some sources—approximately half—spoke for attribution, while the remainder granted interviews only on the condition that their names not be used. When possible, I interviewed sources in person, rather than over the telephone. In the majority of instances, I took detailed written notes of conversations; in other cases, I employed a tape recorder. Following standard reportorial process, I confirmed information whenever possible with independent sources. In questionable cases, when independent confirmation was not possible, information was not used.

I also relied on the work of other journalists and writers, most of whom are personally known to me. When I did not know writers, I checked on their reliability and reputation with others. As far as general background information on the black community was concerned, I found particularly valuable the Urban League's annual report, *The State of Black America*; Ken Auletta's *The Underclass*; Harold Cruse's *The Crisis of the Negro Intellectual*; Charles Murray's *Losing Ground*; Claude Brown's *Manchild in the Promised Land*; Charles E. Silberman's *Crisis in Black and White*; and the Kerner Commission's *Report of the National Advisory Commission on Civil Disorders*. In attempting to understand the history and nuance of Phillips Exeter, I resorted to the written record as well, including Myron R. Williams's *The Story of Phillips Exeter* and a collection of reminiscences edited by Henry Darcy Curwen, entitled *Exeter Remembered*. A number of articles informed my thinking about Eddie Perry. Among them were "Shattered Destinies" by Myron Farber in the *New York Times*; "Why Did Edmund Perry Die?" by Nelson George in the *Village Voice*, and "Death of a Harlem Dream" by Derrick Jackson in *Newsday*. Scores of other newspaper and magazine articles were helpful, in some instances vitally so, in adding to my knowledge about the shooting, police officer Lee Van Houten, the experience of black students in prep school, the drug culture, poverty, violence, police brutality, and education for the disadvantaged. I borrowed liberally from all these sources, in terms of data, background information, and, in several instances, including Van Houten's recollection of the shooting, sourced quotes.

In writing this book, I frequently employed quotations taken from my interviews. With the exception of deleting verbal mannerisms—such as "ah," "uh-uh," "um," "well," etc.—and my own questions and observations, the quotations are as people spoke them. Where editing accounted for substantial gaps in the spoken narrative, it is so indicated by ellipses.

R. S. A.

BEST
INTENTIONS

1

WEDNESDAY, THE TWELFTH OF JUNE, 1985, WAS NOT ONE OF NEW York City's better days. It had rained on and off that morning and afternoon, and all day long the heat—unseasonable for this time of year—had been oppressive. By nightfall the air was thick and soggy, as if a huge wet blanket had descended on the city. Those who could afford to stayed in their apartments, switched on their air conditioners, and waited for the relief the forecast said would come with the weekend.

There were some, though, who could not afford to, or who had errands on the streets that night, and for them life went on as usual.

On the Upper West Side of Manhattan, in an area known as Morningside Heights, one of those New Yorkers was going about his nightly business. His name was Lee Van Houten, and to those who saw him strolling through the shadows along Morningside Drive, his youth and casual attire—sweatshirt, blue jeans, and tennis shoes—would have suggested a student heading back to a university dorm, or an intern on his way to a local hospital. In fact, Lee Van Houten, whose baby face and curly hair made him seem even younger than his twenty-four years, was a plainclothes police officer.

His assignment this evening was to spot and, if possible, apprehend the thieves who had lately been ripping the radios from the BMWs belonging to the doctors at nearby St. Luke's Hospital, one of the three institutions—with Columbia University and the Church of St. John the Divine—that dominate Morningside Heights. Compared with the violent felons the 26th Police Precinct normally handled, the "Blaupunkt freaks," as the police had come to call them, were an almost trifling annoyance. The doctors and their insurance companies, however, had taken a different view. Phone calls had been made, polite pressure had been brought, and finally, an anticrime unit had been dispatched, with Van Houten in the lead.

It was a chancy assignment for any officer, especially for one with only two years on the force. Van Houten, however, had already shown himself to be a good cop. A married suburbanite with a baby on the way and two years of junior college courses to his credit, "the kid," as he was teasingly called by his colleagues at the Two-Six, had a reputation for being dependable in a crunch. If there was trouble—and with Harlem just beneath the Heights, trouble was always possible—Van Houten had but to reach for his radio, concealed in the paper lunch bag he was carrying, and signal to his backup, cruising in a station wagon only blocks away.

Thus far, however, the evening had proceeded without incident. It was nearly nine-thirty, and there had been no sign whatsoever of the Blaupunkt freaks. The streets, in fact, were deserted. It appeared that everyone, law-abiding and criminal alike, had been done in by the heat.

Alone in the semidarkness, Van Houten kept walking. He crossed 115th Street, heading south toward the gothic spires of the Church of St. John the Divine; a moment later he crossed 114th. Across the street, the façade of St. Luke's loomed up. A few paces more and Van Houten would be at 113th.

Suddenly there was an arm across his neck, pulling him backward and down, yoking him like a rodeo steer. Out of nowhere another attacker appeared in front of him. There was a shout—"Give it up! Give it up!"—then the smack of a clenched fist hitting him in the face. The fist struck again and Van Houten went down. As he fell, the bag containing his radio clattered away on the sidewalk. Van Houten clawed at his sweatshirt, trying to grasp the neck chain with his badge. "I'm a police officer," he yelled. The blows kept coming.

Twisting and squirming, Van Houten struggled to his feet. He felt hands going into his pockets. The attacker in front of him was groping for his wallet. The one behind him kept pulling at him. They were black, young, and strong. That was all that Van Houten knew. "Give it up!" the cry came again. "Give it up!" There were more punches, and once again Van Houten was on the sidewalk. His vision was beginning to blur; unconsciousness was closing in on him. Reaching down, he fumbled at his ankle holster. His gun came up. Three shots split the night. Then, all at once, it was quiet.

The attacker who had been holding Van Houten had fled; his accomplice lay face up on the sidewalk, unconscious, a trickle of blood beginning to seep from a small clean hole just to the left of his belly button. Retrieving his radio, Van Houten signaled for assistance, then looked down at the form lying still at his feet. It was just a boy. Lee Van Houten began pounding his head with his fists.

Within moments a cruising blue-and-white was on the scene, the unmarked station wagon bearing Van Houten's backup close behind it. As two of the officers assisted Van Houten into one of the cars for the ride to St. Luke's emergency room, five hundred paces away, a third turned the suspect's body over with his foot, reached down, and handcuffed him behind his back. Seconds later an Emergency Medical Services ambulance screeched up and a team of paramedics began tending to the victim. The white pullover he was wearing was snipped off and he was clad in a pair of rubber ''shock pants,'' designed to force blood to the vital organs. After the attaching of a bottle of intravenous saline solution to his arm, he was loaded into the ambulance and transported to St. Luke's. There, according to a hospital spokesman, everything that could be done was done. It was not enough. Edmund Evans Perry, a wiry seventeen-year-old friends called Eddie, died at 12:55 A.M.

In a city like New York, where there are nearly three hundred thousand serious crimes every year, such events are a relative commonplace, particularly in areas like Harlem and especially among young black males, one in ten of whom, the statistics say, will either meet or cause an unnatural end. As a result, word of these occurrences is usually consigned to the rear pages of the tabloids, back by the stock quotations and the sports scores. There are, of course, exceptions. The day of the abortive mugging on Morningside Drive, for instance, three black teenagers were shot by a Brooklyn grocery-store owner for filching a sixty-five-cent can of Coke. Two of them died on the spot, the third was fatally wounded, and because it was a slow news day, the story made page five of the *Post*.

By comparison, the death of Edmund Perry, late of 265 West 114th Street, Harlem, appeared numbingly routine. From the story police were able to piece together immediately after the shooting, it appeared that he had played a pickup game of basketball earlier that evening on the cement court outside Wadleigh Junior High, not far from his family's apartment. Reportedly, there had been a bet, the loser to take the winner to the movies, and Edmund, who had no money, had wound up on the short end of the score. In search of funds, Eddie and an unidentified companion had walked west, toward the three-hundred-foot slope that is Morningside Park. It is doubtful anyone observed them as they climbed through the darkness. By day the park is a kind of no-man's-land, dividing Harlem to the east from the white neighborhoods surrounding Columbia University to the west. By night it is a spooky place, ventured into only by the brave or the foolhardy.

Shortly before nine-thirty, Eddie and his companion reached the top. Here, along the black granite heights George Washington had once fortified against the British, they began cruising for an easy mark. The one they chanced upon turned out to be carrying a .38.

So the events of that June 12 might have been recorded—another ordinary killing on another humid summer night—but for one peculiar detail, a single bit of information that set the death of Edmund Perry apart from all others. Ten days before, in a ceremony filled with pomp and circumstance, he had been graduated, with honors and the award of a full scholarship to Stanford University, from 204-year-old Phillips Exeter Academy, perhaps the most prestigious boarding school in the land.

It was, as reporters say, a hook, and within hours the story of the killing of the Exeter honors graduate was moving out over the wires. By morning, when the page-one account in the late editions of the *Times* appeared, both television and radio were carrying lengthy reports, and the networks were gearing up features for the evening news.

Word of what had happened spread quickly. In New Harbor, Maine, where the Exeter senior staff was meeting at principal Stephen Kurtz's country house, drawing up plans for the next school year, it came in the form of a mid-morning telephone call. Kurtz, who was in the midst of describing curriculum changes, got up to take it. When he came back, his face was ashen. "Ed Perry is dead," he said hoarsely. "In New York. They say he was trying to mug a police officer." The people in the room looked at each other. For a long moment no one said anything. No one believed it.

In Missoula, Montana, sophomore Eric Bowman, who had argued politics with Eddie the night of the Reagan landslide, saw the story on

CNN. "Wait a minute," he shouted at the screen. "I know that guy! I *know* that guy."

In Devon, Pennsylvania, Warren Kampf, who had lived in Eddie's dorm, was at his summer job when a coworker told him about the shooting. Warren had to sit down for a moment to take it in.

In Chicago, Illinois, Maureen Brown, who had embraced Eddie at graduation, was called from Cleveland by Tamara Horne, who, in turn, had been told by Vicky Hoyt in Detroit. Maureen started gasping. She didn't know if she could breathe.

In Cleveland Heights, Ohio, Becky Storey, who had kidded with Eddie in the Exeter dining hall, was told by her brother, who had heard the news on the radio. Becky told him he must be mistaken. Friends of hers, she said, didn't get shot.

At Phillips Exeter Academy, where the flag was lowered to half staff in mourning, the few remaining faculty members on campus passed each other on the paths without speaking. The mood reminded David McIlhiney, the Academy chaplain, of his student days at Harvard, when President Kennedy was shot. "It was so quiet," he would say later. "So deathly still."

In Sag Harbor, New York, a small former whaling port turned summertime tourist attraction, it was quiet as well, but for different reasons. June is an odd month in this, the place I make my home. The long bleak winter is ended and what the locals call the Mercedes season has not begun. People stick to themselves, reflecting on the months just ended, waiting—not without a little dread—for those just ahead. I, too, had been alone most of that day, struggling with a novel that was not working. By evening I was worn out and depressed and in no mood for the revelations of Dan Rather. Thus I went to bed that night not knowing what had happened to Edmund Perry, which, looking back, is a pity. If nothing else, I could have told my son, Sam, who had just finished his second year at Exeter and had sat behind Eddie every day at school assembly.

The next morning I awoke early and, tiptoeing past the bedrooms where Sam and three of his schoolmates were sleeping, went downstairs and mounted my bike for the daily ride to the delicatessen. Sean, the deli-owner, was his usual hale self as I ordered the regular takeout cups of black coffee and scooped up that day's editions of the *Times* and the *Wall Street Journal.* "Did you see the headline on the *Post*?" he asked as I paid for my purchases. "That's where your kid goes to school, isn't it?"

I glanced down at the stacks of Rupert Murdoch's tabloid. Splashed across the front page was a picture of a smiling black teenager in graduation regalia and a bold-faced announcement: COP KILLS HARLEM HONOR STUDENT.

I picked up a copy, flipped to the inside, and began reading. "Jesus Christ," I murmured to myself.

The story, a wire-service account of the shooting, dressed up with a quote or two from the Perry family attorney demanding the officer's arrest, was shocking, not only because a promising young man had been killed, or had died, while allegedly committing a street crime —poor blacks, after all, were getting killed in street crimes all the time—but because this particular young man had gone to, of all places, Phillips Exeter. Exonians were supposed to be protected from this sort of thing. That, at least, had always been my assumption, and part of the reason I had gone into considerable debt to send my own son there.

As I pedaled home, a copy of the *Post* tucked under my arm, I thought back to the day I had dropped him off at his dormitory, an ivy-covered Georgian edifice erected in honor of a graduate of the class of 1796 named Daniel Webster. "Get through here, Sam," I had said, "and everything will be possible." I imagined that Eddie Perry's parents must have told him much the same thing.

At home I found Sam with his friends, having breakfast on the patio and dressed for an outing at the beach. "You know Eddie Perry?" I asked as I walked into the yard. The boys nodded. "He's dead. A cop shot him in New York. The paper says he was trying to mug him." The boys' mouths dropped open.

As I described what I had read, recounting the police version of events, Sam listened with a skeptical look. "Couldn't be true," he said when I finished. "Eddie was too smart for that. The cop musta' just killed him." I shrugged and went inside. A few minutes later I heard the sound of the station wagon starting up.

The next several days, I did my best to get back to work, but the Perry story kept distracting me. It was hard to pick up a newspaper or turn on the television without reading or hearing about it, with the inevitable comment about how senseless it was. And senseless it certainly seemed to be. For at least as reported by the press, Eddie's personality and background hardly fit the profile of a would-be violent mugger.

He had grown up, the papers said, on a Harlem block better than most—"an oasis," one account called it—and in a family whose roots in the neighborhood traced back five generations. His mother, a day-care worker with two junior-college degrees, was described as a good parent and strict disciplinarian, deeply involved in her church and community, serving the latter as an elected member of the local school board. Moreover, unlike so many other black youths who got into trouble, Eddie had had a father in the house. True, he was an alcoholic, and also true, the Perry family seemed to have had its share of domestic discord, but at least the family was intact, something that could not be said for a lot of other Harlem households.

As for Eddie himself, the reports were all glowing. He had no history of trouble with the police, no record of any violence. "My son carried no gun or knife because he walked with God," his mother, Veronica, told an interviewer. "He always said, 'Jesus fights my battles.'" There were similar testimonials from everyone reporters had interviewed, from his Baptist minister—who remembered him as a church-going boy who went on retreats, served as an usher, belonged to the youth fellowship, did everything, in the minister's words, "except sing"—to his neighbors—who termed him kind, respectful, courteous, and hard-working, "a model," as one of them put it, "for the kids on the block"—to his grade-school principal, who recalled that his classmates predicted that he was "the boy who was going to be the first black president of the United States."

Academically, his record was exceptional. Testing completed in the seventh grade placed his math and reading skills at well above the twelfth-grade level, and in assessing his "ability, self-discipline, leadership, emotional maturity, and initiative," administrators at his Harlem junior high put him in the top 2–3 percent of the school. "His character is of the highest nature," one of his teachers wrote in recommending him for scholarship placement to prep school. "This young man has a great sense of responsibility. He is well-mannered, respectful . . . alert, active, and honest. . . . He has great respect for authority.''

Equally evident was Eddie's ambition. At the age of thirteen, when many of his neighborhood friends were experiencing their first brush with the law, Eddie, according to A Better Chance, a Boston-based organization that places gifted minority students in prep school, was writing of making ''a respectable person of himself in society.'' Having made up his mind that he wanted to become a doctor, he was also building ship and airplane models, because, as he put it, ''a doctor needs a steady hand.'' ''My greatest strength is my faith in the Lord,'' he wrote, ''the faith that tells me that, no matter what happens, He will provide a way. My greatest weakness is trying to understand those who say they love God, but hate people.''

It was that attitude that helped win Eddie a full scholarship to Exeter. Though he was one of only 40 blacks and Hispanics in a total enrollment of 980, Eddie seemed to thrive at boarding school, where he played on the football team, won academic honors, did, in all, so splendidly that he was offered a scholarship, not only by Stanford but by Yale, Berkeley, and the University of Pennsylvania as well. ''Clean as a whistle,'' one Exeter administrator called him, reporting that Eddie's only trouble in four years was missing a few classes. ''A solid citizen,'' George Tucker, the associate dean of students, added. ''A good and popular student.'' ''We gave him a helluva good education and he took it and he ran with it,'' Steve Kurtz told an interviewer. ''He got damn good grades and he deserved them; they were not gifts from the white man. There was no trouble, no violence, no drugs. We know who those characters are here, and Eddie was not one of them.''

Eddie's classmates remembered him similarly. One called him ''a very moral and religious guy''; another, who was black, recalled that Eddie frequently counseled other blacks to avoid theft and muggings, not only because it was wrong, but because, he quoted Eddie as saying, ''it was a disgrace to the black community.'' ''Eddie couldn't have done what they say he did,'' his roommate, a black senior from Brooklyn named Malcolm Stephens, told a reporter. ''He used to talk all the time about how much he hated the thought of jail, the idea of being confined.''

It was impressive testimony, and what made it even more so was

Eddie's plans for later life. Going to Exeter, he informed A Better Chance, had "drastically" changed his impressions of himself. "I now see a growing responsibility I had not noted in earlier years," he went on. "Because I have been fortunate and given this education, I must help to educate and economically advance my race so that we may one day fulfill the wishes of the fathers of this country and make it understood in the U.S.A. and the world that all men are created equal." After finishing college, he told his mother, he intended to come back to Harlem and assist his community. "Ma," she quoted him as saying, "I'm gonna help my people rise."

"He was our shining star," mourned one of his cousins. "Nobody in our family ever did what he did. He was going to change things for us."

How such a boy could have come to such an end was, at least on the basis of everything that had been reported thus far, incomprehensible. The motive the police had come up with—the need for a few dollars to take a neighborhood pal to the movies—seemed not only flimsy but a contradiction of everything that was known about Eddie's personality. Ever since childhood he had been a habitual hard worker who never seemed to lack a way of earning pocket money. Moreover, at the time of his death he had just begun a $175-a-week summer job as a messenger for Kidder, Peabody, a Wall Street brokerage house. If despite it all money was a problem, Eddie could have borrowed it from any number of sources, including a total of forty-eight relatives whose apartments lay between the basketball court and the scene of the alleged mugging. One outside possibility, that an undiagnosed mental illness had driven him to break the law, had also been investigated and just as quickly discounted. Dr. Sidney Weinberg, a nationally known pathologist brought in by the Perrys to observe the autopsy, had examined the body for traces of meningitis or a brain tumor and had found none. The more that was learned about Eddie, the more it appeared that the police might be lying about the circumstances of his death.

In Eddie's neighborhood, where shootings by white police officers were all too frequent, that possibility was being taken as a certainty. At Eddie's funeral, fifteen hundred people packed the local Baptist church, and hundreds more gathered in the streets, many of them wearing red ribbons of protest and mourning. For three sweltering hours they listened as speaker after speaker lauded Eddie and denounced the system that had taken him. "It's time to stop the killing of . . . our talented young brothers," one of several ministers who spoke at the service told the congregation. "It's time to stop. It's time." In the church there were shouts of "Amen!" and cries of "Why Eddie? Why, why Eddie?" "It's the police," Eddie's pastor, the Reverend Preston Washington, charged. "They kill and ask questions later. It's a new form of lynching. The police don't value black life at all."

A few days later, after condemnation of the killing by the whole of New York's black elected establishment, a crowd of a thousand marched in candlelight procession to the police precinct where Van Houten worked, and there heard C. Vernon Mason, the Perrys' lawyer and a candidate for Manhattan district attorney, thunder into the sound system: "Officers of the New York City Police Department, your arms and hands are dripping with blood!"

Elsewhere there were calls for investigation, including one from A Better Chance, whose president, Judith Berry Griffin, demanded that governor Mario Cuomo appoint a special prosecutor. "Regardless of guilt or innocence," wrote Griffin, "we cannot suppress our moral outrage over the brutal killing of another young black boy by the New York City Police Department. The use of deadly force against young-sters like Edmund Perry destroys hope and places into question the values of the very society these children want to uphold. Unwarranted official violence by law enforcement officers must be contained. The needless killing of our young people is unconscionable. It must stop."

The black-owned *Amsterdam News* was talking even tougher. One story in the paper reported that police, in their hunt for Eddie's alleged accomplice, were picking up youngsters and holding them for hours without notifying their parents or lawyers. Another, headlined "Did Police Leave Honor Student to Die?," suggested that Eddie might have survived his wound had the doctors at St. Luke's given him better medical attention. Still another seemed to hint that city-employed pa-thologists had deliberately defiled Eddie's corpse. "In my 40 years as a mortician I have never seen a body as badly mutilated and butchered as this," the weekly quoted the funeral director as saying. "They took his tongue completely out. . . . For no reason at all Perry was cut from his ankle to his head. His whole thigh was open." In an editorial topped by a cartoon showing a New York City police officer going for a gun notched with the name Ed Perry, the editors made their own feelings plain. Eddie, they said, had been the victim of a "racist criminal justice system" with a long history of brutality directed against blacks and the poor, a system that condoned "blatant covering up of crimes committed by policemen." "Edmund Perry had already accomplished what most Blacks would never dream as possible," the editors went on. "Was he hostile, most particularly to whites? Not on a bet! . . . Was the incident a lark? No way! A young Black man of his character and training does not readily take to such folly, especially one who has so much to lose. . . . Let every mother of a Black male child old enough to wear sneakers and carry a basketball and ride a subway or bus be warned: Your child is an endangered species."

The white press, too, was indignant. An article in the liberal *Village Voice* tore into the police account of the shooting and then, after proclaiming Eddie "a future Moses for his people," concluded: "Right now, if you're a young black person, each moment near a New York City policeman has to send a blast of anxiety into your heart. Was Edmund, like so many other victims in this city, just too black for his own good?" In the *Daily News,* Pulitzer Prize–winning columnist Jimmy Breslin was posing much the same question. If a person is "young and black," he wrote, "the disease he has to watch for is liberal spilling of blood onto a sidewalk. . . . Edmund Perry, 17, on his way from Harlem to the sky . . . sought after by name by great universities . . . was unarmed. The youth who fled also was said to be unarmed. Why, then, did a police officer . . . in from the suburbs for eight hours . . . have to shoot and kill one of them?"

The most notable rebuke, however, came from the *New York Times,* which, in an editorial in its June 23 editions, called on prosecutors and police to provide immediate answers. "They have their reasons, in law or politics, for treading slowly," the editors of the nation's paper of record intoned.

But in this special case, silence threatens confidence in the law. For here all New Yorkers have extraordinary reasons to wish for the innocence of the young man who was killed. . . . Edmund Perry was an unusual product of a special Harlem environment. . . . [His] escape to Phillips Exeter Academy and his scholarship to Stanford made him a prized symbol of hope. . . . How could

Mr. Perry have forfeited all that hope and confidence? Why would he put his promising future at risk for a street crime? And, if he did, why did the best secondary schooling fail to stiffen him against temptation? Even if there was no police brutality, the death of Edmund Perry raises painfully troubling questions. The authorities have a responsibility to treat this case with care, and more. How long must New Yorkers wait to learn if it was Officer Van Houten or Mr. Perry who betrayed their trust?

Thirteen days later, as if in response to the *Times*'s questions, a Manhattan grand jury, meeting in secret session, cleared Lee Van Houten of any culpability in the shooting, declaring the killing "justifiable homicide" and "within departmental guidelines." At the same time it handed up a three-count indictment charging Eddie's nineteen-year-old brother, Jonah, a sophomore engineering student at Cornell and himself a prep school graduate, as the accomplice in the aborted mugging. At a press conference afterward, Manhattan District Attorney Robert Morgenthau revealed that a total of twenty-three witnesses, including a "significant number" who had witnessed the actual shooting, had appeared before the grand jury, and that their testimony was "consistent" with the police version of events. "As the father of six children, five of whom have passed through this age group, [Eddie and Jonah's parents] have my complete sympathy," Morgenthau said, sounding genuinely saddened. "It's a terrible thing for a parent to have had this happen. No parent wants to believe that their son or daughter has gotten into serious trouble, but regrettably that's what the facts show."

There, until Jonah Perry's trial, the matter rested. There were no more stories in the newspaper, no more protests, no more marches or editorials. By the middle of July, the incident that had touched so many so passionately had all but slipped from public view.

Nonetheless I remained interested. Sam's going to Exeter no doubt accounted for part of my fascination, as no doubt did Exeter itself, which in its way seemed as emblematic of one world as Harlem in its way seemed of another. There was something more to my curiosity, though, than that.

Basically it had to do with Eddie. By all accounts he had had everything going for him, all the things anyone was supposed to need to climb out of poverty and make it in America. Yet, if what Morgenthau, the police, the grand jury, and twenty-three witnesses were saying was correct—if Eddie Perry had in fact been killed while attempting to commit a street crime—then somewhere along the line something had gone dreadfully haywire, not only for this one seventeen-year-old boy but, by extension, for the country itself.

As the days ticked by, I found myself reflecting more and more on the implications of that possibility as well as on how much everything had changed since the civil rights movement and Martin Luther King. I had written about that movement, witnessed it, and in a very small way—no more than marching in a few demonstrations and wearing a button with an "=" symbol on it—been a part of it. On my office wall was a photograph of one episode from those times. It had been taken in Chicago, during the long, hot summer of 1966. A riot had devastated a large part of the West Side Chicago ghetto that July, and a few weeks later Dr. King had come to the city to cool tempers and lead a march for open housing. As a young correspondent for *Time,* fresh out of Notre Dame, I had marched along with him. I still remembered how it had been that day in Gage Park: the thousands of whites who chanted obscenities and threw rocks at us; the contorted features of the police, as they waded into the mob, nightsticks flying; the black demonstrators, middle-class people, most of them, dressed as if for a church outing; the fear I felt being in the midst of all of it. Most of all, though, I remembered Martin Luther King. A rock hit him in the head that day, driving him to his knees, and I had been one of those who pulled him up and shielded him. I would never forget the look in the eyes of this man who had survived Birmingham and Montgomery and Selma. It was of sheer terror.

Since the death of Eddie Perry, I had glanced at that photograph often: the image of Dr. King, doubled over, head down; a much younger, skinnier me standing behind him, looking horrified and perplexed. It was an ugly scene from an ugly time, but at least then everything was clearer. I knew who the enemy was. I believed that what all the government reports and scholarly studies said was true: that there were two Americas, separated by pervasive white racism, and that if only the racism could be eliminated, life would be wonderful for what were then called Negroes.

Now, the situation didn't seem so simple. Racism hadn't been eliminated, but in many important respects it had been greatly diminished. Equal opportunity was the law, affirmative action the widespread practice. Hundreds of billions had been spent on social programs targeted at every conceivable ill. And yet, according to government statistics, poverty was no less widespread than it had been twenty years before. There were in America today just as many black unemployed, just as many rotten schools, just as many bombed-out slums. For all the work, for all the good intentions, too many of the changes one could see were for the worse: more unwed pregnant teenagers; more fathers deserting the home; more violence, drug addiction, and murder—more, it seemed, of almost everything except hope.

In the tranquillity of Sag Harbor, where the only "social problem" was figuring out how to get downtown during the tourist season, I seldom thought about such things. What went on in places like Harlem had, like any tragedy that goes on too long, lost its capacity to shock. I told myself I hadn't stopped caring—I was still horrified and perplexed—I had merely become inured.

Eddie's death, however, had gotten me to thinking again. It struck home with me, as it appeared to have done with so many people. "Did you read about the black kid from Exeter?" you'd hear at the supermarket or at the laundromat or at a cocktail party, weeks after the story had dropped from the newspapers. "It was awful, wasn't it? How on earth do you suppose something like that could have happened?"

As a journalist, as a parent, as someone who had come of age during a more hopeful time, I wanted to find the answer to that question. Assuming, of course, there was an answer.

2

THE PLACE TO BEGIN, I DECIDED, WAS AT THE END: WHAT HAD HAP-
pened the night of June 12? How had Eddie Perry died?

The story the police told seemed straightforward enough—a clear
case of an officer defending himself against a vicious, potentially fatal
assault. The only problem was that they had produced nothing, at least
publicly, to back it up.

There were sound legal reasons for withholding evidence (among
other things, it helped guarantee Jonah Perry a fair trial), but in the
absence of such items as the forensic and ballistics reports—or, indeed, any hard information, including what the twenty-three still unidentified witnesses had told the grand jury—rumors had begun to
spread. Indeed, Eddie's body had hardly turned cold before a story was
circulating through Harlem that he had been shot execution-style.
Since then, there had been all manner of tales, some claiming he'd
been allowed to bleed to death on the sidewalk, others that he'd been
shot while trying to escape, still others that he'd not been involved in a
mugging at all. There were, in short, a lot of questions and, thus far at
least, damn little else.

The one person who could set the facts straight was, of course, Lee
Van Houten, and I wanted to talk to him first. So, I quickly found, did
many others, and all of us were given the same answer: Lee had nothing to say—at least not to the press.

Considering the civil suit the Perry family was threatening and the
hostile tone of the coverage he had been getting, Van Houten's reticence was understandable. If the story he told his superiors was correct, it was also understandable that he had reacted with deadly force.
Though slim, Eddie was six feet one, and a football-playing six feet
one at that. Jonah, his brother and alleged accomplice, was even
larger—a muscular six feet three, according to published accounts—
and, from the testimony of his prep-school headmaster, who had seen
him tussle with a varsity wrestler and win—possessed of considerable

strength. For Van Houten, five feet ten and of medium build, a beating from either youth, much less both of them, could have been serious or worse. Moreover, the "yoke hold" that had been used to bring Van Houten down was, besides being a favored mugger tactic, well known among law-enforcement people for being highly risky. Applied correctly, the maneuver, which involved putting a clenched fist across the Adam's apple, then pulling back sharply, resulted in unconsciousness. But applied with too much force, it could crush the windpipe and result in asphyxiation. Potentially, then, Van Houten had been in a fatal situation—provided, of course, he had told the truth.

Lately, however, the veracity of New York cops had become highly suspect, especially in connection with shootings of blacks. There had been an alarming number of them in 1985, and though in every case a grand jury had cleared the officer, just as one had cleared Van Houten, something was clearly amiss.

According to a poll taken by a local television station a few months before Eddie's death, the feeling among most blacks was that that something was the cops. When asked whether they agreed with the statement that "police brutality is a common practice" and that it was more likely to be directed against blacks than whites, more than half the blacks questioned responded in the affirmative.* Since Eddie's shooting, those views had, if anything, become even more pronounced. Typical were the comments of Judith Griffin, the A Better Chance president. "You have to be black to understand what happened to Eddie," said Griffin, the well-educated daughter of a prominent Chicago physician. "Whites hear of a cop shooting an unarmed black boy and they say, 'Oh, no, it couldn't be true.' But blacks know it is true. Every black person I have talked to about this has had the same reaction: 'They shot him because they didn't know he was important. They shot him because they thought he was expendable. They shot him because they didn't know they had a reason to let him live.' Shoot first and ask questions later. That's how the police operate. It's like Vietnam. What did it matter if they shot a Vietnamese? They weren't human. The police shoot black children for the same reason."

I wasn't prepared to believe any such thing, at least not until I

---

*When asked whether they agreed with the same statement, only 18 percent of whites surveyed answered yes.

learned more of the facts. I knew, though, that the New York cops, once renowned for the sensitivity of their community relations, particularly in comparison with other big-city police departments, had changed considerably in the last few years. Not only were they far younger (the average NYPD officer was in his mid-twenties and had been on the force less than five years, a circumstance brought on by the large number of new hires since the end of the New York fiscal crisis) and, as a result, less experienced, they also had little feel for the city. Like Van Houten, many of them had grown up in the suburbs and had not had any significant contact with blacks until the moment they made their first arrest.* Moreover, the cops were under enormous pressure. Though their ranks had grown since Ed Koch had become mayor, the number of officers on the street remained well below what it had been in 1960—even as, during the same period, the crime rate was more than tripling, thanks largely to young blacks, whose violent crime rate was sixteen *times* that of whites.† Nor did being a police officer provide automatic protection; violent assaults against cops had reached record numbers as well.

Cops, of course, could defend themselves; they were armed. The question was how they used those arms, and too often during the last

*According to a 1986 report by a subcommittee of the New York State Senate, part of the police department's problems stemmed from the lowering of departmental entrance requirements, which had been undertaken to enlist more minority officers, blacks in particular. During public hearings, the official in charge of examinations for the city personnel department testified that the police entrance test was so easy that "a functional illiterate" could pass it. In its report, the senate subcommittee largely agreed, charging that entrance tests "are based on criteria which may not be consistent with minimum competence." It added that minimum passing grades were lowered "to a level which has permitted candidates with reduced cognitive ability" to start police training. As a result, the subcommittee report went on, the police department was attracting new officers with "lower standards of intelligence, physical ability and psychological soundness."

While disputing many of the report's findings—particularly the assertion that department officials were more interested in meeting hiring goals than in appointing "emotionally stable" officers—the police department conceded that its entrance tests had been made easier, largely to head off a threatened lawsuit by a group of black applicants. Earlier, another lawsuit, filed by a group of black patrolman who had failed to pass the sergeant's examination, resulted in the city's spending $500,000 to design a test confined to job-related skills. When the new, supposedly bias-free test was administered, however, it was passed by only 1.7 percent of blacks—versus 10.1 percent of whites. The disparity in these figures was taken as prima facie evidence of racism, and the city, rather than contest a lawsuit that it calculated it could not win, announced that henceforth promotions to sergeant would be made on the basis of racial quotas—regardless of test scores. The policy, as well as the lowering of entrance requirements, had the full backing of Benjamin Ward, New York City's first black police commissioner.

†As the experience of subway vigilante Bernhard Goetz suggests and survey after survey confirms, "fear of crime" is the number-one concern of New Yorkers, and, considering the data, for good reason. According to statistics compiled at M.I.T., a resident of a city like New York

year the answer had been: wantonly. In one notorious case, several cops had tortured a marijuana-possession suspect with charges from a fifty-thousand-volt "stun-gun." In another, a subway graffiti artist had allegedly been beaten to death while in the custody of half a dozen transit officers (who were later acquitted at trial). In still another instance, a squad from the Emergency Services Division, supposedly the best-trained officers in the department, had shotgunned a deranged sixty-six-year-old grandmother who brandished a knife when they arrived to evict her from her apartment. The cops in the last incident had fired twice. The first shot took off the grandmother's hand; the second removed her head. According to the report of the House Subcommittee on Criminal Justice, whose chairman, John Conyers, investigated these and dozens of other cases, nearly all of them involving blacks, "Racism appears to be a major factor in alleged police misconduct specifically and in police-community relations generally." Perhaps, as was widely being alleged, it was involved as well the night Lee Van Houten encountered Eddie Perry. Then again, perhaps not.

I was impressed, though, by what I was told by a reporter friend who worked the police beat and initially had been suspicious of Van Houten's story. "Sam," he said, "they've got this one cold. I can smell it. You can tell by the way the cops are talking. Almost by their body language. I've been around a lot of bad shootings, but this ain't one of them. They're cool on this one. Really cool."

At least in his description of their demeanor, my friend was correct. When I called the 26th Precinct and asked to talk to one of the investigating detectives, there was barely a beat before a sergeant named Ed Hagerty came on the line, as bouncy as a PR man. Affable though he was, Hagerty did not tell me much that was new. He did say, however, that the police had initially been put on to Jonah Perry through infor-

---

runs a greater risk of being murdered than an American combat soldier did of being killed in World War II.

It is blacks who have the most to fear. According to statistics compiled by *Time*, more than 40 percent of all the nation's murder victims are black, and 94 percent of those who commit those murders are black as well. In one year alone, 1981, the 6,000 or so blacks who were killed by other blacks came close to equaling the number of black servicemen who were killed during the twelve years of the Vietnam War. Whereas in the United States today, a white female has a one in 606 chance of becoming a murder victim, and a white male one chance in 186, a black male has one chance in 29. The group at greatest risk are black males between the ages of fifteen and twenty-four. Of those who die in that age group, one in three will be a victim of homicide.

mation volunteered by residents of the neighborhood. Given the suspicion of the police that existed in Harlem, that was notable in itself. What was even more striking was Hagerty's further revelation that among the witnesses who had testified before the grand jury were at least two of Jonah's relatives. Hagerty would not say who those relatives were, or what they had testified to. Still, it was a portentous piece of information.

Just then, though, my overriding interest was in finding out as much as possible about Van Houten. From what had been reported thus far, his record appeared to be as exemplary as Eddie Perry's. In the two years he had been on the force, no civilian complaints had been filed against him, nor, until the night of June 12, had he ever drawn his weapon in the line of duty. The one incident for which he had received official commendation—for chasing and apprehending a person with a gun—had not involved the use of force. "Van Houten's perfect, absolutely clean," a Patrolmen's Benevolent Association official was quoted as saying. "He looks like a sixteen-year-old kid from Nowheresville who could do no wrong." PBA officials, of course, were paid to say such things. But there were other testimonials to Van Houten's character from sources not so biased, including a Puerto Rican officer who frequently worked and socialized with him. "Lee never showed any signs of racism," the officer insisted. "I would know. He's the kind of guy who, on a dispute run, never takes sides against nobody, never puts his judgment on nobody. He just tries to deal with the facts."

My own inquiries confirmed this portrait. According to a dozen cops, prosecutors, and lawyers, Lee Van Houten was the very model of what a New York street cop ought to be: young, smart, level-headed. If there was a racist bone in his body, no one who had worked with him, black or white, had been able to detect it. "Lee's no wise guy, the way a lot of these young cops are," said a black detective who had spent many hours with Van Houten since the shooting, and who himself had twenty years on the force. "They come on to the force with a lot of John Wayne in them, thinking they are going to clean up the streets. Lee's not like that. To me, he seemed like a nice respectable boy. And I do mean boy. Christ, the kid doesn't look like he's more than seventeen or eighteen. That's why they picked him for the duty that night: he looked like an easy mark. The funny thing is, if he hadn't been so young, this whole thing would never have happened. Someone who's been on the job awhile would have sensed something coming. Not a kid like Lee. If he got a look at them at all, I'll bet he thought to himself, 'They aren't going to do anything to me. *I'm* a police officer.''

Being a police officer had not kept Van Houten from being attacked, and that he was attacked appeared beyond doubt. A number of people, both cops and civilians, had seen him in the St. Luke's emergency room, and all agreed he bore the marks of having sustained a savage beating. "There were a lot of cuts and bruises on him. His arms were all cut up,'' reported one of the detectives who had interviewed him at the hospital. "His face was swollen cheekbone to cheekbone. You could barely recognize him.''

Since that night, Van Houten had been on medical leave, recuperating at his suburban home, where his wife was expecting their first child. One of the few times he had come in to the city was to testify before the grand jury, which itself was a mark in his favor. Under New York State law, grand jury witnesses are granted immunity in exchange for their testimony. Van Houten, however, had waived immunity and, according to the D.A., had testified fully and freely, despite being warned he was a possible target of grand jury action. In contrast, Jonah Perry had declined to testify at all.

Perhaps the most telling point in Van Houten's favor, though, was his behavior since the shooting. Those who had talked to him said that he had been deeply shaken by the incident, as well as by the press accounts that had all but accused him of murder. "The thing is driving him crazy,'' said a cop who knew him well. "Whether he was justified or not, he has taken a life, and he just can't deal with it. I try to tell him that this is the real world and that these things just happen sometimes, but Lee can't take it in. He isn't tough and this thing is really knocking the shit out of him. Every time he talks about what happened, he gets emotional. He tries to block it out. He wants the press, the P.D., everyone to leave him alone. He just wants to forget he ever took a young man's life.''

Nonetheless, there were still a number of questions that needed answering, and the most troubling by far was whether, as an unarmed security guard had told *Newsday,* Eddie had simply been in the wrong place at the wrong time. According to the guard, Eddie was walking by himself down Morningside Drive when he encountered Van Houten, who asked him for a light. As Eddie walked away, *Newsday* reported, "a black and a Hispanic youth slipped through a hole in the fence around Morningside Park and attacked the officer. The first shot was fired, the guard said. Perry then turned around and was hit by the second."

Since the *Newsday* article, nothing more had been heard from the mysterious guard, who was said to work for St Luke's. I tried to track him down myself, but with no success. After several days' fruitless searching, I mentioned the guard and his story to one of the investigating detectives. "Oh, that little shit," he growled. "We know all about him." With that, the detective pulled out a fat file folder marked Confidential and began quoting the guard's signed statement.

I was off on the day of the shooting. The next day, at the scene, I was approached by a female reporter from *Newsday.* I can only remember her first name. It was Frances. She asked me if I knew anything about the incident. I told her I had seen it. I told her I was standing at the corner of 115th Street and saw two people run into the park, one black, the other Hispanic. The reason I told her this was that there had been a lot of police shootings of blacks and I thought I would even the score. I was not a witness. I was off duty and at home. I am sorry I lied to the reporter.

The detective flung the file onto his desk. "That," he said, "is the kind of crap we have been dealing with from day one."

Other questions in the case, however, were not so easily answered—most particularly as to the precise manner of Eddie's shooting and the speed with which he was taken to the hospital. Both were crucial issues, for if, as was being claimed in Harlem, Eddie was shot execution-style or if, as also being charged, there had been a deliberate delay in securing medical help, then a serious argument could be made for brutality, if not outright murder.

A bit of record-checking revealed that neither was the case. According to police department logs, the incident had occurred at 9:30 P.M.

At 9:32, Van Houten radioed for assistance. Within ninety seconds, a radio car was on the scene and by 9:34, according to the records of the Emergency Medical Services, a paramedic team was working on Eddie. Various on-the-scene procedures—snipping off his shirt, outfitting him in "shock pants," attaching him to an IV, loading him into the ambulance, and transporting him, finally, to St. Luke's—had taken, according to hospital estimates, no more than seven minutes. An additional fifteen minutes was consumed in the emergency room, where doctors attempted to stabilize Eddie's condition. Finally, at 10:05, thirty-five minutes after the shooting, Eddie reached an operating room manned by a team of trauma specialists, regarded as among the best in the city. During the nearly three hours they fought to save his life, Eddie was reportedly transfused with twenty-five pints of blood. The bullet, however, had severed two major arteries before imbedding itself deep in the pelvic bone, and the doctors had not been able to stanch the blood loss, in part because Eddie reportedly suffered from sickle cell anemia, a genetic condition common among blacks. In any event, it was clear that Eddie had been accorded first-rate medical care.

As for why Van Houten was taken to the hospital first when it was apparent that his injuries were less severe than Eddie's, the police offered various explanations: that they were following procedure; that moving Van Houten did not entail risk; that it was pointless to transport Eddie when EMS was giving him much the same care he would have received in a hospital emergency room. Finally, though, a senior officer owned up. "It would be safe to say," he admitted, "that the officers were more concerned with the cop than they were with the victim."

It was, perhaps, a natural reaction, but according to Dr. Sidney Weinberg, the pathologist brought in by the Perry family to observe Eddie's autopsy, the decision may have helped cost Eddie his life. "If you can stop the bleeding," Weinberg told me, "then you are in good shape. It's all in the bleeding—how quickly you can stop it. The wound, in and of itself, should not have killed him. That's what troubles me. I keep wondering, 'Did he really have to die?' Time is the whole thing in a situation like this. If nothing happened to stop the bleeding, that may have been the difference."

The path of the bullet that had killed Eddie also troubled Weinberg. From his postmortem observations, he had determined it was downward and to the left, indicating that Van Houten's gun was lowered toward Eddie at the time of the shooting. What Weinberg didn't know, since he hadn't seen the ballistics report, was how far Van Houten was from Eddie when he shot him. If the report showed a lack of fire-and-powder damage, Weinberg explained, it would suggest that Van Houten had fired from a distance of several feet, possibly while standing over Eddie. If that was the case, as Weinberg put it, "Everything would be a different story. That would be wow. That would be holy mackerel."

The answer lay in the ballistics report. Thus far, however, the authorities had not released it, and given their suspicious mood, it seemed doubtful that they would. "Why the fuck should we help you?" one PBA official told me when I called and asked for assistance in getting the report. "You guys have been screwing us up one side and down the other on this thing. You don't seem to realize who the victim is here. It's not the kid who went to Exeter. It's the cop."

The police had been taking a heavy rap from the press, and consciously or not, much of the coverage had a class tinge to it. Eddie was the prep school boy, and therefore innocent. Van Houten was the blue-collar public high school graduate, and therefore guilty. It was small wonder, then, that Van Houten's colleagues were being selective about providing information. Eventually, however, I found one who did not fit the mold, a detective who was not only one of the principal investigators in the case but, better for me, a most talkative one as well.

His name was Billy Carreras and everything about him—the way he looked, the way he talked, the way he handled himself—fairly shrieked cop. "Billy," as one of his partners put it, "is the kind of guy you could make sixteen miles away." Unlike his colleagues, however, Billy was a loquacious sort. "I got my twenty in," he said, referring to his impending retirement. "What the hell." Billy also had the ballistics report, which he shared with me one sunlit afternoon in an office decorated with WANTED posters.

"Got the powder burns, the nitrates, the whole nine yards," he said, looking over the file, which he obligingly left open on the desk. "The kid really got it close. Hardly more than six inches away. No wonder

Van Houten was freaked. Can't be much closer than that unless you had him on the end of a knife.''

Carreras tilted back in his chair and lit a Camel. Watching the smoke curl up to the ceiling, he offered a professional observation: ''Must'a been a helluva fight.''

Finding out what had happened during that fight had been Carreras's principal occupation since the night of the shooting, when he was one of the first cops to arrive at the hospital. He had worked all that night and double shifts for twenty days thereafter, helping piece together the clues that eventually had led to Jonah's arrest. And he had not been the only one. Half a dozen detectives had been detailed to the case, and the full technical resources of the department—including, at one point, round-the-clock television surveillance of the Perrys' block—had been mustered. ''From the moment we saw C. Vernon Mason's business card,'' Carreras explained, ''we knew we were dealing with something more than an ordinary mugging.''

For all the manpower at their command, the police had had a difficult time. ''There's a code over there,'' Carreras said, referring to Harlem. ''You don't rat on anybody. And you sure as hell don't help cops.'' In this instance, however, the code had been broken, apparently out of neighborhood jealousy. ''It's like the Hatfields and the McCoys on that block,'' Carreras put it, ''five or six clans always going at each other.'' A female resident of the block had come forward and pointed to Jonah as Eddie's alleged accomplice. She further claimed that she had been sitting on a stoop the night of the shooting when Jonah had come up and, in front of her and six other witnesses, blurted out, ''We picked on the wrong guy. We got a DT''—street slang for detective.

From that point on, it had largely been a case of finding corroborating witnesses and fitting details together. Carreras was proud of his work, but he took no pleasure in describing it. ''It's a fucking tragedy,'' he said. ''There aren't any heroes in this case. They're all victims: the mother, the cop, even the kids who tried to take him down. It's all a fucking waste.''

Carreras talked on, describing bits and pieces of the case, the experience of being a white cop in a black neighborhood, and parts of his own background. He was born, he said, in the Northeast Bronx and

briefly attended Brooklyn College before dropping out to join the
Army. After a tour in Vietnam, Carreras went back to school, eventually picking up a master's degree in political science. He tried teaching, got bored, and looking for action, joined the police department,
which assigned him to the elite Tactical Patrol Force. "It was an education," he related, deadpan. "We attended riots for three summers:
Brooklyn, Harlem, the South Bronx. Did Columbia in 1968. You
might say it was a chance to see the social revolution, up close and
personal." In 1969, after five years on the job, Carreras won his gold
detective's shield. Since then he had worked the toughest job—homicide investigation—in the toughest areas: Harlem, the South Bronx.
"I've been here so long, I'm used to it," he said with a shrug.

> The conditions are awful, but what's the sense getting upset or
> depressed by it? I'm here, and I have to function. If you don't
> want to make enemies, you'll do fine in a place like this. That's
> my policy: making as few enemies as possible. That way, when
> you walk to your car at the end of the day, you don't have that
> sickening feeling that someone is going to take a shot at you. Of
> course, when it's necessary, you put it on rock and roll and then
> you boogie. But I'm not into any of this Dodge City stuff. I don't
> like violence. The way to get along up here is to treat people de-
> cently, do your best to treat them equally. . . .
> There are a lot of little shits up here, a lot of real bad asses. But
> if you're smart, you learn, and the most important thing you learn
> is that everyone up here isn't a thug. There are a lot of good
> people, and those are the ones you really gotta feel for. They are
> the ones who are really taking all the crap. You ever go into their
> apartments? See all the locks on their doors? They've got their
> houses outfitted like outposts on the frontier. And still these little
> shits break in. Some guy who's working hard comes home, opens
> the door, and the apartment is emptied. Everything is gone, ev-
> erything he owns, and the poor fucker is probably paying for it on
> time.
> You go up to the Perry kid's block and you'll see what I mean.
> I musta been in twenty apartments on that block, and I can hon-
> estly say that I have not found one that is not fit for human life.

They were all well kept. The streets are clean—there are even fucking trees up there, for Christ's sake. You know what that tells you? It tells you these people have pride. They aren't living in the gutter. They're trying. The only trouble is that they are surrounded by these little shits who keep preying on them.

This Perry kid wasn't like that. He wasn't in any trouble with us. No record at all. People on the block say he was a good kid, and I believe them. His mother, she seemed all right, too. Really, a pretty decent woman. I tried to be decent back, but what the fuck do you say? "One of your sons is dead and we're taking the other off to jail?" There's nothing you can say. She's just had her whole life blown away.

I feel for that family. I feel for that kid. Here he was getting high on books and everyone else around him is just getting high. Who the hell is he supposed to talk to when he comes back to that neighborhood? The kids he grew up with have been sharpening their teeth on the curbs of 114th Street.

Carreras kicked his desk drawer closed. It slammed like a gunshot. "It's a fucking tragedy," he repeated. "That's what it is: a fucking tragedy."

"So what happened to Eddie Perry?" I asked. "If he was such a good kid, how come he did something like this?"

"It was the streets," the good cop who was Billy Carreras answered. "The fucking streets ate him alive."

3

"THE STREETS": IT WAS THE PHRASE PEOPLE USED NOWADAYS TO describe certain parts of the city, and the chaos that went on there. No further explanation was necessary. Say "the streets" and, like Billy Carreras, you had said it all.

Eddie's streets, the streets on which he had grown up and come of age, and in the end had not been able to leave, were Harlem streets, and that fact alone gave them a resonance that was unique. Other black enclaves might be larger, some even meaner, but Harlem was the self-proclaimed capital of Black America, and as it went, so, it was said, would go every place like it.

According to every measurable index, the way Harlem had been going for decades was straight down—which had been reason enough for me to steer clear of it during the years I had lived in New York. Whatever one's color, Harlem was not a spot for casual visiting. It had been different, of course, for Eddie Perry. Harlem had been his home.

The block on which he lived, a stretch of West 114th Street bounded on one end by an avenue named for a black hero, Frederick Douglass, and on the other by one christened for a black scoundrel, Adam Clayton Powell, was in many respects a microcosm of the events, good and bad, that had marked Harlem's history during the last sixty years.

The thirty-six five-story apartment buildings that lined it had been built shortly before 1920, just as the Harlem Renaissance was coming into bloom. Though they were no match for the fine old brownstones along Harlem's fabled Striver's Row, they were comfortable enough, and their proximity to Central Park and Morningside Park made them sought-after accommodation for Harlem's burgeoning working class. But after World War II the block, and Harlem itself, began to change. Seeking a better life, tens of thousands of poor, uneducated blacks started moving up from the South. As their numbers swelled, services declined, conditions deteriorated. Older residents who could afford to moved away, taking with them the fabric of what had been a thriving community.

What remained, on 114th and other streets, was an uneasy mixture of hardworking longtime Harlemites, for whom renewal was ever a dream just around the corner, and in far greater numbers, what eventually came to be called the underclass, people who could afford few dreams about anything, including finding a way out. Year after year, it was the latter who grew more numerous. By the 1960s and the start of the War on Poverty, the infant mortality, illegitimacy, crime, and unemployment rates in Harlem were all several times those of the rest of the city, and what had once been Black America's pride and hope was merely another ghetto.

Eddie's block was luckier than most; at a time when, in the rest of Harlem, three thousand apartments per year were being lost to arson, abandonment, and decay, it managed to survive. Its buildings, however, were in an advanced state of disrepair and well on their way to joining their less fortunate neighbors. Then the Kennedy administration stepped in. Eager to demonstrate the federal government's competence in social engineering, and nudged on by the fact that a large number of the block's residents were active in the local Democratic organization, the U.S. Department of Housing took over the entire block and, at a cost of twenty-five million dollars, renovated it from top to bottom. Every building was gutted, its roof torn off, its insides replaced by prefabricated modular apartments, hoisted into place by giant cranes. When construction was finished in 1964, the result was hailed as an example of the Great Society at its most innovative, and Robert Kennedy himself presided at the dedication.*

But before ten years had passed, the buildings were once again on the edge of ruin, and the block had been all but taken over by drug dealers. "If you wanted narcotics," recalled one veteran cop, "114th Street was the place to go." Violence was epidemic; in one instance, a family of heroin dealers was found murdered in their apartment. Then,

---

*Housing programs, such as the one undertaken on 114th Street, have a long history in the United States, dating back more than fifty years. The major effort, however, began in 1964 with the creation of the Department of Housing and Urban Development. Since then the government has spent over $100 billion on housing construction and subsidies, currently benefiting more than fifteen million people. Despite that effort, it is estimated that decent, safe, sanitary housing remains beyond the means of another seven million households, many of them black. In New York, which has spent more than $400 million on low-income housing since the 1960s, the problem is especially acute. In Harlem alone, fully 40 percent of the residents are classified as living in "substandard, unsafe" housing, and the waiting list for public accommodations

in the first year of the Carter administration, the government again intervened. Once more the block was renovated: windows and doors were replaced; new plumbing fixtures were installed; lighting and heating systems were upgraded. The façades of the buildings were repainted and their backyards landscaped. As a final touch, the street was repaved and lined with benches and pale green Zelkova trees, the only greenery for blocks around. To ensure that everything remained in good order, management of the block was transferred to the New York City Housing Authority, which maintained a full-time office on the block, along with two beat patrolmen.

None of which deterred the drug dealers. They remained on the block—which the city courteously swept twice a day—in even greater numbers than before. Many nights the traffic was so thick that cars (a good number of them driven by out-of-state whites) would be double- and triple-parked the entire length of 114th. As the dealing continued, it got bolder. Any day of the week one could come to the block and see customers queued up along the fence outside Wadleigh Junior High, waited on by teenagers who went up and down the line, order books in hand. So brazen was the enterprise that at one point the dealers formed an association and demanded to use the meeting room at Eddie's grade school, claiming they were a "community group." When the principal refused, the dealers went to the school board and attempted to have her replaced.

Life on the block, meanwhile, was becoming more harrowing. Running gun battles were not uncommon, and as bullets whizzed, children crouched behind stoops in terror. Eventually the children themselves became victims. Some were recruited as dealers (one of the lures was riding in a pink Cadillac, which every day ferried them to the local high school), while others became addicted to heroin. In 1977, when Eddie was entering junior high, the body of one boy was found trun-

---

stretches out several years. Such public housing as exists is notoriously unsafe and usually poorly constructed, invariably at several times the construction cost of its privately built counterparts. Largely as a result, the federal government has, since the Ford administration, been gradually whittling back its commitment to public housing. The most radical steps by far have been those taken by the Reagan administration, which since 1980 has allocated virtually no new funds for public housing construction or substantial rehabilitation. As a consequence of these cutbacks (and in some cases the elimination of projects previously approved), the number of federally subsidized housing units during the mid-1980s will amount to half the number provided during the late 1970s and early 1980s.

dled up in a building basement; he had been shot through the head, execution-style. Later police found that his mother had been using the family apartment as a storehouse for money and drugs.

By the late seventies, the trafficking on 114th had become so bad that even the police had given up trying to handle it. They withdrew their patrols and at the same time ended the Police Athletic League sponsorship of the block as a summertime play street. With the police gone and the dealers seemingly in total control, Eddie's block began vying for the title of worst in the city. Then, one memorable night during the winter of 1979, a group of women decided to make a stand.

Armed with a bullhorn, two dozen of them charged into the street, banging on pushers' cars with sticks and garbage-can tops. "Drugs out!" they chanted. "Drugs out!" Flabbergasted at being set upon by a band of angry females, the pushers fled into the night.

Though some of the dealers gradually drifted back, the incident marked a turning point in the fortunes of the block. Seeing what they could do for themselves, a number of mothers organized a tenant association, which began sponsoring activities, such as a blockwide Fourth of July picnic and a Christmas-tree-lighting and community sing. Expeditions were mounted to take the children—there were more of them on 114th, the block's residents claimed, than on any other block in Harlem—on country outings and to Rockefeller Center. By day and late into the night, grandmothers kept watch on kids playing in the street. Even the trees were looked after with care. Let a truck driver inadvertently snap off a branch and, in an instant, fifty people would be around his vehicle, berating him.

Mostly, though, the block developed pride. "I guess it's kind of crazy," said seventy-five-year-old Lettie Gilan, one of the women who had driven the dealers out, "but I still stand in front of the cars of pushers, threatening to break their windows. If I see a kid using drugs, I'm not afraid to let his mother know. If I see people I don't know sitting on our stoop outside, I tell them to get out. I've been here for years and I'm not going to let 'em whup me."

Thanks to women like Lettie Gilan, the police began taking another look at 114th Street. The patrols came back, and the Police Athletic League renewed its sponsorship of summer games. The cops were still not beloved—"When you walk down that street," said one officer, "you can feel every eye on you"—but they were at least tolerated, and as of 1982, the district attorney himself, Robert Morgenthau, began turning up to throw out the symbolic first ball of spring.

During one such expedition, in 1984, Morgenthau was accompanied by *New York Times* reporter Sara Rimer, who later wrote a long, upbeat story on the block's transformation. Among the people she quoted was Eddie, then home on summer vacation after a year of studies in Barcelona, Spain. "It's Harlem," he told her. "It's not the worst place to grow up, and it's not the best place. My mother put ideas into my head that there was something else."

Before going to the block myself, I called Rimer at the *Times* to see if Eddie had told her anything more. "Oh, Eddie," she said. "I'll never forget Eddie."

He was the pride of that block. Everyone I talked to told me, "You gotta meet Veronica Perry's boy. He goes to *Exeter.*" It was hard for me to imagine that anyone on a block like that could be going to prep school, much less Exeter, but it turns out several kids have. Eddie, though, was the one everyone was talking about. It was almost as if he was marked.

So I started walking around, looking for him, and sure enough, there he is, standing on one of the stoops. He's wearing a dark green LaCoste shirt and chinos, and I remember thinking to myself, "Wow, this kid really *is* preppy." I went up to him and said, "Everyone on the block talks about you." It was the perfect line for him. He could have taken it and run with it. That's what I expected, that he'd give me some quotes like, "Yeah, I'm gonna make it out and I'm gonna come back and help my people" or "I love Exeter" or something like that. Instead, he says to me, "I'm not out of here yet. I got some to go before I get off 114th Street." What he was saying to me, in a way, was, "Don't look at me or this place through your little rose-colored glasses."

We talked for maybe twenty minutes, and he was very polite, very articulate, and obviously very smart. But there was something about him that was also very intense and angry and bitter about everything. I remember he made a point of telling me how bad the schools were around his neighborhood, and how he had gotten a bad deal because of that. He also talked about the drugs, how you could still buy anything you wanted to, right on the block. "You grow up here," he said, "and you see people shooting up on the street. It's hard, man, it's hard."

It wasn't what he said, though, that impressed me so much as the way he said it. There was almost something steaming about him. He seemed so unhappy. It was like he was sort of separate from the block, but still of it. You could tell that a part of him couldn't wait to get out, and that another part of him was still struggling with it.

I don't know what he thought of me. Not much, probably. Here I was, another white person, seeing him as a stereotype, the star of the block. And he was right. I was thinking, "Yeah, here is the guy who, at a very young age, was sort of chosen as the one who was going to make it out." You could tell he resented it, but it was all around him. Everyone was looking at him as a sort of cardboard character, when obviously he was much more complex than that.

As we were standing there talking, his father came up. He was carrying this big radio and clearly not doing much of anything. It was strange, seeing the two of them together. They hardly related to each other at all. I thought the father was sort of embarrassed. Here was this *New York Times* reporter talking to his son, who looks so preppy and goes to Exeter, and here is the father, who is not dressed well at all, who is carrying this radio in the middle of the afternoon in the middle of the week because obviously he does not have a job. I guess I just felt sorry for the father. His son had left him so far behind.

When I finished interviewing Eddie, he shook my hand in sort of an odd way. Cold, you know, like he was very hard. But I had this funny sense that he really wasn't hard at all, that the coldness he had was just a cover for him to keep people from knowing he was really shy.

"There are a lot of interesting people on that block," Rimer concluded. "A lot of really admirable people, struggling so hard. But the one who sticks in my mind the most is Eddie. Everyone else on that block that day was sort of telling me what they thought I wanted them to say. 'We really brought this block around. We're all together. We care about each other.' Eddie wasn't like that. He didn't try to charm me at all, and it would have been very easy for him to. It was like he wanted me to know the truth.''

A few days after my conversation with Rimer, I made my first trip to the block, which was in the midst of yet another government-sponsored renewal. The street was just as she had described it. There were the little pigtailed girls playing double-dutch (''We're from 114th Street and we're cute and fine,'' they sang. ''If you look us over, we'll blow your mind''); the grandmothers, posted on stoops, looking over them; the sign on the door of the ''craft lady,'' Miss Pearl (''If you don't want to get your feelings hurt, don't smoke or sell dope in front of my door''); the treasured Zelkova trees and the freshly painted green benches. There, too, was the legendary Tracy Collier, the fourteen-year-old who everyone said was the fastest girl runner in the city; and the ''candy lady,'' Reba Judkins, selling coconut longboys and licorice whips from her cart; and the children's drum corps, rehearsing in the street. There, everywhere I looked, was the picture of life as it ought to be in the city on a summer day.

But there were other sights: the alcoholics drinking from open bottles on stoops; the men idling at midday; the pushers selling ''dust'' and ''horse'' outside the corner tavern; the blank, sudden stares of too many men and women going nowhere. It was those stares that unsettled me most. Everywhere I walked, eyes followed me, as if gauging what I was about, as if asking why I was there. At first I thought I was being mistaken for a cop. Gradually, though, the truth dawned: I was an intruder, a white.

Thus far at least, no one had seemed menacing. On the other hand, they had not seemed inviting either, and getting anyone to open up about Eddie, I worried, would be a problem. Rimer, though, had given me several leads, names of people who might talk. The most important of them was Mrs. Robertus Coleman, president of the block association and the leader of the charge against the drug dealers in 1979. A single mother of five, Mrs. Coleman, who worked as a field installer for the telephone company, was described to me as a tall, imposing woman—and direct and outspoken about her views of the block. It was to her apartment that I headed first.

I found her washing dishes, which she continued to do as we talked. "People don't do enough fighting for themselves," she began.

I'm the bigmouth, so when there's trouble, people come to me. They're calling me all the time, here, at work—always with some problem. Like I'm supposed to solve 'em all.

We do got problems on this block. I'm not saying we don't. Not as many as we used to have, but still some. There's drugs and there's drinking—a whole lot of drinking—and all these children and women with nothing to do. Maybe if people were a little more educated, we'd have less children and fewer on welfare. All they do here now is have children. Every summer, seems like we have a new crop of babies, eight or ten of 'em—and all of them from teenagers. It's children having children, is what it is. I don't know what causes it—maybe lack of education in the home. There's just no training at all. The mothers we got on this block, most of 'em are on welfare. They all got three or four different children from three or four different fathers. The men, they aren't around at all. We have four hundred and fifty-four families on this block, six hundred children, and I don't think there's more than ten or fifteen men. All there is, is women, and they aren't doing nothing. They're dropouts, most of them. They're not motivated enough themselves to motivate their own children. They never go to work. They just go from bench to bench, stoop to stoop, looking to have people do things for them. And complain? That's all they do is complain. To hear 'em talk, you'd think that they hated this block. But they don't—I *know* they don't. You couldn't pay 'em a thousand dollars to get off it. There's togetherness, family, and love on this block, more than there is anywhere in Harlem.

We got our good families here. People who raised their children up right. Edmund, you know, wasn't the only one who went off to prep school. Others did, too. Maybe not Exeter, but they went off, finished college, too.

Mrs. Coleman finished stacking her dishes and neatly folded her wiping towel. "I never did know Edmund and Jonah that well," she went on. "They were never really part of the block. Never participated in any of the activities. Their little sister, Nichol, she was different. She's typical 114th Street, involved in everything. I look out the window, and I see Nichol playing, hear Nichol laughing. She gets into everything she can. The boys didn't."

She shrugged. "I guess Edmund was great. I know he excelled at Wadleigh, excelled at Exeter, too. Him being so well-liked in school, so well-thought-of, you'd think he woulda left a burning candle here. Maybe I'm wrong, but I don't think he has."

Mrs. Coleman gave her spotless kitchen a final inspection. "It's sad he's gone, of course," she said. "But it's not unusual. For a black kid to get killed in Harlem, it's common. You get used to hearing it. Nichol would have been a more tragic loss. I'd miss hearing her voice, seeing her on the street. Edmund being taken was different. It wasn't like a voice was stilled on 114th Street. Truth is, I haven't thought much about the fact that he isn't here anymore. Most of us don't think about it, really. Right when it happened, everyone was shocked: a boy from this block. But then everyone stopped talking about it. Every mother on this block knew it could have been one of their children just as easy."

What Robertus Coleman had told me about the block and about Eddie was repeated elsewhere in the neighborhood, and often as not in the same half-proud, half-defensive tone. There had indeed been other prep school stars from the block, nine of them altogether, and one family alone, the Browns, had sent four children on to college. Their education, however, had not shielded them from the block's horrors. Kevin Wood, a college communications major, recounted seeing people murdered gangland-style and spoke of a friend who committed suicide by jumping from a roof. Johnny Pruitt, a senior majoring in business at Connecticut State College, described eight- and nine-year-old children smoking marijuana and said at least one friend every year for the past fifteen years had died of "angel dust." Pruitt, who wanted to be a social worker, had also seen a teenager shot in the head only the summer before. "The blood shot out of his head and his brains just lay on the ground like bubble gum," he recalled. "I couldn't go to sleep for nights after that."

Pruitt had also known Eddie and had watched him play basketball on June 12. The mood around the court was buoyant, he remembered, and all eyes were on Eddie, who seemed playful and relaxed. Pruitt, though, had been uneasy. "I couldn't help feeling that something was wrong," he said.

> Then I remembered that back about eight years ago there was this guy who was real good. He taught me how to dunk. He taught me that when you play ball, you play to win. You don't just play to be playing. The last day he was alive, he was on the basketball court and he was playing good and everyone was laughing. That night he got shot dead in an argument over a bicycle. I got the same feeling all over again. Everybody was having such a good time that I started thinking that someone was going to die.

Twelve-year-old Kendu Mitchell, an honor student at P.S. 113, had been with Eddie that day as well. The two boys had been friends since the time several years before when Kendu had won five dollars and a bag of Kit-Kat candy bars in a spelling bee, only to have the prizes taken from him by a gang of toughs. Eddie had advised Kendu to begin fighting back. Kendu did, the problems ceased, and he had tagged after Eddie ever since. On what was to be the last afternoon of his life, Eddie had taken time out to teach Kendu how to make lay-ups. "One kid was making fun of my cheap sneakers," Kendu said. "He was wearing the fifty-dollar Adidas. Eddie told me, 'Sneakers don't make the man, the man makes the sneakers.'"

In the days and nights I spent on the block, I gathered many such stories, all of them confirming the popular image of Eddie. He was, according to his friends and neighbors, everything a fine young man ought to be: kind, courteous, sensitive, well-mannered—a joy to his mother, a pillar of his church, an inspiration for the younger ones following in his footsteps. They talked of his ambitions, recounting, as did Roger Pruitt, a high school dropout who had been one of Eddie's friends, that Eddie claimed that one day he would be president, and that when he was, "114th Street won't be crowded no more." He was the special one, they said over and over again, the smart, determined, and ambitious one, who, like a latter-day Joe Louis, brought credit to his block and race.

All this they remembered of Eddie Perry, who seemed far more well known than Robertus Coleman had told me. What they did not remember—or at least did not mention to me, a white man from the world outside 114th Street—was Edmund Evans Perry's ever having been in trouble.

On this point, everyone, from his grandmother to his minister to his chums from junior high, was quite insistent. Not one person—and dozens, of all ages and descriptions, had been interviewed, by me and other journalists who had scoured 114th Street—not one person could recall Eddie's ever having done anything illegal, not so much as pinching a candy bar from the bodega around the corner.

Nonetheless, I wondered. Maybe it was reporter's skepticism getting the best of me, but the stories I kept hearing about Eddie seemed a little too pat and Eddie himself a little too perfect. No one I knew—and surely no teenager—went through life without a miscue. But according to everyone who lived in the Potemkin Village that was 114th Street, Eddie had done just that—not to mention going to Sunday school in the bargain. The worst anyone could think to say of him, and then only in suggestive code words, was that Eddie was a bit aloof, a bit disapproving of the life he saw going on around him. Maybe it was all true. But how then to explain the still unidentified witness who had come to the police department with the tale of another, darker Eddie Perry? I had not been able to find that witness—or, for that matter, anyone who would admit to any knowledge of what had occurred the night of June 12. Instead, I found people who seemed saddened by Eddie's death but not particularly surprised by it. As one of Eddie's friends put it with chilling succinctness, "Edmund died a natural death up here."

That comment—the exact opposite of what I had been hearing from my white liberal friends—stayed with me a long time, as did the descriptions of Eddie's everyday conversations. According to his friends, Eddie talked about anything and everything—except going to Exeter. He seemed, in fact, to go out of his way to minimize his prep school background. He did not talk like an Exonian (though, according to his friend Kevin Johnson, he could do a wickedly funny impersonation of one), dress like one (the Izod shirt Rimer saw him wearing turned out to be favored by a lot of youngsters in the neighborhood), act like one—and if he thought like one, he kept it to himself. "I was amazed at his ability not to become a white kid in a black face," said Eddie's Baptist minister, the Reverend Preston Washington, himself an Ivy League graduate. "He seemed to have a split vision, an ability to make the transition back and forth between here and there. He always remembered who he was and where he was from. He never forgot he was black."

Again I wondered. Perhaps it was possible that Eddie had managed such a delicate balancing act, but at the very least, it must have been emotionally tricky. That impression was confirmed by someone who had managed the balancing act himself, Bill Perkins, the leader of the local Democratic club and a close friend of the Perry family.

Raised in Harlem, Perkins attended the Collegiate School in New York as a member of the first group of students A Better Chance placed in prep school. After graduation he went on to Brown and then took up a career in local politics, where, among other things, he played a leading role managing Veronica Perry's campaign for a seat on the local school board. The night of the shooting, he was the first person Mrs. Perry called, and he was with her at the hospital when Eddie's death was announced.

Smooth, charming, articulate, and tough, Perkins, who currently served as the deputy clerk in the city's board of elections, was counted as a comer in Harlem politics, and when I met him at his downtown office, I could see why. He was a man of bristling ambition.

His tone was wary at first, and it was plain he did not want to discuss the events of June 12. He began to loosen up, however, as he described his own prep school career, and how it was to be one of those selected. "I got in through the Jefferson Park Boys Club," he recalled. "I used to hang out there a lot and they had this test to pick out smart kids that they were going to send to prep school. Well, I took it and I was accepted. My family got a kick out of it. They teased me about the mannerisms I was going to pick up." Perkins smiled and shook his head as if still amazed by his good fortune. He continued:

Getting these opportunities, like Eddie and I had, it's luck, like the roll of the dice. If you're a kid, and smart, you are always looking for a way out, for a way to somehow break the cycle. But when you grow up in these neighborhoods, you think that no one breaks out. It's that way all day, every day. You feel that this is all there is. You see all these people around you who were talented in so many ways once—maybe they were academic stars or big athletes or the leader of the class or whatever—and now they aren't doing anything at all. You think to yourself, If I can just make it through this, then there will be no more welfare. When it actually happens, when you get that chance, you can't believe your luck.

That's the way it was for me. I always wondered, knowing that there were so many other people around me who were so much more talented than I was in so many ways, Why me? Why was I taken? You feel happy to get out, but guilty, too. You feel you don't deserve it. Every day you are in school, every day the rest of your life, you have a sense that you are going to get caught. There are all these traps out there and one of them is going to catch you. You go through your entire life always dodging.

I never talked to him about it, but I know Eddie must have felt that way. He was smart—smart enough to know that there were a lot of people out there smarter than he was. He was the one, though, who had gotten the chance. Why did he get it? There were a lot of reasons: his teacher at Wadleigh, Mr. Plummer, his mother, politics, connections—and plain old luck.

It's a burden for a kid, knowing that. When I was selected, they sent all of us up to Dartmouth that summer to prepare us for life in prep school. There were fifty of us altogether and the *New York Times Magazine* did an article about us. The article had a picture of me in a rowboat on a lake. I felt so embarrassed by that picture. I kept wondering whether my friends at home would see it. I kept wondering what they would think.

At that age you want to fit in with the people around you. The last thing you want to do is stand out. The trouble is, you *do* stand out. The education you get makes you stand out. Eddie did. It wasn't that he looked preppy—he didn't wear taped-up loafers or dungarees with holes in the knees or anything like that—but he was obviously different from the other kids in the neighborhood. His orientation was different. He was more directed, more academic, more defined as a personality. He even spoke different

Spanish. I remember when he came back from Spain, and he'd come over to the political club and we'd bullshit about this and that, and sometimes we'd talk in Spanish. I speak Spanish like they do in East Harlem, where they pronounce *yo* with a hard *y*, so it sounds like *jo*. And Eddie stops me and, with this grin, says, "Listen, Bill, we're speaking Castillian Spanish, not that Puerto Rican stuff."

So he was different in a lot of ways. But at the same time, he didn't want to be different. It's a prove-yourself age, and like everybody else, Eddie wanted to fit in. How do you do it? Well, one way is to talk about coming back to your community, which Eddie did a lot. The only trouble is, these schools don't teach you to come back. Their attitude is noblesse oblige, and that's what they teach you: you can be one of the noblesse; you too can pick up the white man's burden. If you are weak, you will turn out having contempt not only for your own people, but for everyone beneath you. However you turn out, though, it's always a struggle. After you've been to one of these schools, you never completely fit in anywhere.

Perkins paused. "You're not going to have an easy time finding Eddie Perry," he said at last. "He is not a single person anymore. He has become a symbol, a metaphor, a way of explaining everything from Harlem to Exeter to racism to police brutality. The real Eddie is elusive. He is like smoke."

4

PART OF THE LAST NIGHT OF EDDIE'S LIFE WAS SPENT PLAYING BAS-
ketball on what the kids on 114th Street called the Wadleigh pit, a
sunken, cement-surfaced basketball court directly in front of Wadleigh
Junior High. What precisely went on during that game was something
no outsider had been able to determine. Some stories on the block had
it that Eddie played one-on-one against a neighbor boy; others, that he
and his brother, Jonah, played against two boys. There was also dis-
agreement about whether or not there had been a bet and, if so, for how
much. The only things certain were that Eddie played at Wadleigh his
final night and that he lost.

The whole business, including the confusion, seemed neatly symbolic. Basketball was the city game, the quintessential black sport, and
try as he might, Eddie, the prep school boy, was never very good at it.
That he should have been defeated a final time within the shadow of his
old junior high rang with more than a little irony, too. For it was here,
at what was bureaucratically denominated Intermediate School 88, that
opportunity had begun to show itself to Edmund Perry, beckoning him
to be something more.

I was struck by Wadleigh the first time I walked onto 114th Street—
but then, it was hard not to be. From its position at the corner of 114th
and Seventh Avenue, its vast, Victorian façade, obviously grand once
but now soot-stained and crumbling, loomed up over the neighborhood, as if reminding it that both had seen better times. The more I
learned about Wadleigh, whose metal-grated lower windows gave it
the look of a maximum-security prison, the more apt that simile
seemed.

It had been built around the turn of the century, a period of optimism
and opulence in Harlem and, for the New York City Public Schools,
then filling up with the sons and daughters of European immigrants,
the start of a golden age. In the nation there was no school system that
could rival New York's, and in the city there were few that could rival

Wadleigh. Its cathedrallike architecture, replete with Italianate towers and stained-glass windows depicting the muses of Science, Literature, History, and Mathematics, suggested not so much a high school as a temple of learning. More remarkable still was the fact that for sixty years or so, reality matched the image. Designed to educate the brightest girls of Manhattan, Wadleigh turned out such graduates as Agnes Moorehead, Hazel Scott, and Lillian Hellman.

But as Harlem began to decline, so did Wadleigh, and after years of falling enrollment, it closed its doors in the early 1950s. They might have stayed shut but for Harlem's mushrooming population, which, between 1957 and 1964, *doubled* the number of school-age children. Desperate for additional classroom space, the Board of Education in 1958 brought Wadleigh back to life. Its specialness, however, was gone. It was now a regular junior high, open to anyone in the district. In its new incarnation Wadleigh was also almost entirely black.

This last fact entitled Wadleigh, and schools like it, to a host of benefits ordinarily not available to white schools in the city. From guidance counselors and social workers to psychologists and reading-improvement teachers, from group-work programs to "special enrichment" schemes, if a service or a program seemed even remotely beneficial, then chances were that Wadleigh had it.

It was an elaborate, costly effort (during the late fifties and early sixties, New York was annually spending $200 *more* per average Wadleigh student than it was for students attending schools that were largely white); it did not, however, guarantee a good education, and year after year, blacks' academic performance trailed that of whites. So sorry had schools like Wadleigh become that, according to one study, the longer a black child stayed in them, the further he fell behind whites in reading level, IQ, and other test scores.

The question of who was to blame for this was a source of nonstop theorizing and equally nonstop finger-pointing, invariably along racial lines. Blacks, in general, blamed whites for the problem, asserting that since whites controlled the schools through the central Board of Education, it was whites who were responsible for their deplorable condition. No less vociferously, whites blamed blacks, claiming that the cause of poor academic performance lay not in the schools but in the black home, and an overall lack of supervision and educational support. The argument was never settled—in New York today it rages

unabated—but it did produce a number of expensive educational strat-
agems. One, nicknamed the "drawers of water and hewers of wood"
solution, was to shuttle increasing numbers of black students into vo-
cational courses, at precisely the moment the skills taught in such
courses were becoming economically irrelevant. Another was to institute "minimum competency examinations," which, it was later found,
tended to lower educational standards for all. Still another, which resulted in a bitter, racially divisive teachers' strike, was to transfer functional control of the schools to locally elected community school
boards, such as the one to which Eddie's mother, Veronica, would
later be elected. In furtherance of these and a multitude of other efforts, billions were spent (between 1965 and 1980, the federal government allocated more than sixty billion dollars for the improvement
of elementary and secondary education for the disadvantaged) and
seemingly everything was tried, including an educational version of
newspeak (instead of describing their students as "poor" or "under-
privileged," teachers were advised to term them "children unable to
secure much beyond the necessities of today's world because of the
modest finances of the family"). The result, in every instance, was the
same: test scores got worse.*

Wadleigh, which had lost two-thirds of its 1,800-member student

---

*The crisis in elementary and secondary education is not confined to black students alone. The
entire educational system in the United States has deteriorated in the last twenty years, to the
point where, in the words of the National Commission on Excellence in Education, "we have, in
effect, been committing an act of unthinking, unilateral educational disarmament."

According to numerous studies, however, it is black children who have suffered most. Two of
the many statistics that back up this assertion are worth quoting. One is the reading achievement
scores of black nine-year-olds, which in 1980 were nearly 20 percent below those of their white
counterparts. The other, reflecting the same pattern, was the reading achievement of black seven-
teen-year-olds, 62 percent of whom scored in the lowest quartile. The data also reveal that blacks
are systematically shunted into less demanding courses and therefore have less ability to compete
in the marketplace. For instance, according to statistics compiled by the U.S. Department of
Education, only 22.9 percent of all black high school graduates in 1982 took three years of
science. By contrast, the figures for Asian-Americans and white students were 45.2 percent and
33.7 percent respectively. The same situation existed with math, where 38.9 percent of all black
high school graduates took three years, versus 49.5 percent of whites and 68.1 percent of Asian-
Americans. Reviewing the data, a 1986 study by the National Urban League concluded, "Blacks
have lost ground relative to nonblacks at each stage of the educational pipeline."

The Urban League report quoted another study, which explained, at least in part, the spiraling
high school dropout rate, and the reason why blacks, generally, have so little faith in education.
Said the study: "A high school diploma or a college degree is less advantageous for a black man
than for a white. . . . Roughly speaking, a black man has to obtain three or four more years of
education than a white man to rate the same income. Or, put it another way, a black man with
more than an elementary school education will have an income 30 percent less than a white man
with the same education."

body since the 1960s and had stayed open despite renewed efforts by the Board of Education to close it, exemplified these trends. On an average day, a fifth of the student body failed to attend class at all. Of those who did, more than three-quarters required massive remedial work merely to bring them up to grade level. In the end, more than half dropped out before completing high school.

Such teaching as went on at Wadleigh was conducted in a building where paint peeled off the walls and rats patrolled the corridors, and in classrooms where instruction was occasionally enlivened by chunks of the ceiling falling to the floor. The biggest hazard, though, came from the students. Fights were so frequent and vicious—one Board of Education study found that even the best New York teachers spent 75 percent of their time simply maintaining order—that private security guards were brought in.* That cut down on the knifings and assaults; it did nothing to deter the drug-dealing, which was out in the open and rampant. Merely to come to class, students and their teachers had to pass through a gauntlet of toughs, hawking their wares literally at the schoolhouse door. Nor was dealing confined to the young. In May 1985, a month before Eddie's death, undercover police arrested four members of the Wadleigh staff for conspiring to distribute marijuana,

---

*The increasing level of classroom violence, and the destructive impact it has on education, are subjects that have been well (indeed endlessly) documented. What is not so clear is the cause of the violence, which, by the late 1970s, when Eddie was in junior high school, had reached epidemic levels, not only at Wadleigh but at virtually every inner-city school. Various theories have been advanced, from the chaotic nature of the late 1960s and early 1970s to the general permissiveness of society to the intellectualizing of liberal reformers like Robert Coles. To these, researcher and author *(Losing Ground: American Social Policy, 1950–1980)* Charles Murray adds one more: we permitted it.

In 1960, Murray notes, teachers and school systems had at their command an array of sanctions (holding a student back, in-school disciplinary measures, suspension, expulsion) to deal with discipline problems, and as a result, classroom chaos was relatively low. But year by year these sanctions were stripped away by a variety of government policies and legal decisions. "Due process was required for suspension, and the circumstances under which students could be suspended or otherwise disciplined were restricted," Murray writes. "Teachers and administrators became vulnerable to lawsuits or professional setbacks for using the discretion that had been taken for granted in 1960. Urban schools gave up the practice of making a student repeat a grade. 'Social promotions' were given regardless of academic performance." Meanwhile, influential voices in the black community were, as Murray puts it, "claiming that traditional education was one more example of white middle-class values arbitrarily forced on blacks."

The result of all this, according to Murray, who formerly directed a government-funded educational project in Harlem, was that "a student who did not want to learn was much freer not to learn in 1970 than in 1960, and freer to disrupt the learning process for others. Facing no credible sanctions for not learning and possessing no tangible incentives to learn, large numbers of students did things they considered more fun and did not learn. What," he asks, "could have been more natural?"

heroin, and cocaine. One of those so charged, and later convicted, was, as it happened, a teacher.

Given the obstacles, the wonder of Wadleigh was that anyone learned anything. Yet some did. There were still dedicated teachers at I.S. 88, still students who wanted to learn, and for the best of them, like Eddie, there was a means of doing it.

It was called the Special Program, and in twenty-one years it had placed 230 Wadleigh graduates in a total of 72 elite prep schools—a record that surpassed that of any other inner-city school in the country. Of the Wadleigh alumni who had attended prep school, three fourths had gone on to college, and from there into careers as doctors, lawyers, merchant chiefs.

I was anxious to learn more about so seemingly miraculous an undertaking and, more particularly, how Eddie had fared in it. From the data that had been released by A Better Chance, I knew that his grades and test scores were high, and from the people on his block, I knew that Eddie (whom his grandmother had nicknamed "the FBI" in tribute to his habit of pestering her with questions) was nothing if not curious. Even as a child, his minister recalled, Eddie was forever inquiring after the "why" of everything. "He was the kind of kid," said Rev. Washington, "who, in Sunday school, would always be asking you things like 'How do we know God exists? What's the proof for it?' That was Eddie's way. He didn't buy any experience lock, stock, and barrel."

That told me something about Eddie, but not enough. What I lacked—what I needed—was a better sense of him as a student.

Additional information on this score came from teacher Doris Brunson, an attractive, middle-aged black woman who was something of a miracle herself. Born in the South and educated in the North, Ms. Brunson had been at Wadleigh for more than twenty years, turning down numerous opportunities to transfer to calmer settings, as well as business opportunities that would have paid her well above her teaching salary. "I don't want to sound like Joan of Arc," she explained modestly, "but the children have a hold on you. I think of all of them as mine."

According to Ms. Brunson, one of the most special of those children was Eddie Perry, whom she'd taught English in the eighth grade.

"There was something about Eddie's mind," she said. "It was always challenging you."

He was not the kind of student to whom you could say, "We are going to do it this way because I say we are going to do it this way." You would never reach Eddie that way. You would lose him. He wouldn't respect you. You had to explain everything you did, and even then, he was always skeptical. It was just something you could see in his expression, in the way he tilted his head to the side, the manner in which he raised his eyebrows, the smile on his face. He would always ask you things like "Why do I have to know that? Couldn't I do this problem another way? Wouldn't it be just as good to do it my way as yours?"

At first, I wasn't sure I was going to be able to handle this young man. He was always pushing you, always trying to see how far he could go with you. You had the sense that in some strange way he was testing you. But he was always respectful, always well-mannered, and once he knew you had your limits, and that he couldn't go beyond them, you got along beautifully. Still, the skeptical tone was always there. . . .

I remember, once, we were studying Shakespeare in class. Eddie took to it like a duck to water. But he also did some research out of class, looked up some things in critical texts on the plays we were reading. The next day he came in and started asking me questions. It was clear he knew what the answers were; he just wanted to know if I did. I did, and that seemed to satisfy him.

I was lucky that I did know those answers, because Eddie wasn't the kind of boy you could fool. You always had to be honest with him. If you tried to pretend with him, tried to tell him it would all come easy for him, that he wouldn't have problems, that he wouldn't encounter racism at a place like Exeter, he'd see through it in a minute. He knew what reality was. He knew how his people were supposed to be treated. He knew all about the political system and how it worked and what it did to communities like his. He also knew that a school like this one would not have been allowed to exist in a white area.

But there was never any bitterness, never any hostility—at

least none that I saw. Instead, there was a seriousness about him, more than there is with most children his age. When he came back from Exeter, he was even more serious than he had been. You could tell how much that place had changed him. His whole manner was different. His speech was more clipped and precise. He seemed more poised and dignified. He was so sure of himself, so confident of his abilities.

Ms. Brunson stopped herself. "I still can't believe what happened to him," she said, her voice filling with emotion. "The day after he was killed, everyone in the school—the children, the teachers—they were all so stunned. You could feel it all through the building. Someone, I remember, put Eddie's picture up on the main bulletin board. Every time I walked by it, I just felt drained.

"Sometimes," she went on, "I wonder if there was anything more we could have done. Really, though, I don't think so. We were supportive of him when he came home from school, we talked with him, we encouraged him, we praised him for his progress. His community loved him, his church, his family, his school. He had everything a youngster in New York could possibly have. But still this happened."

Ms. Brunson hadn't known why it had happened, but there was one other person at Wadleigh who, I had been told, might. That was the Special Program's founder and director, a forty-nine-year-old black bachelor from West Virginia named Edouard Plummer.

A math and social sciences teacher at Wadleigh since 1963, Plummer had been Eddie's mentor in junior high and had written the recommendation that had helped secure him a place at Exeter. His background was unconventional—he had grown up an orphan and, before coming to Wadleigh, had spent several years in Paris in the company of such black expatriates as James Baldwin and Richard Wright—and so were his methods. Around Eddie's neighborhood, where Plummer was described in tones of awe, almost fear, it was said that Plummer didn't ask his students to produce, he demanded it of them—and woe be to those who didn't. "He has the fervor of a revivalist minister," one of his former students wrote in an article about him, "alternately threatening damnation to those who fall by the wayside and promising salvation to those who keep the faith and follow his gospel.''

When I called Plummer to arrange an interview, the hellfire-and-brimstone side of his personality was apparent. "Meet me tomorrow," he ordered. "Wadleigh. After class." A moment later the line went dead.

When I turned up the next afternoon, the Wadleigh pushers were not in evidence. The security guards, however, were, and it required some moments to convince them I had a reason to be there. Finally Plummer appeared and escorted me to his classroom, which was dominated by a portrait of Martin Luther King, Jr., and a poster that proclaimed: Fight Back with Merit.

As I took a seat at one of the desks—the same one, Plummer informed me, Eddie had occupied—Plummer walked to an open window overlooking 114th. The sound of a ghetto blaster turned to top volume floated in. "I always tell people who come here one thing," he announced, looking over the street. "Everything depends on attitude. If you have the right attitude, you can go to Harvard. If you don't, you'll end up in the city jail." He spun around and fixed me with a drill sergeant's glare. "I could have reunions of my graduates at both."

His mood lightened as he began talking about the program he had created. It had begun, he related, during a vacation to the South of France in the summer of 1964, Lounging on a beach one day, Plummer picked up a copy of *Time* and found in it an article extolling the wonders of a new organization called A Better Chance. Impressed—"By golly, I thought to myself, it really *can* be different"—Plummer wired *Time* for more information and, on his return to New York, started drawing up plans for a program that would produce ABC candidates. "I had seen too many bright kids going down the drain, because they had nothing to look forward to," Plummer recalled. "Just look around this neighborhood—that's what they had to look forward to. I wanted to show them there was something else."

He encountered problems, at first, from the parents ("Most of them didn't know what prep school was"), from some of his faculty colleagues ("'Let them do what they please,' they were saying. 'They aren't here to learn'"), from Wadleigh's white principal ("He all but laughed at me," Plummer recalled), and, not least, from those who accused him of "skimming the cream" from the community. But Plummer pressed on and, with the help of several faculty volunteers, managed his first year to place sixteen children in schools such as Dalton, Putney, Westover, and Lawrenceville.

From that effort grew the special program. Open to those whom Plummer deemed to have the requisite determination, drive, talent, discipline, and ambition, it consisted of twice-weekly hour-and-a-half sessions presided over by Plummer and Ms. Brunson. During those after-school lessons, and at a six-week summer session, students were drilled in reading, math, and test-taking abilities. They were taken to the gym to learn about leadership and sportsmanship, to the theater to learn about culture, to the library to learn the mechanics of doing research. After completing the Secondary School Aptitude Test in the fall, they were also given instruction on how to handle prep school life: which fork to use at dinner; the proper way of addressing teachers ("'It's 'yes' or 'no' and a complete sentence, not 'em-em' or 'uh-uh'"); the clothes they would need ("I always tell them to pack long underwear, because it's going to be cold where they are going"); the rules they would be expected to follow; the art of getting along with white roommates. Nothing, seemingly, was left to chance, not even learning how to waltz. "They may not ever waltz in prep school," Plummer explained, "but someday they are going to be at the White House, at some diplomatic reception, and the orchestra is going to start playing a waltz, and I am going to be looking down from heaven and I am going to be smiling."

It was a demanding regimen—"We don't have time for children who don't care," said Plummer. "If they don't want to do the work, it's fine and good-bye"—and the program was not without its critics. "You know what the perception of black children is," Plummer said. "All these children are good for is singing and dancing and shooting baskets. These stereotypes are so ingrained even blacks believe them. We hear it all the time: 'The children will be misfits. They won't be prepared. They won't fit in.' I have an answer for that and it is this: 'Black people have always felt out of place, so what's new? And how is placing sixteen kids out of ten thousand taking away "the cream of the community"? And if they are the crème de la crème, then what the hell have the New York City schools been doing with them?'"

Plummer was rolling now, the thoughts coming in long staccato bursts. ''I operate on the basic premise that children are not responsible for the positions they are in,'' he declared, his thick, precisely groomed moustache twitching.

It's the adults who put them there. When I see a child who is talented and gifted and wants something, then I think he should be given a helping hand. If people hadn't helped me when I was growing up, I wouldn't be where I am. I had ambition and desire, but they opened doors for me. They helped me financially, spiritually, and mentally. Now I think I have an obligation to give something back. . . .

We're not doing anything revolutionary here. All we're doing is working small-scale, one-to-one. But nothing else is going to change things for blacks. No big mass movements are going to solve our problems. No one thing is going to sweep us all up. I watched the social revolution and struggle during the sixties and I tell my children today, ''All those people who were criticizing and everything—what were they doing? They made noise, but they had no sense of direction. They had emotion but no substance.'' That's what we've got today: a great deal of emotion but no substance.

You take all our so-called political leaders. You never see them here. They never come into the schools and ask me, ''What can we do? How can we support your program?'' They aren't concerned—not one of the black leaders or politicians or ministers. The only reason they got involved in the Perry case is because it made the newspapers. If Edmund had not gone to Exeter, he could have been a black spot on Main Street. He would have been just another young nigger shot in Harlem.

Plummer got to his feet and started pacing restlessly. ''We don't kid ourselves,'' he went on.

We know it is not going to be easy for a child from Wadleigh to go to one of these schools. And we don't kid our children. We tell them about the problems they are going to run into, the fact that certain people may not like them, and they may not like certain people. We admit to them that they will encounter racism at their schools. Racism is a part of this society, and the schools are just a microcosm of it. We tell them that when they go off to places like Exeter, they are going to be with students who have never seen blacks before except on TV. They are going to be assuming that everyone from Harlem carries a knife and has a mother on welfare. They don't know that there are middle-class values in Harlem—we just don't have the money to match them. But we also tell our children that they mustn't blame all whites. People are just people. There are good and bad in every race. Human nature didn't make Hitler what he was, and it didn't make Martin Luther King what he was. Human nature doesn't make anyone. It's what you do with your gifts.

That's the attitude we try to instill in our children. We try to build up their ego, their sense of value and self-worth. We try to reach into children and make them see themselves as larger and better than even they realize. At first, they may not even believe it themselves—that's how conditioned they've been by the environment. But we keep working and working at it. One of the things we do is let them know that there have been successes ahead of them. We get the older ones to come back and talk to them. We tell our children, "He sat right in that seat over there, and look what happened to him. Here is his business card. This is what he does. He is married. He has children. He has executive rank at his place of employment. He travels. He has his own car. He does this, he does that"—you make them see that it can be done.

Will it be tough? Of course it will be tough. But we believe our children have the capability of handling it—*they've shown* they can handle it; they've *proved* they can compete with whites—*if* they have discipline.

I believe, and I try to teach my children, that discipline is everything. The first day they come into this class, I give them a list of thirty rules and have them write them out in their copy books. And then I make sure they obey them. Because if they can't stand up to the pressure they get from me, how on earth are they going to stand up to what they are going to feel in prep school?

. . . Right from the beginning we tell them: "You are going to
be independent and make your own decisions. You are not to do
anything that is going to jeopardize your situation. These other
children you are going to school with, if they get kicked out, they
are going to put on their Bermuda shorts and go into daddy's
business. What are you going to walk into? You've got to work
for everything. You are there for a reason, not for a season, and if
you lose that opportunity, you are not going to have a second
chance. Your mother and your father can't put up fifteen or
twenty thousand dollars to get you into another school. So you are
not to become involved in drugs, alcohol, stealing, or cheating."
And they don't. Until this incident with Edmund, none of our
children had ever gotten into trouble. They knew that if they did,
they would have to answer to me.

We had been talking for more than an hour, and it was the first time
Plummer had mentioned Eddie's name. From the expression on his
face, even that brief reference seemed to pain him. He continued to
appear troubled when I asked him what kind of student Eddie had
been. "He was aggressive, in a way," Plummer replied, choosing his
words carefully.

Not physically aggressive, intellectually aggressive. Aggressive
with a positive attitude. He wanted to know a great many things.
. . . Sometimes you could think his personality was brittle, but he
was also very disciplined. That's the first thing that impressed me
about him: how disciplined he was. All Harlem boys are supposed
to be bad, have a big void when it comes to buckling down and
obeying rules. But not Eddie. He was never any trouble at all.
    That's the kind of student Exeter is looking for: someone who
is bright, who is aggressive, who knows how to work. I took him
to see other schools, too—Lawrenceville, Hotchkiss—but you
could see how impressed he was by Exeter. He told me he wanted
to go there because during the summers he'd been in New Hampshire on the Fresh Air Fund. But there was more to it than New
Hampshire. It was Exeter. It was a challenging place, and Eddie
was a boy who loved challenges. I'll never forget the look on his

face the day he got in. He just beamed, just lit up like a flashlight. "I am going to prep school," he kept saying. *"I'm* going to prep school."

. . . On vacations home, when he'd come over to our classes and tell the children what it was like, trying to give them a sense of what they would have to go through, I'd sometimes ask him, "Was it worth it, everything you had to put up with here?" And he'd say, "Oh, yes, Mr. Plummer, it was worth it. It was worth all of it." He said he was getting along beautifully with everybody. I had no idea anything was wrong.

Plummer turned and walked to the window, where the music of the ghetto blaster still drifted in. "Sometimes," he said softly, "you wonder whether it is worth it. I had one boy, years ago, even brighter than Eddie. Hundred and thirty IQ, ninety-ninth percentile on the SSAT [Secondary School Aptitude Test]. His mother wouldn't let him go away. I said, 'Oh, hell,' but there was nothing I could do. He wound up just coasting through high school, doing nothing, finally getting strung out on drugs. Then one day—it was eight years after he left here, the same day he would have graduated from college—someone called me and said, 'David is dead. He OD'd on drugs.'"

Plummer stared down at the street. "I don't know what happened to Eddie," he said. "Maybe it was just a foolish moment of indiscretion, a stupid chance. All I know is that when I came to school the next morning, his sister, Nichol, was outside waiting for me. 'Something bad happened to Eddie,' she said. 'Eddie is dead.'"

5

COMING OUT OF WADLEIGH, PLUMMER AND I NEARLY COLLIDED
with a stout black woman going in. It was Eddie's mother, Veronica
Perry.

As Plummer introduced me, explaining the story I was doing, Mrs.
Perry eyed me suspiciously, as if trying to figure out what I was actu-
ally up to. Her look softened when Plummer added that I had a son at
Exeter.

We shook hands, and for a few moments we chatted about the may-
or's race (it was primary election day, and Veronica had come to
Wadleigh to vote) and how C. Vernon Mason was likely to do against
Morgenthau. Finally I asked if I could call to set up an interview.
Veronica immediately agreed. "You know," she said as we parted, "I
can't blame God for taking my boy. No I can't. Ed is on high now.
Praise God. Praise Him!"

It was not what I expected to hear from a mother whose son had
recently been shot to death under what could at best be called controversial circumstances. I particularly did not expect to hear it from Veronica Perry, who had come off on television and in the newspapers as
a bitter, emotional woman, intent on extracting revenge on whites in
general and the New York Police Department in particular. Shock, no
doubt, accounted for some of her behavior, as, I suspected, did the
advice she was getting from political types, who were, as one of them
told me, "urging her to renew her commitment to the black struggle."
Nonetheless, the stridency of Veronica's pronouncements—and the
eagerness with which she made them—left me unsettled. Her grieving
seemed too public, almost as if she was rather enjoying the sudden
celebrity her son's death had brought her. It was largely for that reason
that I had delayed contacting Mrs. Perry until now. Time, I hoped,
would allow some of the bile to drain away, allow her to talk more as a
mother and less as a spokeswoman. But there was no waiting any
longer. A few days later after our encounter at Wadleigh, I called her

at the Lenox Hill Head Start Center, where she worked as an assistant teacher. Very pleasantly, she said she would meet me at her apartment the following Sunday.

By then I had learned a fair amount about Veronica Perry. I knew, for instance, that she had grown up in a family whose Harlem roots could be traced back four generations, and that Veronica's immediate branch of the family consisted of one mother, two fathers, and twenty-two children, only fifteen of whom were still alive. One of her siblings had been killed in a hit-and-run accident, another had been shot to death in an argument, and still another had died of medical complications linked to drug abuse. Of the survivors, at least one was a heroin addict, and yet another had shot a man to death. I knew also that Veronica herself had not had an easy time of it.

As a child, she later told me, she contracted rheumatic fever, slipped into a coma, and nearly died. Experimental medication saved her, but she did not fully recover her health until she had spent several years as a virtual shut-in at a rural foster home. When she returned to Harlem, her mother, a hotel chambermaid, enrolled her at Wadleigh Junior High, and, like a number of her classmates, Veronica was soon caught up in radical black politics. She was a frequent participant in rallies staged by Muslim leader Malcolm X and later fell in with the Black Panthers, who in the late sixties maintained a heavily fortified headquarters a few blocks from the apartment where Eddie was to grow up. According to her friends, Veronica's involvement in such activities was intense and would remain so, coloring her views of politics and race; it did not, however, affect her performance in school. She did well academically, both at Wadleigh and later at Brandeis High School, and had ambitions of going on to college. But in the absence of the scholarship programs that would later benefit both her sons, those plans were put aside. Instead, at the age of eighteen, Veronica married Jonah Perry, a southern sharecropper's son then making his living as a Harlem numbers runner.

The couple moved to Brooklyn, where Veronica gave birth to her first child, a son she named Jonah. Two years later, Edmund was born, and three years after that, a girl, Nichol. By then, however, the Perrys' marriage was beginning to come apart.

The problem, according to family friends, lay with Jonah senior.

After the move to Brooklyn, he got a job as a stockboy in a hardware store, rose rapidly to become store manager, and, by the time of Nichol's birth, was laying plans to buy a part of the business. But the pressures that came with Jonah's rapid rise extracted a toll. He began drinking, socially at first, then compulsively. As his habit descended into alcoholism, he lost his job and became alienated from his sons. Finally, in 1974, Veronica obtained a legal separation and moved the children to Harlem, where they settled in a cramped, third-story walkup at 265 West 114th Street.

By day Veronica worked as a clerical assistant. By night she studied at Bronx Community College, from which she won a two-year degree in practical nursing in 1978. Her diploma allowed her to secure a relatively well-paying job at a local hospital. Soon, though, Veronica decided that what she really wanted to do was work with children. Returning to night school, she got a second degree—this one in special education—and was eventually hired as a teacher's aide in a federally funded Head Start program. Shortly thereafter, Veronica's life took two dramatic turns.

The first was getting back together with Jonah senior, who rejoined the family in 1980, much gentler though no less alcoholic than before. The second was becoming deeply involved in local community affairs, as the outspoken leader of the P.S. 113 PTA, which was then in the midst of battling a city-mandated shutdown of after-school programs. Veronica played a leading role in the fight, which eventually succeeded, and was subsequently elected PTA president. The emotional cost, however, was high. Shortly before Christmas, 1980, Veronica suffered what she termed a breakdown and was hospitalized for several weeks.

After her discharge, Veronica resumed all her activities with the same energy as before. By 1982 she had become sufficiently well known in the district to make a long-shot bid for a spot on the local community school board. It was a bitter, uphill campaign, marked by charges of racism and gossip about the circumstances of Veronica's hospitalization. But Veronica worked hard and scored a decisive upset victory. Soon after her election, she was in the thick of school-board politics, which were then centered on a proposal to create an "alternative school" for the benefit of gifted children. Since the overwhelming majority of the children in the district were black, while those tested as "gifted" were largely white, feelings on the issue ran high— particularly after a stormy meeting during the course of which a group of white parents threatened to withdraw their children from school unless the board approved the special education scheme. The board itself was nearly evenly split. The deciding vote turned out to be Veronica's, and it went against the alternative schools.

Nonetheless, Veronica was not universally popular among blacks in the district. Some of the resentment could be traced to her independent, frequently confrontational style. "Veronica doesn't behave like a black woman in politics is supposed to," one of her friends said. "If you're a woman in Harlem, you're supposed to do what the sisters did for Adam Clayton Powell: cook that chicken, keep Adam in those nice suits and cars so he can go up and talk to white people. Veronica doesn't play that role. She acts like a man." Another added: "Veronica is a very frustrated lady. If she had been born twenty years later and male, life would have turned out a lot different for her. She would have been the one going off to prep school. So she's resentful, and that makes a lot of people resent her." According to others, some of the hostility directed at Veronica derived from the way she raised her sons. As one woman who knew her put it, "For those boys to get as far as they did, she had to be telling them, 'You're gonna be better than that riffraff and those niggers out there. Don't you be like so and so. Don't you do like such and such. You're gonna go somewhere.' Right from jump street, those boys got the message that they were better than the other kids on the block. And that's not the kind of thing that wins you a lot of love."

Loved or not, it was clear that Veronica was respected. One and all commended her for her devotion to the school board and her church, and even the most envious of her neighbors acknowledged that she had been a fine parent under trying conditions. Whether it was getting them off to church on Sunday, or enrolling them in special programs after school, or seeing to it that they escaped the city during the summer under the aegis of the Fresh Air Fund, there seemed to be nothing that she wouldn't do for her children, including giving them a deep sense of their history and race. "She is not one of these stereotypical welfare mothers who sit around having babies," Bill Perkins said. "She's a tough chick and she hustles over obstacles for her kids. That's one of the reasons she got involved politically. When Veronica started out, she was a woman who didn't have anything in her pocketbook but dust. She knew that politics and the connections she would make would give her access to people who would help her kids. About some stuff, she's fairly naïve, but not about that.''

Veronica's shrewdness also impressed the authorities at Exeter, particularly admissions director Jack Herney, who encountered her several times during recruiting visits to Harlem. ''There are a lot of parents who live their lives through their children,'' said Herney, ''and Veronica Perry did more than most. I remember when I would come down to show films of the school. She would be there, talking to the parents, telling them the plusses and minuses about going to Exeter. But the thing I remember most was her reply when one of the parents asked why she had sent her son away to school. She said, *''We* have our ambitions.''

Since the death of those ambitions, Veronica's mood had been swinging wildly. In the hours immediately following the shooting, she seemed composed and in control—devastated, to be sure, but still able to cope. ''The thing that impressed me,'' said Peter Noel, an *Amsterdam News* reporter who was with Veronica both at the hospital and at her home, ''is how strong she seemed. Other mothers in that situation would have been under heavy sedation, but she was sitting there, sweating it out. She would read Eddie's yearbook aloud and smile and say nice things about him. Then she would pick up the Bible, read a psalm, and press it to her chest and say, 'Lord, why have you done this to me? I've been a good mother, and I think I understand, but make me understand more. If it had to happen, give me a reason why. Give it to me now. Tell me why you took my son.' Then she would begin to cry, but only for a little while. I'll tell you that lady was strong. I've been with a lot of mothers whose sons have been shot, and I've never seen anything like this.''

By the next day, however, Veronica's composure had vanished. At a press conference at C. Vernon Mason's office, she lashed out emotionally at the ''lunatic'' Lee Van Houten and at the ''white men [who] hated to see [Eddie's success]. . . . That's the only way I can figure it,'' she went on, chest heaving, breaths coming in short gasps. ''They wanted to wipe him out . . . because he was so good." Finally she crumpled altogether and had to be led out of the press conference in tears.

According to Veronica's friends, her emotions had been fluctuating that way ever since. One day she would seem peaceful and religious, praising God and looking to the Bible for strength. "Our God is a good God," she would say. "I know it's not Him who is punishing me, but Satan who is testing me. I know he's steady after me." Other days she would seem morose and agitated, saying nothing about God, only damning the cop who had "premeditated and took a gun and killed my baby." She was similarly divided talking to reporters. To some she spoke of the Lord, proclaiming, "I don't feel any hatred or malice. I'm overjoyed my son is with the King." Of others, she demanded, "Who is Lee Van Houten to be judge, jury, and executioner for a mugging? He is nothing but a twenty-four-year-old white boy from the suburbs. If that's what the police officers are about today—young rookie, trigger-happy—then we don't need them."

Knowing of her emotional history, some people in the neighborhood were keeping a watchful eye on her. As I mounted the graffiti-covered staircase leading to her apartment the Sunday of our scheduled meeting, I wondered what frame of mind I'd find her in.

There turned out to be no reason for worry. Veronica greeted me cordially at the door and beckoned me inside, where, it developed, a modest celebration was going on. The occasion was the baptism that morning of Veronica's niece Thomasina, a young mother of two, who was living with the Perrys pending her assignment to public housing. Veronica introduced me to her guests, and then to her daughter, fourteen-year-old Nichol, a smiling bundle of nervous energy. I had been told by people in the neighborhood that Nichol, whom Veronica was thinking of sending to live with relatives in rural Virginia ("Got to get that girl away from Harlem," she said), was the most typically teenage of the Perry children, and she quickly proceeded to live up to her reputation. When I asked her about school and whether she planned to follow in her brothers' footsteps, she screwed up her face, let out a "yuck," and with that, bounded out to play. Finally Veronica guided me to a weathered, beaten-looking man sitting quietly in a chair in a corner of the room. "And this," she said, "is my husband, Jonah."

Mr. Perry, whom I took to be in his late fifties—later I would learn he was barely past forty—smiled wanly, gave my hand a limp shake, and motioned me to a seat in a velour easy chair. While Veronica retreated to the tiny kitchen to continue work on the feast she had been preparing since six in the morning, Jonah senior and I sat looking at each other, saying nothing. Several long moments passed. I felt uncomfortable with the silence and unsure how to break it. Jonah senior, however, seemed quite at ease.

 Gradually I allowed my eyes to wander around the room. It was furnished with pride and care, like any middle-class household, though some of the items were a bit shopworn. Instead of a real fireplace there was a fake one, with a plastic ''marble'' mantel and a hearth that glowed red with the turn of a switch. Next to it were a series of bookshelves, groaning under the weight of a three-decade-old edition of the World Book Encyclopedia and a gold-painted bust of John F. Kennedy. A few feet away, dominating the room, stood a large floor-model color television set, atop which rested a Bible, opened to the Song of Solomon. On the opposite wall were two portraits of idealized black children, painted on velvet and rendered in the wide-eyed manner of Keene paintings. Beneath them was a basket filled with magazines. I could spot the titles of only two: the Exeter *Alumni Bulletin* and *The Workers Vanguard*. The cover of the former announced a new endowment campaign, the latter, an article titled ''Apartheid Terror.'' But it was the pictures of the family that held my eye. They appeared to be everywhere, on walls, on shelves, on virtually every surface, and most of them were of Eddie. There was Eddie at junior high graduation, Eddie at camp, Eddie in Spain, Eddie playing with Jonah, Eddie doing this, Eddie doing that, and in these pictures, at least, always smiling.

My snooping was interrupted by Veronica's return, bearing a steaming platter of ham, pork chops, and corn bread. Grace was said, a celebratory bottle of champagne uncorked, and glasses filled. Mrs. Perry offered a toast: ''Here's to the family and the future.'' We took a sip, and then Thomasina proposed a toast to God, ''who brought us all together''—''who saved us all,'' Veronica added.

As we ate, Veronica, who had recently returned from a few days visiting a sister in California, reminisced about vacations past, including one a number of years before in Washington. "I had this rabbit coat on," she related. "Most people wouldn't say it was much—it was just rabbit, but that was fur to me. That was *mink*. And I was over at the White House, touring around, you know, and somehow, I got into one of the president's press conferences. On the way out, I tripped and fell down, and all these security people hurried over to help me up. 'Madam Ambassador,' they said, 'are you all right?' Isn't that something? They thought I was an ambassador. I guess they figured that in the middle of the day all black women are either out working or at home, watching their kids. They didn't know I was just on vacation. They just saw that I was a black woman, so they thought I was an ambassador from Africa. Then I went out to the street. I was walking around and some young black boys came up to me and said, 'That's some coat you have, sister. Where'd you get that coat?'—like they were going to take it away from me. I just sort of glared at them and held that coat tight around me and said, 'I'm from Harlem, U.S.A.' They said, 'Oh, you're a home girl—are you tough?' And I said, 'No, just ready.' Isn't that something? You can be in the White House and they think you are an ambassador, and ten minutes later there are people out on the street looking to rip you off. I guess it's just a matter of perspective."

We laughed and Veronica kept talking, spinning stories of her minister, her days in high school, her first trip to Exeter. It was apparent she was enjoying herself, and apparent as well that she was used to being the center of attention. After an hour of stories and a dessert of homemade chocolate cake, Veronica announced that a postprandial stroll through Central Park was in order. As we got up, she took me to the bookcase and began describing the pictures of Eddie. Pointing to one of him with the Exeter basketball team, she said, "He wasn't good enough to make the team. He was the water boy. But he practiced with them everyday. He was better at football. Won his 'E' his senior year. His sister has it in her room." She gestured at a framed award. "This is for science. Eddie won it in junior high. He wrote a paper on why the cockroach lasted so long. He concluded it was because of its adaptability." She beamed at the memory and picked up another certificate, this one for academic achievement. It was dated June 29, 1985, seventeen days after Eddie's death. "I have so many of his awards," Veronica said. "I think I am going to put them up." She extracted a shoebox from one of the shelves. It was filled with postcards Eddie had written. "Eddie was real good about writing," she said as I leafed through the box. "There's this box, and four more just like it in the closet." I picked out several of the cards.

The first was postmarked from a small town in New Hampshire and had been written during one of Eddie's summers with the Fresh Air Fund. Eddie reported that he had "played with snakes" and that the food was good.

Another, showing a bucolic view of the south of France, was written several years later, during Eddie's school year abroad as an Exeter junior. Recently, he recalled, he had met a "beautiful, black French-speaking goddess." She was engaged, he added, but he was "working hard to break them up." Catching my smile, Veronica said, "Eddie loved girls so much. He told me once, 'Mom, I love 'em so much, if I had been born a girl, I woulda been a lesbian.'"

I laughed and pulled out another card, sent from Exeter for Mother's Day. The front of it showed two white children tugging on their mother's skirts. Above the card's legend—"If kids could choose their mothers, one thing is true: you'd need a bigger house, because they'd all choose you"—Eddie had written, "Pretend all these people are black, OK?" Inside, he had included a poem of his own composition, calling Veronica "the lady of my dreams." He closed with a postscript saying how lucky he was to be her son.

"He was lucky," I said as I finished reading. Veronica shook her head. "No," she replied, solemnly. "I was the lucky one."

While Veronica gathered up her nieces I walked to the television, where, tucked beneath the Bible, I noticed several other letters. Leafing through them, I realized at once that they had not been written by Eddie. One began: "I would just like to tell you that I agree that this was a racial incident—your son mugged the cop because he was white. I'm glad your one son was killed and only wish that the other nigger was killed, too."

A moment later, we trooped downstairs to a day that was warm and sunny and a block that seemed alive with children, many of whom called out to Veronica by name. "They all know me," she said proudly. "And I know them. This is a Perry block, it is. We got thirty of our children right here.'' A youngster scooted up to Veronica and gave her a hug. She kissed him on the cheek and patted him on the head. ''Roots is what makes it for you,'' she went on. ''There's forty-eight Perrys right around here. More on 111th Street. We may not have much, but we have each other. That's our strength. Always been.''

The recitation of family history continued as our little procession made its way slowly up the block. ''My grandmother, Paige Edwards, was the first of us who came here,'' Veronica recounted. ''She's eighty-four now, and lost her leg a while back. But she's still active. Still lives right on this block. She grew up in the South, outside Richmond, Virginia. Her mother was a slave, and they were working the land, living in one of the master's houses. Sharecroppers is what they were. It was hard for black folks, back then, living in the South. She came up here to make a better life.'' She pointed to the building where her grandmother lived. ''Ed used to go and visit her all the time. He wanted to hear what it was like for her, about growing up in the South, the KKK, having a mother a slave and all. One of the reasons, I guess, is that when Ed was growing up was the time when Dr. Martin Luther King and the Kennedys were getting killed. I remember he came home from school one day and said, 'Mama, white people are the devil.' I asked him why he thought that, and he said, 'Because they kill all the people who are trying to help us. God is going to get them.' I told Ed you can't judge people just by the color of their skin. There were just some people who felt power by holding black people down. 'Sides, there's some white in all of us. Just look at my color. I'm light—our whole family is mixed. I told Ed how that happened, way back in slavery times. When the master wanted a black girl, she had to go.''

Veronica shrugged, as if the truth of the story was self-evident. Then, as we turned down Seventh Avenue to walk the final four blocks to the park, she began talking of her adolescence and the things that had led her to become politically involved. ''When I was at Brandeis,'' she began, ''the principal there was a white man and he didn't care about us one bit. He'd have us there in assembly, arms folded across his chest, looking out and glaring at us. He said, 'If you don't get an education, one of two things is going to happen to you. You're either gonna be like those people out there cleaning up the streets, or you're gonna be in jail. You do what you want to do. I'm still gonna be picking up my check.' After that assembly I went up to him and said, 'I'm gonna get my education, and I'm gonna show you. I'm gonna make something of myself.'

"That's what I tried to do: make something of myself. Maybe if it had been different I woulda gotten farther. . . . Maybe I'd be eating in fancy restaurants and traveling to Spain and learning about different cultures and people, but that wasn't in the cards for me. I did all right, though. I went to college. I was the only one of my mother's children who graduated. People ask me how I did it, and I tell 'em like that commercial, I got my degree the old-fashioned way. I earned it.' "

Veronica laughed at her own joke. "I'm not like all these other women you see in the neighborhood," she went on, "spending all their time drinking, getting high, collecting their checks, going out for their boyfriends, doing nothing for their community, doing nothing for nobody. That's not for me. When I see something wrong, I speak up. I get involved. . . . That's why I ran for the school board. I knew what they were going to do to Harlem. I heard all this talk about 'planned shrinkage.' They had already closed the hospital, and they were gonna close the schools. If you don't have hospitals and you don't have schools, you don't have a community. I couldn't let that happen. I had to do something about it. Some'll tell you I'm a bigmouth, and maybe I am. But the way I see it, people who don't look out after anything, who only think of themselves, are really missing out on life. . . .

"It's hard being involved," she continued. "The meetings are long, and it takes you away from your kids. I remember once I came home from a school board meeting late at night. Jonah was fourteen or fifteen years old and he was angry. He yelled at me, 'You're not a mother to me. You're not sensitive to me. You're never around when I want to talk to you. The only person I have to talk to is Jesus.' Hearing Jonah say that—'The only person I can to is Jesus'—made me so happy. I laughed so hard. I said, 'Son, that's the only person I think I can talk to, too.' "

Veronica sighed. "Maybe I coulda spent more time if I wasn't always doing for others," she said. "But that's just me. I can never say no. I even took a college course once on how to say no. I thought that might be the answer to my problem. But I didn't finish it, because I couldn't complete the paper. Because while I was looking out for me, I was looking out for everybody else, too. Especially those kids. The number-one thing in my life has been those kids. They were the shining stars of my life.''

We had come now to the northern edge of the park, an area of incongruous, startling beauty. I was about to comment on it when, quite unbidden, Veronica began revealing the story of her breakdown. ''It happened in December 1980,'' she said, in a flat, reportorial tone. ''That was about the time Ed's father was calling on me, seeing about getting back together.'' She let out a small laugh. ''I guess that would have been reason enough to have a breakdown,'' she went on. ''But that wasn't it, really. No, the real reason I had the breakdown is that I saw the system for what it was. I was going crazy in my head, trying to figure out how to get my kids out, to protect them from the system. I knew it was going to grind them down. So I talked to God, and God talked back to me. He told me that there were going to be major changes in my life, that I was going to be in a position of power—a leadership position. He didn't say how it was going to happen. He only said that it was going to happen. I wouldn't understand it, but He would see me through. It was the first time I felt the presence of the Lord—and that's why I cracked up. When I told the doctor what had happened, that God had spoken to me, he didn't know what to do. Poor man. I guess he'd never met anyone who claimed that God had talked to 'em.''

Veronica looked at me, as if waiting for a response. I could think of none. As we seated ourselves on a bench in a playground overlooking a large pond, Jonah, who had barely spoken a word all afternoon, piped up to announce he was returning to the apartment. He walked away, taking Thomasina with him; Veronica's nieces scampered up the rungs of a nearby jungle gym. Still keeping a watchful eye on them, Veronica pointed at a small hill on the other side of the pond. ''That's where we had our cookouts every Fourth of July,'' she said. ''We had our little place all staked out.'' For a brief instant, her eyes misted. She went on, ''I taught the boys how to swim in this pond. Taught 'em how to iceskate, too.'' She paused. ''They were such good children. Both of them were. Never caused me any problems at all.''

"Tell me about them," I coaxed. "Tell me what they were like."
Veronica began to speak, as much to herself, it seemed, as to me.

I was so blessed with those boys. They was always trying to
please me. Both of them used to talk about how they'd take care
of me when they got out of college. Eddie said that he was going
to take me to La Pierre for lunch. Jonah'd say that a hundred
thousand dollars would be chump change in their pockets.

People ask me how I got to be so lucky, having kids who didn't
give me any trouble. Sometimes I wonder that myself. I think
maybe it's 'cause they saw first-hand how dreadful things could
be. Maybe they saw that I was dealing with enough. When the
other kids would try to get them into trouble, they would say,
"Hell, no, we can't do that. Our mother would find out." And
the kids knew they were telling the truth. I would find out—and
they were terrified that I would find out. As much as I let them go
and have their own way, they knew that I had limits. They also
knew I wasn't afraid to use the belt. I used it on them a lot. The
way I judged it, if they aggravated me, then something was
wrong. They had it coming. . . . I always told them, "If you tell
me first, we'll handle it. We'll deal with it. But we can't deal with
it if I don't know about it." That's what they always did, because
they knew that if they didn't, if they lied, they were going to be in
bigger trouble.

Ed was always good about that. He could talk to me about
anything. School, boys and girls, sex—whatever was on his
mind. Once he even talked to me about oral sex and homosex-
uality. Can you imagine kids talking to their mother about stuff
like that? But Ed did. . . .

He was such a good boy. Oh, he'd get into scrapes now and
again, but those things just happen. He never went looking for
trouble, never in his life. Ed was a talker, not a fighter. He
wouldn't run from a fight—Ed wasn't a punk—but he'd rather
talk his way out of it. He'd say, "Let's talk it out, and if we can't
talk it out, then we can always duke it out." Usually, it worked.
He'd cut 'em with that sharp tongue of his. He told me once that a
boy up at Exeter had called him colored. "Who are you calling

colored?'' Ed said to him. ''You have red hair and green eyes and white skin. I'm brown all over: brown hair, brown eyes, brown skin. So who's the colored boy?'' They never called him colored after that.

Sometimes, though, he'd have to fight. I had to take him to the hospital once, after he got into a fight on 110th Street. He was helping out one of his friends against a big black man. He didn't have any choice. Mostly, though, he was a negotiator. That's why what the police say is so unbelievable. If the man had said, ''I'm a police officer,'' Ed would have raised his hands and said, ''Take me,'' He wasn't physical. He was smart. He knew that cops shoot little black boys. . . .

He was so gentle, Ed was, so sensitive. He always had a way of sensing when I was down, and then he'd do something to cheer me up. That lamp you saw in our house? The blue papier-mâché one? That was one of the things he did. Made it for me in school. There's a heart on it that says, ''You light up my life.'' That's the kind of things Eddie was always doing for me. I remember once, when I was feeling kinda low, he sent me a letter from Exeter. He wrote, ''Don't do what other people try to convince you is right. Do what you think is right, because it always is right.''

I wanted the best for Eddie, the best for both of my boys. Hard as it was, much as I missed them, that's why I sent them away to school. I knew what the schools were like here, the terrible shape they were in. You just look at Wadleigh. How are kids supposed to feel good about themselves in a building like that? When they go to school in a building like that, they get the feeling that people don't care about them, so they don't care about themselves. I didn't want that to happen to my sons. I wanted them to get the best education possible. . . . I knew it wasn't going to be easy for them. I never fooled myself about that. Before they went off to prep school, I told them they were going to be different. They were poor, and all these other kids were rich. They could do things that they couldn't do. I said to them, ''They are bringing you up here because they want to learn about black people. They want to learn about their world. You have to teach them, and you have to learn about their world. You have to learn about it, because you have to fit into it. . . . Like it or not, it is their world. If you are going to play the game, you have to be in it. Maybe you can change the rules of the game later, but first you have to play it. You gotta pay the cost, if you're gonna be the boss.

You never had to fight Ed about that. He not only wanted to go to high school, he wanted to go to the best high school. He never missed a day at school. He never forgot who he was, either. His grandmother told him before he went away, "I don't want you to come back talking all that white stuff. If you do, I'm gonna let you know about it. Don't you ever forget where you are from." They never did. Not Ed, not Jonah. Neither of them adopted the white world. They stayed black. In fact, Eddie came back from Exeter blacker than he had been.

Ed was never one to talk about race, though. For a long time he didn't even like to talk about politics. Wasn't interested in it at all. I remember when I decided to run for the school board, before Ed went to Spain. Ed didn't like it one bit. "Ma," he said, "are you really gonna run?" I said, "I'm gonna run and I'm gonna win. I wouldn't run if I didn't think I would win." He shook his head. He said, "Politics isn't for you. You are too sensitive and honest. They are going to be scheming and doing a lot of dirty deals. It's gonna corrupt you."

But I ran and, praise God, I won. When Ed came home his attitude was different. He had gotten real political over there, because he knew that politics had to do with everything that was going on in society. He started going with me to the business meetings of the school board, because he was really interested in how the process worked. . . . Sometimes we'd argue—Ed always said we never had any arguments, just the loudest discussions in New York—and Ed would say I was too idealistic, that I didn't understand the way things really were. He used to say that rich people don't even consider helping poor people. For them, poor people don't even exist. "You think you are going to help these little people do something," he'd say. "You can't. The rich folks won't let you." I never agreed with that. I said to Ed, "You can't cry about it, you have to do something about it."

. . . After Spain, Ed began to see I was right. He really grew up over there, put on four inches in a year. I used to say, "I sent a boy to Spain and they sent me back a man.'' Ed used to say it different. ''Ma,'' he'd say, ''it was the women—they just stretched me.'' There were a lot of women over there, and a lot of leisure. Sometimes, I thought, too much leisure. It was hard for him, coming back to Exeter after all that freedom. He couldn't get used to all the rules. It was driving him really bonkers—he couldn't wait to get out. He felt he was grown up, that he had learned all he could. He wanted to move on. He said to me, ''I'm alienated when I am up here. I want to come home, because home is where I have roots.'' But he knew he had to stay and finish. I always told my children, ''I don't care what you do, but I want you to do it a hundred percent.'' I can't stand people who lay around and only give fifty percent, hoping or waiting for someone to do the rest. ''You have to give it all,'' I'd tell Ed. ''You have to give a hundred percent.''

Ed wasn't afraid of giving it all. He wanted it all. That's why he was going to California to college. He thought he had seen enough of the East Coast. He wanted to see the West Coast because he wanted to know how the whole country worked. He thought of going to Berkeley, but he chose Stanford because he heard that that's where all the shakers and movers went, the people who really ran the country. Ed decided he was going to be one of them: a shaker. . . .

He always had big ambitions. I remember when I was sending him to Head Start, and what his teacher, Mrs. Goldfarb, said to me one day when I came to pick him up. ''Do you know what your son told me he wants to be?'' she said. I knew how much Ed liked to play with trucks and buses, so I said, ''What? A truck driver?'' ''No,'' she said, ''he told me he wants to be president of the United States.'' Wasn't that something? Here it was, black people just getting to be able to vote, and he wants to be president of the United States.

Veronica halted. She let out a deep sigh and smiled. ''It's strange all the things that come back to you, how you remember 'em so well.''

I was just thinking now of a conversation I had with Ed, about ten days before he died. I was going out to a school board meeting and Ed, I 'member, was sitting on the washing machine. He said to me, "How do you keep coming back? How do you keep getting over? How do you make it? All the things you went through, with my father, with your illness, with the nervous breakdown, how do you keep going on?" I told him I depended on Jesus. When things get over my head, when I couldn't handle it, I called on God. He said, "So that's your bridge. That's how you get over. Jesus is your bridge."

I 'member, too, the night it happened. I'll never forget that. I'd gone to another school board meeting and my friends had walked me back to the bus. I remember how happy I was, because I had told the kids I would be home by eleven and this time I was actually going to make it. I was going to come home and sit down and all of us would eat and talk. It was gonna be so nice.

But then I came back and the streets were quiet. I thought that was strange, it being a hot night and all, but it never dawned on me that something like this had happened. Then my brother Quentin and an elderly lady who was new to the block called me over and told me that my son had been shot. They didn't have to tell me which one, I knew it was Ed—that boy was so accident-prone. I asked them, "Who shot him?" And they said, "The police." I said, "Oh, wow, no!" They were looking at me so strange.

I immediately went into prayer. I didn't know what else to do. When I don't know what to do, I call on Jesus. He always knows what to do. And Jesus did know what to do. He put Bill Perkins's number in my head. I called Bill and he called Pam [Green, a Democratic district leader] and Peter Noel of the *Amsterdam News* and they all came down to the hospital. When Peter saw what was going on, he called Vernon.

The nurse came down at eleven-thirty and said, "Your son is holding his own." That relieved me. I was a nurse, and I know that when someone tells you that someone is holding their own, it's gonna be all right. Everyone thought it was going to be all right. They never did tell me anything different until they dropped the bomb on me. . . .

I was furious when Eddie died. That's all I was: furious. I got on the phone and started calling up some people I knew, people I knew could get me some explosives. I wanted to blow up the freaking city. I was scheming to do that, I was so furious.

I was picking up the phone to make that call, and Jonah saw me. He didn't know what I was doing, but he must have sensed it. He said to me, "Mama, don't do that. Put down that phone. Don't be scheming that way. You always told us that God has a reason for everything. How can you be scheming to do that, when you don't know what the Lord has in store? 'Member what you told us when we were children? 'You gotta let go and let God?' You gotta do that now. Let go and let God." My son really had me in a box that night. He was reminding me of what I had taught him, and he was right. . . .

I don't have any bitterness or malice toward anyone now, not even that police officer. That's just the way it is: the more good that comes your way, the more you have sorrow and care. I knew something terrible was going to happen. I just didn't know what it was. The thing I can't understand, though, is when they say that police officer didn't do anything wrong. The Lord says, "Thou shalt not kill," and he killed. That's wrong. Some in the neighborhood say that the police had a quota, and he was just filling it. Maybe they're right.

But I can't complain. Ed lived a full life. He always wanted to be first, and he's first now. He's up there in heaven, checking things out for us. God had it all planned out. The trouble is, we didn't know what the plan was. We didn't know that He was going to take something away from us that is more precious to me than life itself. If I'da known what was going to happen, I would have had Him change the game plan. I would never have given up Eddie.

Veronica Perry looked at me, and at the children playing in the park. And then, very quietly, she began to weep.

6

I WAS A LONG TIME REFLECTING ON MY CONVERSATION WITH Veronica Perry, and the more I reflected on it, the more I was disquieted by it.

It was not that she had been reticent or had tried to conceal things from me. Far from it. If anything, she had been *too* talkative, discussing matters like her "breakdown" and "scheming to get explosives" with all the casualness of describing a trip to the grocery store. I was jarred by that, as I was also jarred by the fervor of Veronica's religious and political beliefs. Both were extremely intense, almost linked ("They took our baby," she had told a friend after Eddie's death, "but we're gonna get 'em with God's love"), with seemingly little room for compromise or give. Even her admonition to Eddie that he must not judge all whites harshly, because there was "good and bad in every race" had been coupled with a story about white slave-owners raping defenseless black women. The truth of the story, as I saw it, wasn't the point. It was, rather, how it and Veronica's other teachings—her tales of whites conspiring to destroy the neighborhood, for example—had shaped Eddie, who was, I was repeatedly told, "very, very impressionable." Had they left him racially proud? Or had they rendered him racially angry—angry enough, possibly, to have vented that rage on a seemingly innocuous white boy on a darkened city street?

Another thing I found myself dwelling on was what Veronica had said—and not said—about her older, surviving son, nineteen-year-old Jonah. Apart from revealing that Jonah was "macho," operated "on perceptions instead of what reality is," and felt slighted by her political involvement, Veronica hadn't really talked about him, which, up to a point, was understandable. Eddie was the boy who had been taken from her, and it was about Eddie that I had asked the bulk of my questions. All the same, I came away with the impression that for Veronica, Jonah was the decidedly lesser child. Which, as it happened, is largely how Jonah had been portrayed ever since the shooting. Very little had been reported about him, nor had Jonah himself said very much, save a few comments protesting his innocence. The latter circumstance at least was not surprising. He was, after all, under indictment on charges that, if proven to be true, could result in a long jail term, and no doubt he was under instructions from his lawyer to say nothing.

Nonetheless, the relegation of Jonah to the status of a bit player in a drama of which he seemed so integral a part was odd. For whatever Jonah's connection to the circumstances of Eddie's death, he had been closer to him than anyone else. They had grown up in the same house, attended the same grade school and junior high school, gone through very much the same experiences, including attending prep school. But there, I discovered, the similarities ended.

Jonah was born on September 3, 1967, at Kings County Hospital in Brooklyn, not far from where the family was then living. When Veronica moved the family to Harlem in 1974, Jonah, then seven, entered P.S. 113. At some point around that time—just when was not clear—he suffered an injury that left him noticeably swaybacked and puffchested and prevented him from playing contact sports such as football. The handicap, however, was a minor one and in no way affected Jonah's performance in school. He did well at P.S. 113, and even better at Wadleigh, where his outgoing personality helped win him election as president of his class.

It was that personality, in fact, that was Jonah's most frequently noted characteristic. "Sweet," people called it; "gentle," "easygoing"—especially in comparison with Eddie's. "Jonah's a much more regular guy than Ed," said an Exeter student who knew both boys well. "More laid back, easier to be with. It's like Eddie smart and Jonah cool." But Jonah was not cool all of the time. Strapping, broadshouldered, and muscular, he was also possessed of a temper. "If you hit my son," as his mother put it, "he'll hit you back."

The violent side of Jonah, however, was seldom in evidence. In describing him, people focused instead on his niceness and likability. He was a good boy, the residents of his neighborhood said, a churchgoer who worked hard, kept his nose clean, looked after his invalid grandmother, and found fun in going to the movies and chasing girls.

It was perhaps because he was such an average, likable kid that

Jonah's smarts were seldom mentioned—save to be contrasted negatively with Eddie's. Whereas Eddie was possessed of a burning curiosity about almost everything, Jonah's mind, as his minister phrased it, "had a more utilitarian bent." Nonetheless, Jonah was bright enough and, like his brother, won admission to Plummer's special program class, where his grinding persistence gained him a credible record. "Jonah was quieter than Eddie," Plummer recalled, "not as mentally astute, and certainly not someone you would describe as the leader type. Once he got his feet wet, though, he wanted it. He did his work, he turned in his assignments, he took criticism well. In fact, he responded well to everything. There were no problems with this guy at all." Terming Jonah "a willing worker who struggles hard to overcome all obstacles," Plummer recommended him to ABC, which in the fall of 1980 placed him at Westminster, a solid if undistinguished prep school in Simsbury, Connecticut, a countrified suburb of Hartford.

At Westminster, where he was one of 15 blacks in a student body of 335, Jonah seemed to blossom, though not without some initial difficulty. He was taunted his freshman year (according to his mother, some students called him Sambo and Jabbar), and on one occasion a white student, who had been riding Jonah about his race, punched him in the mouth, chipping a tooth. Later the same year, another name-calling incident climaxed when, according to Veronica, Jonah cracked a cinder-block wall with his fist. After that, Jonah's tormentors left him alone, and freed from their harassment, he began to excel. He did especially well at extracurriculars, captaining the track team, playing on the basketball squad (where he won a trophy his senior year for "sportsmanship and effort"), acting in student dramatic productions, serving as a campus tour guide and as a panelist at alumni functions. "There wasn't a nicer kid," his track coach said. "He was very outgoing and genuinely popular," added Westminster's headmaster. "He was the guy who broke up fights. He was a healer kind of person."

According to his teachers and classmates, though, the quality that stood out most about Jonah was his good nature, and with it, his ease about being black. W. Thompson Pruitt, who as Westminster's drama coach directed Jonah in such productions as *Guys and Dolls* and *The Mad Woman of Challiot,* and who sometimes gave him rides to New

York, recalled that Jonah frequently talked about the contrast between living in Harlem and going to school in Westminster. In Harlem, Pruitt quoted Jonah as saying, many of his friends "were either involved in drugs or had had some brush with the law," while at Westminster, which was almost all white, "the kids thought nothing about spending a lot of money." "The remarkable thing," said Pruitt, "was that Jonah seemed to be so much at home in both worlds." Jonah's student friends noticed it, too. "In a predominantly white school, some of the black students feel resentment or bitterness, but Jonah wasn't that way at all," said Gretchen Peterson, who shared a mailbox with Jonah and ran on the track team with him. "He was never bitter—he was always laughing about stuff. One day he got all this mail from Yale and Princeton and I joked with him. I said, 'Hey, Jonah, I didn't know you were that smart.' He said, laughing, 'No, I'm just black.'"

Being black did not hurt Jonah with college admissions officers. He applied to Cornell his senior year and, despite a middling academic record, was admitted on full scholarship as a major in electrical engineering. Even that accomplishment, however, was shaded by thoughts of Eddie. "You know why I went to Cornell?" Jonah said to a friend after his brother's death. "Because I knew Eddie would try and do better than me and I wanted to make sure he saw what I did and picked an Ivy League school. Eddie always thought that I was good with girls and a better athlete. But Eddie was better. I always knew that Eddie was smarter than me. Maybe he was just too good for this world to stay alive."

According to family and friends, the rivalry Jonah described had existed since childhood, when the boys had been nicknamed Jealous Jonah and Electrifying Eddie. Whatever the activity, if Jonah did it, Eddie would follow and do it better. If Jonah entered a poetry contest, Eddie would enter it as well, not only writing a better poem ("If I lived in Egypt," one of the stanzas went, "I wouldn't want a lion's face, or anything else to replace my face"), but having it selected for a special exhibition at the Metropolitan Museum of Art. If Jonah took up photography, Eddie would *build* a camera and proceed to take pictures with it that would become part of an exchange with children in upstate New York. If Jonah started a paper route, Eddie would get one with more customers. If Jonah talked of being an engineer, Eddie would

build a model solar house that would win a city commendation. If
Jonah attended a good prep school, Eddie went to the best. If Jonah
squeaked into Cornell, Eddie would get offers all but begging him to
come to Yale and Stanford. On and on it had gone in that way, Eddie
the favored, Eddie the bright, Eddie the talented and promising—Eddie everything that reliable, average Jonah was not, including being his
mother's prize.

It was a humiliating position for any older sibling, particularly one
with Jonah's pride and sensitivity, and on numerous occasions it had
resulted in fights. One of the most serious of them, according to police,
had occurred the previous fall, when in full view of several neighbors,
Jonah had administered a beating to Eddie, then left him on the sidewalk. "They used to be always scrapping with each other," Veronica
told me. "Always fussing and bickering. Between the two of them,
ruckusing all the time, the house was always in an uproar. Once, Eddie
got so mad at Jonah, he punched holes in the bedroom wall. You can
still see where he had to plaster 'em up. I used to wonder why brothers
couldn't get along. My friends said it was natural, just sibling rivalry.
Well, they were rivals all right. What Jonah did, Ed just went out and
did it better. He did the same thing as Jonah, plus something more."

Despite all the friction, the brothers had been close, especially after
Eddie's return from Spain. In conversations with friends, Eddie, who
had taken to wearing Jonah's Westminster jacket his senior year, spoke
frequently and warmly about his brother, who, he said, served as a
model for him. Jonah lauded Eddie, in turn. He once told a friend,
"Agewise, I'm the older one, but, in a lot of ways, it's really Eddie
who is. I'll settle for something. Eddie goes for the best."

In what was to be the final summer of Eddie's life, the brothers had
planned a number of adventures together, including a projected car trip
to California. They were going to be tight that summer, they told
friends, tighter than they had ever been. Then came the night of June
12.

According to a statement Jonah gave police at the hospital, the evening began with the pickup game of basketball on the cement court of
the Wadleigh "pit." Afterward, he and Eddie played a game of cards
on their front stoop, then went inside and downed a wine cooler.
Sometime after nine they walked back downstairs and, Jonah claimed,
went their separate ways. Eddie, who wanted a hamburger, headed

west, toward Morningside Park and a Columbia student hangout called
the College Inn. Jonah himself turned in the opposite direction,
crossed the street, and walked a few doors down to the apartment of his
grandmother. There, he said, he spent an hour or so talking and watching television. Around ten-fifteen, Jonah went on, he left his grandmother's apartment and started off in search of Eddie. As he neared the
base of Morningside Park he heard gunshots. Still unaware of what had
happened, Jonah kept walking, until he encountered a neighborhood
drug dealer named Reese, who informed him that his brother had been
shot by the police and was now at the hospital. A few minutes later,
Jonah himself arrived at St. Luke's.

Such was Jonah's story, and initially the police believed it. "I have
talked to a lot of people over a lot of years," said one of the detectives
who took Jonah's statement, "and I can tell you, this kid was good. If
it had been me in that spot, I would have been shitting in my pants. But
not this kid. This kid was cool. I believed him. Everyone in the room
did." The police began having second thoughts when Jonah, who had
agreed to help them hunt for the mysterious Reese, said that he first
wanted to talk to C. Vernon Mason, and then disappeared from the
hospital. He returned within the hour, but by then the police were
suspicious. "If my brother had just been killed," said one investigating officer, "I would have been doing everything possible to find out
who was involved. And if the cops hadn't helped, I would have been
taking shield numbers and filing civilian complaints. But Jonah didn't
do that." What heightened police suspicions even more was Jonah's
reaction to the announcement of his brother's death. "He was carrying
a radio or something and he started banging it against a wall," one
detective recalled. "Then he started pounding the wall with his fist. He
was yelling and carrying on, and all the while his mother is sitting
there, just devastated. You would think that he would be trying to
console her. But instead he was off into his own trip. It was a weird
reaction, like he was disgusted with himself. Right away, a little light
bulb went on in my head. It was like Peter Falk scratching himself on
Columbo. I said to myself, Wait a minute. Something isn't right."

Within forty-eight hours the cops had reason to believe their hunch
was correct. They had a witness who quoted Jonah as putting himself
at the scene of the crime.

According to police, the witness, whose identity was being kept secret, told them she had been sitting on a West 114th Street stoop with half a dozen friends around ten forty-five on the evening of June 12 when Jonah approached from the direction of St. Luke's. Before anyone could say anything, Jonah allegedly blurted out that he and Eddie had gone to Morningside Drive to rob someone and had "run into some static." "We picked on the wrong guy," Jonah supposedly told the witness. "We got a DT"—street slang for detective. With that, Jonah returned to the hospital and there learned that the static his brother had encountered had been fatal.

For the police, the witness's story was the major break in the case, and three weeks later, having gathered what they claimed was corroborating evidence, they arrived at the Perry apartment with a warrant for Jonah's arrest. On the way to the lockup Jonah appeared calm. One of the officers who accompanied him recalled that he talked about growing tomatoes and going to Cornell.

Since then, Jonah's only public comment about the incident had been to call the charges against him lies and to suggest that everyone connected with the case, including Van Houten, take a polygraph test. Whether or not Jonah himself was telling the truth would ultimately be decided by a jury. In the meantime, many of his friends were prepared to accept his protestations of innocence. Jonah may not have been the smartest person in the world, they said, but he was savvy enough to have spotted a plainclothes cop from a block away. Moreover, Jonah's story of being with his grandmother rang true; his attachment to her was deep and well known. Also suggestive of Jonah's innocence was his behavior since the incident. Apart from the emotional outburst at the hospital and another at his brother's funeral, he had seemed extraordinarily, almost eerily, composed, as if he had nothing either to fear or regret. But the most powerful argument in Jonah's favor was his nature. He was, his friends said, a gentle soul, and not at all the type to be involved in a vicious mugging. If anyone had jumped a police officer, they reasoned, it would have been hotheaded Eddie.

Others were not so sure. It was true, they conceded, that Eddie was more fiery than his sweet-tempered brother, but it was equally true that he was far more shrewd and calculating—too shrewd to have been involved in anything as dangerous and senseless as a mugging. If by some long chance the brothers had done what the police alleged, then

Jonah must have gotten them into it. He was not only the dimmer of the two, and the far more physically powerful, but also the one far more disposed to use force. Eddie talked his way out of tough spots; Jonah bulled his way through.

I wanted very much to talk with Jonah myself but had not been able to discover his whereabouts. Some sources had him returning to Cornell, where his academic career had been a rocky one (according to the detectives who examined his college records, Jonah's grades were mostly C's and D's),* while others placed him in Harlem, where his mother had secured him a summer job at a child-care center. Hoping to find which version was true, I gave his lawyer a call.

Jonah had a new one now, C. Vernon Mason having left the case to pursue his electoral ambitions full-time. His place had been taken by a black associate of William Kunstler named Alton Maddox. Like his mentor, Maddox had a reputation for turning criminal trials into political crusades, and as a result, his selection as Jonah's counsel had not pleased everyone. Indeed, several of Veronica's friends had urged her to drop him, in favor of Jay Topkis, a senior partner in a blue-chip Manhattan firm and one of the most successful trial lawyers in the country. Though Topkis had offered to handle the case gratis, he happened to be white, which disqualified him with Veronica. She explained, "I don't want to make it look like I am turning against my own by bringing in white folks to defend my son."

So Maddox it was going to be—provided he was on hand to try the case. For thanks to the workings of what he called "the racist criminal justice system," Maddox was currently under indictment himself, having been accused of assaulting two court officers. The charges had

---

*Jonah's relatively poor academic performance in college is typical of many black students. According to a study cited in a report by the National Urban League, black college students, as a group, perform at an academic level less than half that of their white counterparts, even when differences in high school grades and SAT scores are taken into account. Partially as a result, 35 percent of the black students who enter college drop out before graduation. Of those who remain, few go on to advanced study. During Jonah's sophomore year at Cornell, for instance, not a single black student was admitted to the graduate programs in the physical sciences. At the University of Illinois, black enrollment in graduate programs dropped 40 percent between 1974 and 1985. Throughout the country, blacks, who account for 12 percent of the population, account for less than 3 percent of those holding doctoral degrees. At Harvard Law School only a few black students have graduated in the top half of their class during the last five years. A national study (Robert Klitgaard's *Choosing Elites*) found that in the late 1970s, black law school admittees had median test scores on the Law School Aptitude Test at the eighth percentile of the overall distribution of test scores among law students.

grown out of an incident that had occurred the previous summer, when Maddox was defending one Willie Bosket, who was on trial for attempting to rob at knife point a seventy-two-year-old blind diabetic. The twenty-one-year-old Bosket was no stranger to courtroom procedures, having by his own admission committed more than two thousand crimes since the age of nine, including two murders, twenty-five attempted murders, and one especially grisly incident in which he cut a man's eyeball out with a knife. On this particular day, Bosket took exception to a court officer's laying a hand on his shoulder as he was being led out of court. A fight ensued, and before it was over, according to court papers, Maddox had leapt onto a court officer's back and hurled his briefcase in the direction of the judge.

Over the phone, Maddox made no mention of his own difficulties, which were soon to come to trial, but dwelt instead on the troubles he was having getting the New York police to tell him anything about Jonah's case. Claiming that he had been subject to "hostility and harassment" and that others in Jonah's neighborhood had been the victims of "intimidation" and "coercion," Maddox said that the police were engaged in "some hanky-panky," by thus far withholding Van Houten's personnel and medical records. This, he hastened to add, did not surprise him. "Basically," he said, "you have an alien population controlling and patrolling these neighborhoods. It's not just this precinct, it's all the precincts in the city. They all have a reputation for widespread brutality." As for what had happened the night of June 12, Maddox claimed not to know. "There may have been some kind of confrontation," he speculated. "Maybe Jonah and Eddie saw this white boy walking along and asked him, 'What are you doing in this neighborhood?' Maybe that happened. Maybe one thing led to another. It can happen in a situation like that, but that is just my suspicion as a black person." He paused. I waited for him to tell me that Jonah was at his grandmother's house, at the soda shop, praying in church, anywhere but the scene of the crime. Instead, Maddox plunged on. "One of the real problems with growing up in a neighborhood like Harlem, then getting removed, and coming back, like Jonah and his brother did, is that you forget how you are supposed to act. You come back and you act a little more assertive than people who grew up in that neighborhood. When you act assertive, it can get you into trouble with the police."

Other than what the police themselves had told me, Maddox's statements were the most damaging testimony against Jonah I had yet heard. If this was the view of the man charged with defending him, I wondered what Jonah had to say for himself. Unfortunately, however, Maddox claimed not to have any idea where his client was.

I was thus back at square one, with no notion how to move off of it. Despairing one night with Karen Emmons, a young reporter who'd been helping me with research, I suggested, half-jokingly, that she give it a crack. Karen, who was nothing if not dogged, did, by calling Jonah's house, in hopes of tracking down the phone number of his grandmother. A male voice answered. "Jonah?" she guessed. It was indeed.

He was not anxious to talk, explaining that he was about to head off to the movies. Karen, who could be as charming as she was persistent, asked to tag along, promising she'd ask nothing about the case. Jonah agreed, and, an hour later, they met on a street corner in Times Square. This is the report Karen brought back:

"In the flesh, Jonah appeared far more pleasant than in his unsmiling newspaper photographs. In fact, he seemed rather boyish, with a warm, engaging smile that puffed up a pair of cherubic cheeks. He was also, I noticed as we bought our theater tickets, heavily into expensive fashion. The shirt he was wearing was silk, the bag he was carrying was leather, by Vila, while his wallet was a number crafted by Louis Vuitton.

"The movie we saw was Michael Cimino's *Year of the Dragon,* an unrelievedly violent police epic with heavy racist overtones. Afterward Jonah complained that it had shown 'too many people dying for no reason.' While watching it, however, he seemed to enjoy himself, laughing uproariously as each Chinese villain was dispatched.

"From the moviehouse we repaired to a nearby Roy Rogers for french fries and hamburgers. As I took my first bite, I looked across the table. Head bowed low, Jonah was saying grace. A moment later he began to talk. His tone was easy, unselfconscious.

Before Eddie went to Spain, we had a rivalry. I did good, he did better. He always took what I did a step farther. But that was Eddie. He always wanted the best—the best prep school, the best college. . . . He was more religious about doing well. He felt the pressure to do well and he accepted the pressure wholeheartedly. It was part of his personality. He would sacrifice more than I did, some wants and needs that I wouldn't. He said to me once, "I know you do a lot of things easily, but you're just coasting. You got a lot of talent. You're just skating across that ice, when you could be driving a Cadillac across it.

Maybe Eddie was right. But I always thought there's a lot more to life than studying and getting A's. Eddie was the type who liked to work for the future. I like to work for today. All I want to do is make it, and make a lot of money. . . .

I got a little bit of a brain, though. I can do all right. And there's some things I always did better than Eddie. Like girls. I was getting into the social scene and clothes and girls when I was eleven. Older girls were always chasing me. Girls fourteen, fifteen, they were always messing with me. Eddie, though, he was fourteen before he got his first girlfriend, and that was only because I got her to be Eddie's girlfriend. The girls Eddie did get were never as good as mine. They were ugly. Stupid, too. . . .

I've always been popular. The kids respected me at Westminster. I'm popular at Cornell, too. They wanted me to join this fraternity, and I thought about it, but I'm not gonna now. I'm too popular. . . . People are looking up to me now, you know. That's what's happened since Eddie's gone. At home, I've always been pretty much the man of the house. There were times my mother would come to me with problems she wouldn't let Eddie know about. She knew I was the man.

Now, though, I gotta do more. Eddie's death is a message to me from God that I gotta work harder than I do. I'm a model now for other people. If I strive, maybe it'll be better for my little cousin. The eyes are on me now. There's a lot of pressure to be good. And I'm gonna be good. I have a chance to make a little money, to give my family a new outlook on life. People are hooked on the idea that there's only one way to live in the ghetto. But I can show them that there's more. That's what I'm gonna do. I got a expression about myself: "I can sell myself for me." And that's what's gonna happen. The change is all on me now. . . . I

want to buy my mother a house, maybe in the suburbs or wherever she wants it. The second thing I'm gonna do is get my father
a cab company. Basically, he's an alcoholic, roaming the streets.
But he has his aspirations, and the biggest is running a cab company. That's what I'm gonna get him. Maybe what I'd do is get
the company in his name, and he would benefit from it, and someone else would run it. Whatever, I'm the man of the house now.
That's what I am.

''Jonah shifted restlessly in his seat. It was obvious he was anxious
to go. A few minutes later we said our goodbyes on the street.

''Short as our meeting was, I came away from it understanding why
people thought Jonah so likable and charming,'' Karen concluded. ''I
also came away feeling that there was much that Jonah Perry knew—
much that he would never, ever say.''

7

JONAH HAD PROMISED KAREN THAT WHEN THINGS SETTLED DOWN, he'd try to find time to talk to me. Whatever the reason, that time never arrived, and I was not to see Jonah myself until months later in a Manhattan courtroom. I regretted not meeting him, not least because there was much I wanted to ask him, including what he and Eddie had thought about prep school.

It was, obviously, a crucial period for both boys, and it had come about largely through the efforts of A Better Chance, one of the minority-assistance programs that had proliferated during the sixties. What I knew of A Better Chance, in turn, came largely from a few conversations with former ABC officials (who said the organization had gone into decline in recent years)* and from an expensively printed ABC press kit, which featured a host of testimonials from successful ABC graduates, all of whom were quoted as saying that ABC had changed their lives. The life I was most interested in, though, was Eddie's, and on that subject, ABC, apart from denouncing the police and proclaiming Eddie "an uncommon child with an uncommonly fertile mind," wasn't saying much, apparently because no one at the organization had

*The decline of A Better Chance in some respects mirrors that of other civil rights organizations founded during the 1960s. According to a number of sources, among them the admissions officers of several leading prep schools, ABC's problems began with the economic recession of 1973. With their donations falling, prep schools began cutting back on minority scholarships and, at the same time, began pressuring ABC to send them better-qualified—and richer—students. At first ABC resisted, fearing (correctly, as it turned out) that moving away from the poorest students would dilute its base of community support. But as the economy continued to worsen, ABC's resolve began to weaken. It crumbled, finally, in 1978, when, after a bitter internal debate, the organization abandoned its poverty criteria altogether. Henceforth, theoretically, anyone could become an ABC candidate, regardless of income or race.

While far from total, the shift away from the ghetto was a profound one strategically, and it had two immediate impacts. One was that the federal Office of Economic Opportunity ceased all funding; the other was that ABC's pool of community volunteers began drying up. Inevitably, the situation also produced discord within ABC. As the dissatisfaction grew, key staff members began leaving, including its president and chief fund-raiser, William Boyd, who resigned in 1981.

Boyd's place was taken by Judith Griffin, who early on decided to shift the fund-raising emphasis away from white-controlled foundations and onto the black middle class. The immediate result was that ABC's financial position greatly worsened. Teetering close to bankruptcy, the known him very well. During my talk with Plummer, however, he mentioned that several years before, when Eddie was in the eighth grade, a young woman had done a film documentary about A Better Chance, in which the Wadleigh program had been featured. Other than remembering that Eddie had been one of the film's stars, and that the woman had herself been an ABC student, Plummer was vague on the details. He did, however, have the woman's name—let's call her Carolyn Jones—and a telephone number for her in Brooklyn. The chance to see Eddie on a television screen—almost alive, as it were—excited me, and though the number was dated, I decided to give it a try.

Luckily, the number was still a good one, and after several days of back-and-forth between telephone-answering machines, Carolyn and I finally got in touch. I explained to her what I was doing, adding that I would like to see her film. Carolyn, however, was guarded. She wanted to know precisely who I was, what my employment history had been, and most important of all, what "line" I was taking on the Perry story. I did my best to reassure her, but Carolyn, who had made the documentary for a film-school course, was not easily convinced and said she would spend several days "checking me out" before deciding whether or not to show me the film. "Look," she explained, "I got

---

organization began slashing programs, including a well-thought-of orientation course, which, under Boyd's administration, had been whittled back from six weeks to two, and was now trimmed down to a day. Also eliminated were the stipends ABC had formerly provided prep schools to help cover the costs of ABC students. The students themselves also felt the pinch. Whereas once they had been visited twice a year by an ABC staff member, what counseling they received now was provided largely by volunteers and letters from the home office. The letters, written by Griffin, had a marked political tone. "Whatever your influence will be on others in the future," one read, "simply by being one of a small number of minority students at your school you have allowed other students the privilege of knowing and interacting with you. . . . You must not lose sight of the richness of your own culture, tradition, history and values. None of us will gain if, in the process of being educated, you forget to distinguish between striving to succeed and merely striving to imitate those around you."

The one area that did not shrink under Griffin's stewardship was accommodations for the ABC staff. New offices were established in Washington, New York, and San Francisco and the national headquarters was moved to a lavish complex overlooking Boston Common. When a white visitor inquired about the reason for the shift, Girffin snapped, "We take pride in our surroundings. We don't want to give our children any impression or feeling of poorness. Our kids deserve what everyone else's children deserve."

Such comments did not sit well with all of ABC's member schools, a number of whom were already unhappy with the quality of students ABC was providing. Over the years, the largest and most prestigious of them, Exeter included, had established their own recruiting networks. Now they began relying on those networks more and more. As they did, ABC became increasingly irrelevant. "It is a sad, sad story," commented a black lawyer who had worked closely with ABC through the years. "There was a time when a lot of us were really enthusiastic about ABC, who saw it as a real vehicle for change. Now that's all gone. The organization is just drifting."

mine. I'm set. But what about all those other Carolyn Joneses coming up out there? I don't want to say anything that will mess it up for them.''

A week passed after that conversation, and I began to worry that I had failed Carolyn's background test. I was disappointed, not only at the prospect of not seeing Eddie on film, but at not talking further to Carolyn. From what she had told me about herself on the phone, her background had been truly horrific, a ghetto version of a Charles Dickens novel, save that this one had a happy ending. That she had survived and was currently enjoying considerable personal and professional success was the result of a number of things, not least of them the chance to go to a well-known New England prep school. Though she made it plain that her experience at school was far from being an entirely happy one, she had, as she put it, "gotten mine," and for that she was grateful. As Carolyn phrased it, "People ask me what I woulda been doing without school. I always tell them, 'Fifteen to life.'"

I wanted to know more about this remarkable young woman, more about the troubles she had had in school, and especially more about how her experience might relate to Eddie's. But I doubted I was going to get that opportunity. Then, just as I was about to give up, Carolyn called and invited me to meet her at her apartment. Apparently, I'd passed her test.

A few days later I drove to the Bedford-Stuyvesant section of Brooklyn, where Carolyn was living in a loft above an abandoned, boarded-up store. I pounded at the door and presently heard the sound of multiple locks being turned and unbolted. Finally the metal door swung open, to reveal a bare wisp of a woman with skin so black it was almost blue. "Hi," she said, flashing an enormous smile. "I'm Carolyn."

Three long flights of stairs later, we reached what could easily have passed for student housing. The place was crammed with books, shelf after shelf of them. There were also a few photographs of Carolyn taken on location, a modest array of Conran's-style furniture, and an oversized, compulsively friendly dog named Bear. As Bear licked whatever of me he could, Carolyn switched on the videocassette recorder and drew up a pair of director's chairs.

"I'm sorry if I seemed suspicious," she apologized, as she pulled a tape down from one of the crowded bookshelves, "but a lot of my life is tied up in this thing." She ran her hand over the cassette, as if caressing it. "There is a lot that I wanted to put in it that I decided to leave out. Some of the stories those kids told, about how it was for them . . ." She paused. "Well, you know how it is for black folks now—everyone looking for an excuse to get them. I didn't want to give them that."

Carolyn inserted the tape and pushed the play button. The machine began to hum.

Whatever footage Carolyn had omitted, her cuts did nothing to detract from the documentary's power. It was an affecting film, filled with stories of promise, struggle, and success. The film's most enduring image, however, was that of a chubby-cheeked black boy, face smiling, bright eyes dancing. "My name is Edmund Perry," he proclaimed. "I attend Wadleigh I.S. 88 Intermediate School. I live at 265 West 114th Street. My age is thirteen and I will be going to Phillips Exeter in the fall. It is located in Exeter, New Hampshire. Since the first or second grade, I told myself that I would be coming to this school. In the third grade, I told myself that I was going to the top fourth-grade class. When I made it to the sixth grade, I told myself I was going to Mr. Plummer's class. When I made it here, I told myself I was going away to school. I don't have any more goals yet, but I'll put some up there pretty soon."

I froze the screen on that image and stared at it a long moment, reflecting how different it was from the pictures I had seen of Eddie taken in his senior year. Those photographs were of a young man who had grown up, a young man who still had his goals but, for reasons I was still trying to discover, no longer smiled.

"Edmund was the crown prince of that class," Carolyn said. "You could tell it, just by the way Mr. Plummer looked at him. He treated them all as equals, but Eddie was first among equals. He was Mr. Plummer's pride and joy, and Eddie knew it." She smiled at the screen and looked back at me. "I'll never forget something that happened that day. The shoot was over and we were packing up our equipment, and I feel someone tugging on me. I look down and it's Eddie. He was so small then, just a little bit of a thing. And he says to me, 'Am I going to be all right up there? Are those white kids going to be picking on me? Are they gonna call me nigger?' He wasn't afraid—you could tell that—he was just curious. And I told him, 'Don't you worry, Edmund. Everything's gonna be fine.' That's the last thing I told him: 'Everything's gonna be fine.'"

Carolyn's comment was the beginning of a conversation that was to stretch out for more than four hours. It was a rambling, frequently emotional talk, touching on Eddie, ABC, her own experiences at prep school, and, time and again, the travails of being young, gifted, and black. This is some of what she had to say:

> When Edmund died, and there was all this criticism, and people were jumping up and down, and ministers were saying, "They gotta stop killing our people," and they were threatening to fly Jesse Jackson in on the next jet, I said to myself, "Wait a minute. I know what's going on. I know exactly what's going on—'cause the same thing happened to me." The only difference is Edmund got shot. . . .
>
> You gotta understand how it is for kids like Edmund and me— how it is for us to grow up in one environment and then be sent off to school in another that is totally different. You gotta understand the kinda things that does to your head. Because if you are like Edmund and you grow up in a place like Harlem, you are taught that you are powerless, and deep down you know you are powerless. But still, it's only a vague notion. You talk about "the man" all the time, but you almost never really see "the man." Then you go off to an elite boarding school, and "the man" is right in front of you. It's one thing to hate something in the abstract, to be aware of some system that is keeping you down. It's quite another to be face to face with that system. You are caught up in a situation where everybody says you should be happy, where you think you should be happy, and instead of being happy, you find there are tears in your eyes because you are so angry. That was one of Edmund's tragedies. He was in an environment where he was constantly being reminded how powerless he really was. . . .
>
> I remember the first night I went to dinner at school. To my

right was an heiress to a cosmetics fortune. To my left was an heiress to a department-store fortune. Across the table from me was an heiress to an oil fortune. And they were all talking about the places they had been, the things they had bought, the vacations they were going to take, as if I wasn't even there. Finally, one of the girls—it was the department-store heiress—tapped me on the elbow and said, "You better be nice to me, because I'm paying for half your scholarship." I almost got sick to my stomach. I didn't say anything, I just got up from the table and walked out. It was two weeks before I could bring myself to go back into the dining hall. What had happened was that I had met "the man" face to face.

It would have been easier for me if they had just come right out and called me nigger. That kind of personal racism you can deal with. Someone calls you nigger and you can smack him in the mouth, and if you are bigger than him, he's gonna know not to call you nigger again. Edmund had dealt with that kind of racism all his life—we all do—but before he went to Exeter, he had never, ever in his life dealt with institutional racism. That was something he couldn't fight against. How do you hit an assumption? How do you tackle history? How do you get your hands on an environment? You can't—you can't even begin to come to grips with it. That's what makes it so insidious and hard to deal with. And the thing is, it's never personal. It's just *there*. . . .

I'm not saying that all white people are evil or racist. I'm not saying that at all. Most white people, at least most of the ones you meet at places like where Edmund and I went to school, are actually quite well-intentioned. They just don't know any better. I remember a white boy in one of my classes. He said, "Blacks don't have to be on welfare. Instead of spending all their welfare checks, all they have to do is invest a little each week." This kid meant it. He wasn't trying to be mean, he was trying to be helpful. I finally had to tell him, "Look, asshole, there ain't no Merrill Lynch office in my neighborhood."

If you're black, you get that kind of stuff all the time—and it's not just in class. There was a faculty member once who gave me a present. Now anyone who knows anything about me knows that the present I like best is a book. But that's not what this faculty member gave me. Oh, no. What he gave me was a very sexy dress, off the shoulder, slit up the front. Like the white boy, he was trying to be nice. I wonder, though, how he would have felt if someone had given his daughter a dress like that. I guess he just thought that anyone from a quote-unquote deprived background has gotta know about sex. *You know those niggers—they just love to fuck.*

The first few times something like that happens to you, you think it's your fault, that you are sending out some kind of strange signals that people are picking up on. But as it keeps going on— and it does keep going on—you finally realize that you personally have nothing to do with it, that you are being treated in a certain way simply because you are black. And the thing is, it's constant; there is no way to get away from it. Because if you do something like close the door to your room, people will start saying, "Is she being angry? Is she being militant?" You can't even afford to be moody. A white girl can look spacey and people will say, "Oh, she's being creative." But if you walk around campus with anything but a big smile on your face, they'll wonder, "Why is she being hostile?" You always have the sense of being examined. When your mama works for 'em, works for 'em, she can at least go home at night. But when you're at prep school, you're always on—like a twenty-four-hour-a-day cultural attraction. . . .

Kids would always be asking me about my hair. *"How do you keep it up? What happens when it gets wet? Can I touch it?"* It never dawned on them that I found these questions offensive. Why would it? If you are a kid born with a silver spoon in your mouth and grew up on a big estate with servants, then no one has ever said no to you in your life. That's the problem with the white wealthy in this country: they don't know any limits. If you are black, you are there for their pleasure. To provide them with *"an experience."* Sometimes I think that that's how these scholarships are sold to white parents. *By God, their kids are going to be well-rounded. They're going to have Rossignol skis and Lange boots and a black roommate for "an experience."*

If you're smart, you learn to go along with it. In the beginning I wasn't smart. The first week I was at school, a kid I had never met in my life walked up to me and said it was my fault she almost didn't come back to school, because black kids were taking all the scholarships. I slammed her against the wall. For a week no one would talk to me. What I had done was violate the code, the unspoken law that says that everything is fair so long as it is done in the right tone of voice, with the proper English and absolutely no sign of emotion. I caught on quick, though. The next time I had an altercation with a kid I became quite preppy and just walked away. I had learned that I couldn't threaten to kick her ass and kill her mama. That doesn't play too well with the country-club set.

What's even harder than going to one of these schools, though, is coming home from one. After you've been in that pressure cooker, all you want to do is be alone and have some time to clear your head and figure out what it all means. But you never get that time. Because there will always be someone saying they want you to come over to the Baptist Church on Sunday or the Boys Club on Thursday and give an inspirational speech to the young people. You do it, because you have to do it. Because you are *expected* to do it. Because you are a symbol for the neighborhood.

The trouble is, you really aren't a part of that neighborhood anymore. After you see the kind of wealth that Eddie saw at Exeter or that I saw at my school, you know that there is more to life than hanging out on street corners, having babies, and getting welfare checks. You've been living in an entirely different world. Instead of jiving down on the street corner, you've been getting turned on to Nietzsche and Thoreau. Still, you gotta fit in with your friends. How do you do it? I'll tell you how you do it. You gotta snort more coke, smoke more reefer, shoot more baskets, and give up more poontang. You've got a week to prove you are black, before you're on that bus Monday morning, heading back for class.

A place like Exeter can't help you make that transition. Exeter is there to teach you mathematics and English and how to be a leader. It doesn't teach you anything about being black. It teaches you just the opposite. It teaches you that you are omnipotent—

and for a black kid, that can be dangerous. Because it's one thing to stroll across campus with your head held high, the way leaders are supposed to, and it's quite another to walk down 114th Street that way. You are sending out a totally different signal. What I am saying is that the kind of behavior that can get you elected student-body president at Exeter can get you shot in Harlem.

So those are the kinds of problems that Edmund had to deal with. I don't know whether he was able to deal with them or not. But if he did, he did it by himself. Because that's how it is when you are from Eddie's neighborhood. When you come into the street, you don't say, "Let me share with you what I am feeling today. Let me tell you how your behavior is affecting me today." If you're black and male, you are supposed to be strong. You're not supposed to need any help. It's a screwed-up system, but at least you know where you stand. . . .

When you go away to one of these schools, though, you are always getting double messages. One message is "I want you to talk to me and tell me everything that is going on," while the other message is "Don't tell me anything that will freak me out, because I will have to deal with it." You end up being caught between a rock and a hard place. If you go to people and tell them the truth, which is that you are going to bed every night thinking of slashing your wrists, that's bad form, that's embarrassing the school, that's going to cause hard feelings. And if you are black, that is the last thing in the world you want to do. You know that you are there on scholarship, which means that you are there on probation. Scholarships are renewed every year, and you may not be invited back. So are you going to say anything that will rock the boat? You bet your ass you won't. . . .

Basically, black kids aren't supposed to have problems, and if they do, they aren't supposed to talk about them. Instead, they are supposed to be good little niggers, sit there and be grateful. So they suffer in silence. Or they talk to other black kids. When I was at school, a black girl dropped out semester break of her senior year. She had been playing surrogate mother for all the other black students. That wasn't her job—her job was to get an education—but that's what she had been doing, and finally she just got overwhelmed.

I'm sure Eddie was overwhelmed, too. I'm also sure he didn't talk to anybody. How could he? He was supposed to be a race-horse. He was supposed to be an Exeter *man*. But there were clues to how he was feeling. All you had to do was take a look at his face. But did anyone at Exeter do anything? They did not. And you want to know why they didn't? Because *that* would be racist.

Liberals are so hung up trying not to be racist that they are always missing the basic point, which is, yes, blacks are different, but, no, you don't have to take care of them. Conservatives, at least, are more up-front about everything. They operate under the premise that you *can't* do it. Then you can lean back and say, "Wanna bet?" And if you do do it, you get their grudging respect. But that ain't the way it is with liberals. They never say you can't do it. They say, "*You* don't have to do it. *We'll* do it for you." That's the way it is in society, and that's the way it is in these schools. They don't expect you to keep up academically. They just expect you to tread water and hold your own. Black kids aren't stupid—if they were stupid, they wouldn't be in these schools in the first place—they know what's going on and they know it's racist. But after a while they begin to believe it, and after that happens, liberals really do have to take care of them, because they have forgotten how to take care of themselves. . . .

Maybe, deep down, white people don't want to see what we can do for ourselves, because then we would be competing with them. Maybe that scares them. I don't know what's going on in white people's heads; I got enough trouble figuring out what's going on in my own head. Somewhere along the line, though, the system has gotta get fixed. I'm not saying we have to throw out the baby with the bathwater—get rid of ABC and the scholarships. Hell no! But I do think we have to sit down and examine the premise of what we have been doing. The way it is now, ABC basically sends black kids to wherever there is a slot. It's a racist assumption: if they are black, they can adapt. What works for one black kid will work for all black kids, because there is no diversity within the black community. Well, maybe Eddie would have had a better time of it if he had gone to a school in Connecticut, so he could come home on weekends. Or maybe he would have done better if he had been in a situation where he could have gone to school six months and worked six months. Or maybe he would have been fine if he had been in a school that would have allowed him to channel some of his rage into community service. Maybe nothing would have worked. The point is, those questions were never asked. Nobody ever wondered about his individual needs. He was a person who was being used by a whole bunch of people, black and white.

So am I surprised by what happened to Edmund? No, I am not surprised. The only thing that surprises me is that something like this didn't happen sooner. You teach people to be schizophrenic, and they will become schizophrenic. You keep treating them in a way that encourages them to act out, and they will act out. You give people the kind of information Edmund got, over and over and over, and they become the expectations you have for them. That cop had nothing to do with what happened to Edmund. That poor litle schmuck was just the representation of the people who had been controlling the strings on him all his life. Of course he went crazy. He had to go crazy. That's what they had taught him, wasn't it?

I said nothing, only looked at the screen, where the image of Eddie Perry was still staring out at me. A moment later I thanked Carolyn for her time and what she had told me.

On the streets, darkness was beginning to gather. I walked the few blocks to my car quickly, uneasy about being a white man in Bedford-Stuyvesant at night, and uneasy, too, about what I had heard. It was a depressing assessment, far more depressing than I had expected—or wanted—to hear. Carolyn, however, had been all too convincing. As I drove the hundred miles to the security of Eastern Long Island, one thing she had said in particular kept turning over in my mind. It was the contents of a dream Carolyn said she had been having ever since prep school. In it, Carolyn is lined up with a number of whites for the start of a race. The whites are ready to run, but Carolyn is having trouble getting ready. The coach approaches, demanding to know the problem. "Can't you see?" Carolyn tells him. "I only have one leg." "You people are always lying," the coach snarls. "Get into line." Carolyn does, the gun goes off, and miraculously, she wins the race. "I won! I won!" she exults. "You can't have won," the coach says. "You only have one leg."

8

IT IS AN EXETER TRADITION THAT, BEFORE GRADUATION, SENIORS may take a page in the Academy yearbook to sum up what the last four years have meant to them. For the about-to-become alumni, it is a chance for a final say, an opportunity to tell others who might one day read it, "Yes, this is how it was."

In 1985 there were dozens of such pages in the *Pean,* as the Exeter yearbook is called, filled up with scores of pictures and hundreds of recollections. Some students left lyrics of songs; others, stanzas of poetry; still others, personal good-byes to friends and thanks to the moms and dads who had made it all possible. Then there was page 195, Eddie Perry's page.

It featured three pictures of Eddie: one, togged out in a running suit, looking pensive; another, leaping exuberantly into the air with a black classmate; the last, in an Exeter football uniform, left index finger pointed skyward, signifying "We're Number One."

The page also had four quotations.

One was taken from the lyrics of a song by the black "rapper" Melle Mel:

> You search for justice, and what do you find?
> You find just us on the unemployment line . . .
> You find just us sweatin' from dawn to dust.
> There's no Justice, there's Just Us . . .

Another was drawn from Martin Luther King's "I Have a Dream" speech:

> I have a dream that my four little children will one day live in a
> nation where they will not be judged by the color of their skin, but
> by the content of their character.

The third was a thank-you to his mother.
Finally, Eddie addressed Exeter:

Good-bye Exeter, you taught and showed me many things . . .
God bless you for that. Some things I saw I did not like, and some
things I learned I'd rather not know. Nevertheless, it had to be
done because I could never learn not to learn. It's a pity we part
on less than a friendly basis, but we do. . . . Work to adjust
yourself in a changing world, as will I.

ME (Eddie Perry)

During the weeks I spent in Harlem, I looked at that page a number
of times, puzzling over the meaning of it. Apart from a handful of
interviews and the scattered recollections of a few classmates and
teachers who had been quoted in the clips, it was the only solid indica-
tion I had about Eddie's time at Exeter, and sad to say, it didn't tell me
much. The yearbook quotes made it apparent, however, that all had
not gone well for Eddie at school and suggested that, possibly, there
had been racial trouble. The specifics, though, were missing. What
were the things Eddie had seen he hadn't liked? What had he learned
he'd rather not have known? Why was it, finally, that he had left what
by all accounts was the educational opportunity of a lifetime on "less
than a friendly basis"?

No one I had talked to thus far, including Carolyn Jones, had provided a completely satisfactory answer to those questions. I was hoping that Exeter would.

Which was why, not long after my talk with Carolyn, I went to a
midtown Manhattan law office, where, open on the coffee table in
front of me, was the same yearbook I had looked at so often. This
particular copy belonged to the office's occupant, a graduate of the
Exeter class of '44 named Michael Forrestal.

Mike Forrestal was president of the Exeter board of trustees and, as
witnessed by the photographs of the great and powerful that adorned
his office, a most distinguished personage. His father, James Forrestal,
had been Franklin Roosevelt's secretary of the navy and, until he
hurled himself from an upper story of the Bethesda Naval Hospital in
1949, Harry Truman's secretary of defense. According to the listing in

Who's Who, Michael himself had had a glittering career. After graduation from Exeter and Princeton he was commissioned a naval officer
and dispatched to occupied Berlin, where he was an aide to the Supreme European Command's tripartite naval commission. He was then
posted to Moscow as an assistant naval attaché. When that stint was
complete, he spent two years at Averell Harriman's side, helping to
draw up the Marshall Plan, before returning to the States and law
school at Harvard. In the years since, Forrestal had divided his time
between lawyering and government service, including three years as a
senior member of the White House National Security Staff during the
administrations of John F. Kennedy and Lyndon Johnson. His bene-
factions were numerous—in addition to being an Exeter trustee, he
had been chairman of the Metropolitan Opera Guild; a member of the
board of directors of the Metropolitan Opera Association and of the
National Opera Institute; executive secretary of the advisory commit-
tee of the Kennedy Institute of Politics at Harvard; a trustee of the
Institute of Advanced Studies at Princeton—and so were his mem-
berships and clubs: Foreign Relations, Racquet and Tennis, Links, the
Metropolitan in Washington, Travellers in Paris. Low-key in manner,
unpretentious in style, Michael Vincent Forrestal was in many respects
the embodiment of the Exeter ideal.

As I gazed about his office, Forrestal was finishing up a consoling
phone call with Sally Rockefeller. Someone close to Ms. Rockefeller—I wasn't able to gather who—had recently been hospitalized, the
result of being thrown from his horse during a fox hunt. In the gentlest
of tones, Forrestal was doing his best to assuage Sally's concern.
"There, there," he soothed. "Everything will be fine. Don't you
worry about a thing. Feel better? Great. Talk to you soon. Much love.
Bye now."

Forrestal replaced the receiver and flashed a satisfied smile; the reas-
surance had apparently worked. Crossing the office, he gave my hand
a hearty shake and settled in a chair beneath a photograph of himself in
smiling conversation with a former Soviet premier. Coffee was signaled for. It arrived a moment later, in bone-china cups. Forrestal
stirred at it with a silver spoon and stretched himself out. Over his
shoulder, through his corner office window, I could just make out
Harlem, shimmering in the distant haze. I asked Mr. Forrestal how he

had heard of Eddie's death. "A fellow called early the next morning," he answered, in a perfect mid-Atlantic accent.

Actually, it must have been the middle of the night, because as I remember, the call got me out of bed. His name was Miller . . . Marshall . . . Mason—yes, Mason, that's it—and he said he was an attorney, representing the family. He told me he wanted the Academy to pay for the costs of the funeral. He also wanted the Academy to bring to New York any of the students who wanted to go to the funeral. And he wanted us to bring pressure on the mayor. There was some talk about lawsuits. He was quite exercised about the whole thing. Anyway, I put him off.

I hadn't known the boy, of course, but my reaction, I guess, was the same as anyone's in the city. Shock. I thought to myself, "Here we go again. The police have really mucked it up this time." I assumed it was a grotesque accident.

When I called Steve [Kurtz, the Exeter principal], though, I was sort of surprised by the reaction. It was not the kind of violent outrage that one would expect from a New England liberal community. They were stunned, yes, but also strangely passive. It got me to wondering what this boy had been all about.

A few days later Steve and I went to the funeral, and I must say, I have never experienced anything quite like it. It was a community event almost, rather than a private memorial service. There was a big crowd, everyone was jammed in—you had to elbow your way into the church—and I remember it was very hot. I remember, too, that it was very quiet. Outside there seemed to be as many people as there were inside. I expected the police to be out en masse, but there were only four or five officers and they were very unobtrusive. They handled themselves, I thought, quite well.

There was a restrained political aura to the service. Most of the eulogies were by public figures of one sort or another, but they only really edged on the problem of blacks and white police. The minister himself was very eloquent. A Williams man, you say he is? It doesn't surprise me. He certainly was up on his classics and his Bible.

It was uncomfortable to be a white man in that crowd. There was nothing overt—everyone was very well-dressed, as I recall—just a stoniness on people's faces.

Forrestal sipped at his coffee. He appeared to be reflecting on what to say next, the way of putting it, the advisability of saying it. Finally, he spoke.

Steve, you know, has been really rocked by this. A lot of people at the Academy have. But I wouldn't want to change any of our admissions policies because of what's happened. This was an awful, freakish accident, but it doesn't call for us giving up. It might call for a little more care. But do we still want to have blacks? Of course we want to have them. The idea has been and, I think, will continue to be that when you have a group that represents eighteen percent of the population—and I am talking now of both blacks and Hispanics—then they ought to be represented at Exeter. We're not like Scarsdale High or St. Paul's—not that there is anything particularly wrong with either Scarsdale or St. Paul's. It's just that we try to be different. We make a conscious effort at representing a much deeper cross section. . . .

It's always been hard with blacks; they don't come to the school easily. In fact, when I was going to school there weren't any blacks at all. But during the nineteen sixties there was a very powerful effort made to recruit them. I know a couple of them from that era, and I'm afraid they have had a terrible time coming back to the real world.

So we know that they have problems, very special problems. But they aren't the only ones under pressure. We've had suicides there, too. The whole place has gotten too artificially competitive. Too corporate. It's different than it was in my day. There is all this drive to succeed, and there is no real safety valve.

Forrestal peered into his coffee cup; a faint frown crossed his face. "Something," he said, "must be done about that."

We talked a few minutes more, exchanging tidbits of campus gossip, until Forrestal's secretary stuck her head through the door and gave her eyebrows a meaningful arch. In the corridor Mr. Forrestal once again pumped my hand, wished me luck in my investigations, and then, in one of those ironic understatements that is a hallmark of an Exeter education, said, "You know, this is not the sort of thing that is supposed to happen to an Exeter man."

Indeed it was not, and, as I would soon discover, Michael Forrestal was not the only Exonian who was mystified—or distressed—that it had. The entire "Exeter family" appeared to be lying low on the subject of Eddie Perry, saying little about him and even less about the circumstances of his death, except that it was all a terrible, inexplicable tragedy. One could sympathize with their shock, as well as their reticence. Having an alumnus gunned down while allegedly in the act of commiting a street crime—it would be an embarrassment for any alma mater, especially one so "different," as Michael Forrestal put it, as Phillips Exeter.

It was hard, even for Exonians, to put into words exactly what that difference was. The Academy's long and storied history no doubt accounted for some of it, though only some, since other schools possessed equally legended pasts, and one, arch-rival Andover, was three years older. The roster of Exeter graduates, which through the years had included men as diverse as Frank Stella, Dwight MacDonald, and the Gettys, *fils et petit-fils,* was also cause for pride—not to mention a goodly share of the Academy's $125 million endowment—but other schools, too, had their distinguished alumni, and though Exonians would be loath to admit it, some—Groton and Hotchkiss come to mind—were even more impressive. The Academy's physical plant, which sprawled across 880 lushly landscaped acres, and included—in addition to twenty-three tennis courts, ten baseball diamonds, assorted track, crew, and lacrosse facilities, and a football stadium seating six thousand—forty major buildings, among them a Lewis Kahn–designed library with room for 250,000 volumes; an art gallery; a theater; a state-of-the-art science center; a music center; a well-equipped hospital; a cavernous indoor track facility, and a gymnasium housing two 25-meter swimming pools, two hockey rinks, twelve squash courts, and three full-length basketball courts, was a marvel, as well, but even that could be matched elsewere. Princeton, for instance, was said to be nearly as nice.

Harder to duplicate, surely, was the Exeter's superb 123-member faculty; its college-level curricula (besides the basics, there were courses such as Cultural History of Central and South America, Ornithology, Electromagnetism and Field Physics, Advanced Filmmaking, the Florentine Renaissance, Multivariable Calculus, and half a dozen foreign languages, among them Russian and Chinese); its seminar style of teaching, and, not least, its student body—980 boys and girls, drawn, in Eddie's senior year, from forty-four states and twenty-four foreign countries, and possessing, it was said, the highest average SAT scores and the largest number of National Merit Scholars of any student body in the country.

Daunting as all of this was—and even Exonians professed to be a little awed by the place—the Exeter difference could not be explained simply in terms of history, bricks and mortar. Rather, it was an attitude, an unspoken assurance, a sure knowledge that Exeter was the best and that being the best, those who partook of it were not only more fortunate, not only brighter and more blessed, but somehow, in some way, forever marked and protected.

To understand how all this came to be, one has to go back some, back all the way to the third day of April, the year of Our Lord 1781. On that date, at a site fifty miles north of Boston and ten miles west of the New Hampshire port of Little Boar's Head, in the town of Exeter, county of Rockingham, a Calvinist minister's son named John Phillips established what he described as "an Academy . . . for the purpose of promoting piety & virtue and education of Youth."

The original Academy was a modest affair, no more than a single wood-frame building, a lone headmaster, and an initial enrollment of forty boys. But Phillips, a Harvard man who had tried his hand at teaching and the ministry before making his fortune as a banker and land speculator, had considerable ambitions for it. Not only would his fledgling school instruct youth "in the English and Latin grammar, writing, arithmetic and those sciences wherein they were commonly taught," he wrote in his bequest, "but more especially to learn them the *great end* and *real business* of living."

Phillips, who knew a thing or two about education (with a cousin, he had already founded another prep school, in neighboring Massachusetts, that eventually came to be known after the hamlet of its location, namely, Andover), and who confessed to a "painful anxiety" about "the growing neglect of youth," had very definite notions how this was to come about. Instructors, he decreed, were to "frequently delineate . . . the deformity and odiousness of vice, and the beauty and amiableness of virtue." They were also to "spare no pains" to convince students "of their numberless and indispensable obligations"— and if their pupils didn't get the message, "bring them under such discipline as may tend most effectively to promote their own satisfaction and the happiness of others." But above all, Phillips went on, in a passage that was to become the Exeter credo, "it is expected that the attention of instructors to the *disposition* of the minds and morals of the youth under their charge will *exceed every other care;* well considering that though goodness without knowledge is weak and feeble, yet knowledge without goodness is dangerous, and that both united form the noblest character, and lay the surest foundation of usefulness to mankind."*

For all of John Phillips's high-mindedness, Exeter's first one hundred years were not especially notable. The Academy had its fair share of distinguished graduates, such as Daniel Webster, Lewis Cass, and Leverett Saltonstall, but also its fair share of disasters. Fires and fiscal mismanagement were constant plagues, and with few exceptions, headmasters were hardly sterling. Matters began to improve toward the end of the nineteenth century, when the likes of Booth Tarkington, Amos Alonzo Stagg, and Morgan Bank heir Thomas Lamont were schoolboys; and by the advent of what was then called the "Great War," Exeter was showing signs of living up to the inscription etched in granite above the Academy Building door: *Huc venite pueri ut viri sitis*—"Come hither, boys, that ye may become men."

---

*According to contemporary accounts, Phillips was a man who practiced what he preached. One writer of the time described him as "a vigorous old Puritan . . . simple in his habits and far-seeing in his plans," while a governor of New Hampshire commended him for being "of a liberal spirit," as witnessed by his willingness not to "decline fellowship with Christians of a different creed." "He had a strong aversion to everything that had the appearance of splendor, pomp and parade," the governor added, "always preferring the useful to the showy." There were less flattering assessments of Phillips—one of his neighbors recalled that he would "not give a boy a cherry from his trees unless the favor were asked with a low bow and the most reverent tone" and that "the failure of a little girl to make her accustomed curtsey on meeting him in the street would overshadow his face with a frown, which hours of sunlight could not dissipate"—but on his shrewdness there was general agreement. He was known, for instance, to have disapproved of the recently completed American Revolution, but according to the governor, he was "solicitous" about keeping such opposition to himself, "and studiously avoided conversation upon the subject, and, as far as he was able, anything related to it." Phillips's discretion was well-advised, as at the time, more outspoken Tories were being conveyed from New Hampshire riding atop a rail.

The process by which that transformation was accomplished was, then as now, a ferociously difficult one, and Exeter made no bones about expecting its students to produce. "The Phillips Exeter Academy insists first of all on honest labor," a turn-of-the-century headmaster wrote. "Every boy, high or low, rich or poor, must show actual performance. Not to learn one's lesson is a breach of trust. It is believed that the ordinary boy between fourteen and nineteen years old is well able to do hard work and is the better for it."

Hard work there was—harder, Exeter boasted and its students agreed, than at any other school in the country. "We went at it without limit," recalled China scholar John King Fairbank, a graduate of the class of '25, "and I, for one, have been coasting ever since." But despite its triumphs—and, later, a graduate of the class of '31 named Richard Salant would credit it for making him president of CBS News—the Exeter method of instruction was no different from that of any other prep school, a few of which had achieved even more distinction. Then, on a memorable evening in 1929, Exeter's principal, Lewis Perry, went to a Broadway play with New York philanthropist Edward S. Harkness. As they were standing on the curb, trying to hail a taxi, Harkness, whose endowments had already created the "house system" at Harvard and the "college system" at Yale, turned to Perry and said, "Lewis, I want to do for Exeter what I have done for Harvard and Yale, and if you will get up a scheme, I'll give you all the money you need to put it into operation." Harkness had only one condition: that the scheme Perry devised be unlike any other.

After a year of study and a number of proposals, Perry finally devised a plan: the creation of a seven-by-eleven-foot oval table—the Harkness Table, it came to be called—around which would sit no more than a dozen boys, who would learn their lessons not by rote but through argument, discussion, and interchange.

It was a radical proposal, and to put it into operation, Exeter would have to cut class size by two thirds and more than double the faculty. New classroom buildings would be necessary, new dormitories, new facilities of every kind. When the bill for everything was totaled, it came to five million dollars. Harkness was happy to pay. With the new method of teaching, he wrote to Perry, "the whole educational system in our secondary schools [will] not only be changed, but changed enormously for the better."

The Harkness Plan failed to spark the revolution its benefactor had predicted, but it changed Exeter forever. Teachers loved it; educators poured in from around the country to study and marvel over it. But the biggest raves came from students, like Arthur Schlesinger, who attended Exeter in the early thirties. "We sat around tables and talked back to masters," the Kennedy historian said decades later. "Education became not a performance, but a process. . . . So far as the training of the mind was concerned, Exeter could hardly have been more effective for me."

Exeter's unique style of teaching still had that effect on students fifty years later. One could drop into an Exeter class, as presidential education commissions were wont to do, and find not a roomful of unruly adolescents but a small band of intent young scholars, decked out in the required coat and tie, thrashing through the meaning of, say, Anouilh's *Becket,* or critiquing, sometimes viciously, a classmate's essay on the campaigns of Peter the Great. Seated at the head of the table, a teacher, who often as not held a doctorate in his field, would occasionally offer comments or ask questions. As the discussion picked up, his presence would seem increasingly irrelevant. Now and again he might even leave the class, not be missed until the bell had rung.*

Remarkable as the Harkness Table was—and every year, a third of the seniors who sat around it went on to Harvard, Princeton, and Yale—it was not without its drawbacks. It encouraged conflict, put a premium on verbal skills, and, in the end, produced students who tended to be a little glib, if not a little arrogant. Novelist John Irving, a "faculty brat" graduate of the class of 1961, noted the latter characteristic in *The World According to Garp,* a book set largely at what he slyly calls the Steering School. "Everyone got the picture," Irving writes. "Not only were certain kinds of arrogance tolerated by the

---

*Outsiders who witnessed such performances were invariably amazed. One public high school teacher, who spent three days at Exeter, picking up pointers for his students back in Maine, later reported an incident that astonished him. "I was passing between classes," he wrote. "Two students were walking behind me, 'preps,' probably, the Exeter term for freshmen. I slowed my pace, curious to hear an unguarded conversation. *They were talking about Pericles.* (No kidding.) Obviously, they had just walked out of a history class and they were wondering, rather heatedly, if Pericles' heroism would have stood up to the battlefront. And then another strange thing happened: one kid answered the other with a quotation from Shakespeare—the one about cowards dying a thousand deaths (I had to look it up). Finally, when one fourteen-year-old said, 'Let's drop it; history is boring,' his partner replied, 'No, it's not. I find it really interesting!'"

society of the Steering School, certain kinds were encouraged; but acceptable arrogance was a matter of taste and style. *What* you were arrogant about had to appear worthy—of higher purpose—and the manner in which you were arrogant was supposed to be charming.''

On the whole, Exeter students were charming; it was one of the things that set them apart from other teenagers, and the Academy's adults worked hard at maintaining the difference. Over and over again they pounded it into their charges' heads that they were not like others their age, and that because they weren't, more was expected of them. Not only more work (at Exeter, five hours of homework per night was the norm), not only harder play (all students were *required* to play a sport every season), but more responsibility—to themselves, to their school, to their family and country.

The experience was intense—''like a war,'' said one graduate; ''after you come back to the real world, nothing else is quite as interesting''—and it could be intimidating as well. ''When you are sitting around a table,'' said a forties-era scholarship student from Cleveland, ''and the kids sitting with you have names like Dulles, Rockefeller, and Lamont, and you're discussing a public policy question, and you begin to hear them use the word 'we,' as in '*We* are going to do such and such,' you begin to realize what this place is all about. They aren't just going through lessons. They're debating how they are going to run the world.''

There were, in fact, such students at Exeter, and seriously or not, such discussions did go on. But despite the rooms stocked with personal computers and stereo systems, the holidays spent skiing in Gstaad and sunning at Newport, Exeter was not only for the rich and famous. In writing the Academy's charter, John Phillips had stipulated that the yearly interest from his endowment was to be set aside for ''the charitable purpose of paying the board of poor scholars, whose talents and character entitle them to publick patronage, while they are preparing for college.'' Over the years, Exeter attracted those ''poor scholars'' from literally every state in the union. ''Exeter is a national and democratic institution,'' the Academy catalogue boasted. ''It is our goal to maintain this democratic diversity as one of the most effective ways of teaching tolerance and respect for what a person is and what he does rather than for what he has been given.'' What the catalogue didn't mention was that until the 1960s, virtually all of this "democratic diversity" derived from "poor scholars" who were white.

The inability to attract black students was a problem that existed at all prep schools, and over the years Exeter had tried numerous ways to correct it. None of them, however, had met with any notable success—nor had the lack of it occasioned any notable worry. But with the civil rights movement coming to a boil, concern over Exeter's "whiteness" began to increase, fed in part by the publication of an enormously influential book by former Harvard president James B. Conant.

Titled *Slums and Suburbs,* Conant's book catalogued the horrors of inner-city schools such as Wadleigh, contrasting them vividly with those that served affluent suburban whites. According to Conant, money alone could not correct the disparity, since money alone was not at the root of it. Rather, said Conant, the problem lay with "the status and ambition of the families being served." Upper-middle-class white families had both, and surrounded by it, their children learned. Poor blacks had neither—at least not in sufficient supply—hence their children didn't. The solution, Conant seemed to suggest, was to take the latter and put them under the care and tutelage of the former.

It was a controversial (and according to its critics, racist) message, but, in the climate of the times, it found a wide and receptive audience, particularly among prep school headmasters. In 1963, twenty-three of them, Exeter's principal included, met in Boston to create an organization for the specific purpose of luring talented minority youngsters to their schools. They called it, A Better Chance, ABC for short.

With a network of volunteer recruiters strung out across the country, funding from foundations and the federal government, and a splashy advertising campaign ("Which future would you rather he have?" asked the headline of one ad, which showed two pictures of a young black man: one, in prison garb, behind bars; the other, in pinstripes, behind a desk), ABC drew in thousands of applicants and by the early 1970s was placing hundreds of black students in prep school every year. There were some well-publicized failures along the way (in one case, an ABC honors graduate was arrested during the course of an armed robbery), and more than a quarter of the ABC students who entered prep school withdrew before graduating, but they were overshadowed by the success stories of those who had made it. "ABC was an idea that cut across racial, political, and class lines," said William Boyd, ABC's former president. "It wasn't like a program that gave a thousand dollars to some unemployed person and hoped for the best. We were dealing with the best; the results were almost guaranteed. Everyone loved it. It sold like hot pancakes."

At few places did it sell better than at Exeter, where by 1973, the high-water mark for minority admissions, there were more than eighty blacks and Hispanics on campus—nearly a tenth of the student body.

Just as quickly, however, that figure began to recede, driven back by the pressures of the recession and the internal disarray at ABC. The small number of blacks who remained at the Academy were, as one black instructor put it, "almost invisible, like ghosts."

But in 1980, Eddie's last year at Wadleigh, two circumstances combined to begin to reverse the downward trend. The first was a pick-up in the economy, which fattened Exeter's endowment and made possible an increase in scholarship money. The other was the appointment of John David Herney as Exeter's director of admissions.

A native of a small town in upstate New York, Herney had attended prep school himself on scholarship and was eager to make the same opportunity available to increasing numbers of minority students. Exeter's trustees had agreed with his arguments, and with their blessing—and a fresh infusion of scholarship cash—Herney set off on his first recruiting trip. His first stop was Wadleigh Junior High; the first applicant he talked to was Eddie Perry.

My own acquaintance with Herney dated from several years earlier, when I brought my son to his office, seeking admission and financial aid. Both were granted, and I had had warm feelings about him ever since. When I called him at Exeter, however, and said I wanted to talk to him about Eddie, there was an unmistakable hesitation in his voice. Finally, though, Herney consented, and the next day I made the long drive up to New Hampshire.

I found him at his office in the admissions building, a white clapboard structure that had been erected a decade or two before the American Revolution. Herney was togged out in his usual L. L. Bean uniform: horn-rimmed glasses, rep tie, chinos, and black tassled loafers.

With Eddie in mind, I began by asking how Exeter went about selecting black students, who, I had already been informed, scored, on average, 40 percentile points lower than their white counterparts.* Herney smiled, as if guessing where I was heading. "You really can't trust the SSATs where minority kids are concerned," he answered.

A lot of people have been saying for a long time that the tests are culturally biased. And the fact is that not all failures have low SSATs and not all successes have high SSATs. If a kid is from a background where the family does a lot of reading at home, and he gets a low SSAT, then that is a bad sign. But if that isn't the case, the SSAT doesn't mean much. In Harlem, a thirty-fifth percentile verbal score on the SSAT means nothing.

With a kid from a place like Harlem, you have to go more by

---

*The consistently poor performance of blacks on such standardized tests as the pre–high school SSAT (Secondary School Aptitude Test), and its college-entry counterpart, the SAT (Scholastic Aptitude Test), is not a phenomenon confined to Exeter. It is, as researchers like Charles Murray and Glenn C. Loury have documented, a national problem, affecting all sectors of the black population, whatever their background or educational plans. In 1980, for instance, the average SAT score for blacks was 330 on the verbal test (the SAT scoring range is 200 to 800) and 360 on the math test—more than 100 points lower on each test than the average score for whites. Moreover, more than 70 percent of the black test-takers scored less than 400, generally agreed to be the cut-off point for ability to handle college-level work. The same year an even greater disparity showed up in the Defense Department's Armed Forces Qualification Test (AFQT). On that examination, the average white score was 2.3 *times* that of the average black score. Likewise, there was a wide gap in the results of the 1981 Graduate Record Exam (GRE), a test that is taken by virtually all college seniors seeking to pursue advanced studies in the humanities and the sciences. Here, the average black score on the mathematics component of the test was 171 points lower than the average score of whites. While economic deprivation explains some of the difference in test results, it does not explain all of it. Whites (and for that matter Asian-Americans) from households with the same income as blacks continue to significantly outscore blacks on all standardized tests. In the 1982 SAT, for instance, blacks from families with incomes in excess of $50,000 per year scored 60 to 80 points below whites with comparable backgrounds.

Why blacks score so poorly is far harder to get at, though over the years much of the blame has been placed on the alleged "cultural bias" of test questions. Various attempts have been made to overcome this problem, but none have produced convincing results. One such effort, underwritten by a grant from the National Institute of Mental Health, was dubbed BITCH (Black Intelligence Test of Cultural Homogeneity). It amounted to a vocabulary test of ghetto slang, and it proved, in the words of Charles Murray, "that blacks know more ghetto slang than whites do." A more thoroughgoing effort was undertaken by the Ann Arbor, Michigan, public schools, which since 1979 have been using "Black English" as the principal medium of instruction, the theory being that black students would do better if they were taught in their own "culturally distinct patterns of speech." In the six years the program has been in operation, black test scores have shown no notable change.

Increasingly experts are coming to the view that the root cause of poor academic performance among blacks is not so much cultural bias in testing as it is persistent feelings of mental inferiority. As a black education writer, cited in a publication of the National Urban League, puts it: "Differences in scores have little to do with ability and a lot to do with what may be the biggest barrier to black education: a subtle, often subconscious cycle of self-doubt and an avoidance of intellectual competition."

things like grades and teacher comments, but you can't trust those all that much either. It's human nature: some teachers will gold-plate a student's record, make him seem a lot more than he is. Grades are even less reliable. In some of these inner-city schools, sixty percent of the student body is getting As. What it comes down to is that you gotta trust your instincts. You gotta go by feel. That's why the interview is so crucial.

Herney stopped and looked over his glasses. "Now I suppose, you want to know about Eddie." I nodded. Herney hesitated a moment, then resumed.

Eddie, you know, was the first kid I ever interviewed. The very first. I suppose you always tend to remember the first time you do anything, and I sure remember Eddie. He had a very impressive background. His grades were excellent, his teacher comments were terrific, and he had also done well in the SSAT, scoring a lot higher than black kids usually do. Another thing that impressed me about him was that he told me he was taking a special course downtown. When I asked him how he got there, he said he just hopped on the subway. That told me something. On the other hand, I talked to another kid in Harlem the same day who had never seen the Hudson River. His whole world was his neigh-borhood. That told me something too.

All in all, Eddie seemed like a great kid. You just had a sense, talking to him, that he was very independent and self-confident, a kid who had a good sense of his identity and how to maintain it. The thing that really turned me, though, was what he said when I asked him a question that I often ask students, to get a feel for their ambition and direction. That is, "What do you expect to be doing twenty-five years from now?" That question stops a lot of kids, but Eddie didn't miss a beat. Right away, he said, "I want to be a doctor and come back and help my community. It's good," he said, "but I want to make it better. I want to make it proud."

That, I thought, was a hell of an answer. It's the kind of ambi-tion we are looking for in kids: someone who is looking to do something not just for himself but for his neighborhood.

So Eddie was the kid I took, not the kid who hadn't seen the Hudson River. Was it a risk, taking him? Of course it was a risk. But we are taking a risk with all these kids, and we know it. If you accept diversity, you have to accept the consequences. There are kids here from different life-styles and backgrounds, and, yes, different capabilities, too. Even though they may be innately bright, they may not have gone to a super, terrific day school that prepared them very well. So they are going to have problems— and not just in the classroom. When black kids come to a school like this, it's very difficult for them. They don't feel fully a part of this place, and yet they are different than the kids back home. They have one foot in each camp and both feet in neither.

There are white kids and white adults here who understand that there are special problems for kids like Eddie, and we do what we can. But we can't do everything. We want to treat these kids as adults. We don't want to oversupervise them. And we certainly are not wittingly trying to impose the gamut of white middle-class values on them, because, frankly, some of those values are not worth having.

As for Eddie himself, and how he did after he got here, I really don't know that much. My job was getting him in here. Apart from that, we didn't have that much contact. Once in a while I'd see him through the window, walking across campus, and I'd wave, but that was about it. Everything I heard, though, was good.

Herney pursed his lips, then looked down at the tassles on his gleaming loafers. "You understand there is urban violence," he went on. "You know that these kids live in environments different from yours and mine. But you never expect something like this to happen to someone you know. It surprised me. Shocked me. Especially it happening to Eddie. He was—how should I explain it?—he was, I thought, a kid who had things in some perspective."

9

THE PHRASE HERNEY USED—"HAVING THINGS IN PERSPECTIVE"—
was one that, in the coming days, I would frequently hear applied to
Eddie, particularly in his first two years at the Academy. He was, said
those who had taught and coached him, mature for his age, serious,
studious, determined—and not at all in awe of the strange new world
that was Phillips Exeter. "I thought he was extraordinary," one of his
first-year teachers put it. "A lot of kids who come here are really
intimidated by the place. The surroundings, the responsibility, the
work—it just overwhelms them. But Eddie didn't seem to have any
trouble at all. He fit right in. If you hadn't looked at his records, you
wouldn't have known he was from a place like Harlem. He was a most
unusual kid."

So it appeared, virtually from the day Eddie settled into a single
room on the fourth floor of Cilley Hall, one of the largest of the Exeter
dorms, and presided over by three faculty "houseparents," among
them a soft-spoken Yale Divinity School graduate named David
Daniels. Then one of three blacks on the Exeter faculty, Daniels, an
ordained Pentecostal minister, was close to Eddie, closer, his colleagues said, than any other Exeter adult.

"Eddie arrived at Exeter with excellent study skills," Daniels
recalled.

That's unusual for anyone who is thirteen years old. It's especially unusual for someone who is from—let me phrase it this
way—a weak junior high school. For most of these kids, Exeter
is the first time they've really had to sit down and work, and it
takes them a while—sometimes a semester, sometimes two or
three—to learn how to do it. And that can be devastating to a
kid's ego. Because when they start getting bad grades, they don't
see it as a problem with studying. They see it as a problem with
intelligence.

Eddie, though, wasn't like that. This guy, this Mr. Plummer, had instilled in him a sense of discipline. He knew how to sit down and study when he had to. So in the evenings, when you'd find most of the other preps running around with each other, doing all the things thirteen-year-olds do, you'd never find Eddie with them. Instead, he'd always be in his room, his nose in a book, studying. I asked him once why he didn't hang out with the other kids, and his answer was remarkable for a kid his age. "Because," he said, "what they are doing is immature."

To me, that answer seemed to sum up what Eddie was all about during his first year. He knew what he was at Exeter to do, and he was doing it. In a way, he was showing people that he wasn't the stereotype of an ABC kid who had been recruited from the ghetto knowing nothing. He was letting them know that he had come to Exeter educationally equipped, that he was ready to compete with them on the same level.

Eddie's preparation, his readiness to compete, was also evident to his teachers, who, in describing him, used words like "bright," "feisty," "aggressive"—"the kind of kid," as one of them put it, "you love having in class." "I was immediately impressed by him," said Anja Greer, who taught Eddie first-year mathematics and saw him frequently outside of class.

He was more successful, more savvy, more quick-witted than most of the black students—just more self-possessed. He spoke up in class. He wasn't afraid to be wrong. Also, his disposition was good. There was never any hostility or bitterness. In fact, he always seemed to be cheerful, in class or out of it. Really, I'd never known a kid from the inner city who seemed more comfortable, who adjusted so well.

I asked him once, "Eddie, how in the world do you ever survive up here?" He said, "As a black kid, you have to have soul and have to believe in yourself. No matter what signs the school is giving you, you have to know inside yourself that you are succeeding. If you don't believe in yourself, you're going to crash."

You never had the sense that Eddie was going to crash. You

always had the feeling that he was going to make it. He knew who he was, and he wasn't going to lose it. You could tell it, just from the way he talked. Most black kids will drop their slang when they come here. But not Eddie. He used the word "ain't" as if it was his personal stamp of where he came from. I remember we had a nickname for him. We called him Eddie from the city because the fact that he was from the city was so obvious, from his walk, his talk, the clothes he wore. Eddie liked the name. He had a sense of humor about himself. He didn't seem to be the type of student who took himself too seriously.

By the end of the second semester of his first year, "Eddie from the city" was on his way to establishing a B-minus average, a rare accomplishment for a male black student, and sufficient at Exeter to qualify him for academic honors. He was also opening up more to Daniels.

It took me a while to get to know Eddie, but that's not all that unusual. Initially, most new students, especially most preps, have the image of the adult in the dorm as the person who is there for disciplinary or spying reasons. They will be very cordial with you, but they will not volunteer any information. Some time has to go by for them to begin to trust you, for them to realize that you are not prying but only interested in them.

Eddie was typical in that when I would come into his room and ask him how it was going, he would answer the question, act a little annoyed, and not say anything more than what he thought was necessary. But where the other preps would seem nervous when I'd ask them something, Eddie would act cold. I thought that was understandable. After all, he was in a new place, away from home, and here is this person knocking on his door for reasons he couldn't figure out.

Sometime before the end of the first semester, though, he began to warm up to me. Partly, I suppose, it was the passage of time. And partly, I guess, he had realized that I was not trying to do him any harm. Whatever it was, we began having good conversations. I heard about Mr. Plummer and about Jonah being at Westminster and about his sister at home. He was proud of Jonah, because Jonah was a hard worker, but he was worried about his sister. She wasn't a hard worker, and Eddie was concerned whether she would be able to go off to prep school and a good college and all that. Mostly, though, I heard about his mother. Eddie had a real affection for her, like a lot of black students do for their mothers. The fact that he was in love with her and that she was in love with him really came through. I remember him saying that he wanted to do well so he could go back and make life easier for her.

Eddie continued to do well during what Exeter called lower year, and his teachers continued to extoll him. "Intellectually, Eddie was voracious," said Michael Drummey, who taught him second-year English. "He wanted to get everything out of class he could. He was on top of everything we were doing. The kid was an exciting tenth-grader, a real hard worker. He had a sparkling intellectual daring."

It was also during his second year at Exeter that Eddie tried out for the junior varsity basketball team. He failed to make the squad, which was dominated by talented whites, two of whom would later be named high school All Americans, but his determination impressed his coach, Malcolm Wesselink. "Eddie was one of the last kids I cut," said Wesselink.

There was a lot of flash to his game—he could dribble between his legs and all that—but in a lot of ways, he just wasn't fundamentally sound. The problem, basically, was that Eddie played a city game. The playground kind of game looks great—there's a lot of whoop-de-do, a lot of sticking your nose in and skinning your knees, a lot of dog-eat-dog—but it doesn't translate real well to any kind of system. That's what Eddie was like. He was great one-on-one, but he couldn't catch a pass. It's not that unusual; there's a lot of kids who play the street game who can't adjust to the system, and Eddie was one of them. He also wasn't a physical kid. A lot of kids will get down on the floor and fight for the basketball, but Eddie wasn't like that. He wasn't tough at all. . . .

After I cut him, he asked if he could stay and practice with the team so he could try to get better. I've had kids ask me that before, and it never works out. So I tried to discourage him, told him I couldn't make any promises. But Eddie said it was okay. He just wanted to play. I had my doubts—he was kind of a cocky kid, you know, and I was wondering, when it got bad, how he would handle it, when he would finally say, "To hell with it." But he never did. Instead, he worked out the whole year. He did a good job, too. Never asked for anything; did all the things I told him to, and always very politely and respectfully. It was always "How are you doing, coach?" and all that. I have to say, I was impressed.

I guess the kids were too, because they treated him like a regular member of the team. They invited him to the team dinner, and when I'd have them over to my house, he'd come along with everyone else. Even though he wasn't that good on the court, he was sort of the center of everything. He was funny and nice, kind of a show-off, in a way, and everyone seemed to get along with him real well. There were no strained feelings with anybody. People accepted him.

Apparently buoyed by that acceptance, Eddie began socializing more and developed a friendship with Dave Lemos, a white classmate who was one of the stars of the Exeter hockey team. Twice during the year, Lemos brought Eddie to visit his home in the nearby town of Dover, and both visits went well.

By and large, however, Eddie was cautious in his dealings with whites, revealing little about himself and even less about his background. Wesselink, for one, was unaware of the fact that he had come from Harlem—"Being at Exeter, seeming so educated, I thought he was from some nice East Side neighborhood"—and wrote off Eddie's urban "slickness" to adolescent role-playing. "There was an air about him, an attitude," Wesselink explained. "It was like he was trying to play a role at Exeter, trying to be something maybe more than he was, like he was trying to play the black kid from the city. There were a lot of things that gave you that impression: the way he walked through the halls of the gym, the way he talked to people, the way he played basketball. He had that sort of strut that kids have when they are trying to look badder than they are. Personally, I didn't think much of it. A lot of kids at this place are into playing roles, and I assumed that that's all it was with Eddie. I never found out anything different, because I'm not the sort of person who goes chasing after people's problems. Anyway, Eddie was pretty standoffish. Not mean, just cold."

David McIlhiney, the Exeter chaplain and one of Eddie's instructors prep year, also noted Eddie's aloofness. "I tried to get to him," McIlhiney said, "tried to get him to talk about something more than academic matters and things that were happening at school. But Eddie was not the kind of boy who gave much of himself to you. There was a wariness about him; he was very guarded."

One of the few times Eddie did let his guard down, the purpose was to mislead. The incident had come after a trip home to Harlem, during the course of which Eddie had fallen from his bicycle while riding through Central Park. The spill had torn a deep gash in Eddie's leg, requiring a number of stitches. When Eddie returned to Exeter sporting a big bandage and a nasty-looking wound, he informed his classmates he had been injured during a fight on the streets. "Ma," he later explained to his mother, "what's so exciting about a boy from Harlem falling off a dirt bike in the park?"

With his black friends, Eddie had less reason to pretend, if only because most had come from backgrounds similar to his. Nonetheless he continued to come on strong, especially with the girls. "He could be obnoxious at first, really pushy," said Stephanie Neal, an ABC classmate from Cleveland. "The first time I met him, at the square dance they have for preps, I had a terrible time getting rid of him. He was all the time following me around. Later that year I started going out with someone else, and Eddie didn't like it one bit. He was really jealous. He said, You have to make a decision between him and me now. That's the way it has got to be. Now, what is it?' That's the kind of person Eddie was. If he had something to say, he said it."

Jessica Ortiz, an ABC student from Manhattan, had much the same experience with Eddie—"He was coming on too confident, trying too hard to put up a front"—and, like Neal, attributed Eddie's aggressiveness to his neighborhood. "Harlem kids are like that," she said. "A little too cocky, a little too cool. And that's how Eddie came across. Even though he was up here, it was like a part of him was still in his neighborhood." So seemingly "street" did Eddie appear that

Ortiz was surprised to learn he was bright. "Eddie fooled me," she said. "Acting like he did, I didn't think he was smart. Then one night we were talking about grades, and he asked what I got in biology. I said, 'Grades? Who are you to be asking me about my grades?' Then he told me what his grades were. He had A's. I said, 'Ohhh.' So I asked him, 'How do you do it?' And he said, 'Instead of walking around like a lot of folks, I just go to my room, sit down, and knock it out.'"

Eventually, both Neal and Ortiz came to count Eddie among their best friends, as did André François, a Haitian-American from North Miami Beach, Florida. The friendship, however, was slow in developing and came only after Eddie had subjected all of them to long testing and evaluation. "Eddie was not the sort of student who got along with everybody," said François. "He kept to himself more than most kids. He didn't take to belonging to any group. I guess you could say he was a little defensive."

According to François, much of Eddie's defensiveness, especially with whites, sprang from his neighborhood. "Kids at Exeter just aren't used to Harlem blacks," as François put it.

They have these weird feelings about them. Eddie used to say that many of the students had the attitude that blacks were people who were just looking for welfare and didn't look for work. That bothered Eddie. He was proud of his home. He knew that neighborhood helped get him where he was. He always used to say that when he got out of college, he was going back to help his people. They had given him this opportunity, and he was going to pay them back.

Eddie was always talking about Harlem, the friends he had there, the fun, the things he did, his family, everything that went on. A lot of black kids talk about their home. This is the first time most of us have been away, and, face it, a lot of us are homesick. After a few weeks, though, it usually tails off. But not with Eddie. He talked about Harlem all the time. It was almost like he was sort of afraid, like if he didn't talk about it, didn't keep reminding himself of where he was from, this place would change him.

Occasionally, Eddie's regard for his home could lead him into conflict, particularly when the talk around the Harkness Table turned to race. "Sometimes Eddie would be fighting the whole class," said one of Eddie's black classmates. "The kids would be saying these crazy things, and he would have to jump up and say, 'This is not my attitude. I live in the ghetto. I know poverty. I see people struggling.'" Another friend remembered sitting in a class with Eddie during a discussion of Social Darwinism. "All the other students just sat there," he said, "accepting survival of the fittest as a fact. Ed got up and started shouting, 'What about the people who didn't get a chance at education?' He always argued that since whites had the power, they were the only ones who could help his environment."

Eddie's racial sensitivity did not go down well with all his white classmates. One recalled being in an English class with Eddie during a discussion of *Huckleberry Finn* and being startled when Eddie denounced the book as "racist garbage." "That kind of stunned me," the student said. "I mean, Jim is the most attractive character in the book. All the whites are pretty lousy. But for some reason, Eddie was relating himself to it, and he was really ticked off. He was talking on, not making much sense, and the teacher was really riding him, saying 'I can't understand you, Eddie. I can't understand you.' The teacher was right—sometimes, it *was* hard to understand Eddie—but that only got Eddie more frustrated. He was babbling, talking in this sort of black stutter, like he was really nervous. I don't know why he was so upset. The book didn't make any difference."

Another white student, who shared several classes with Eddie, urged him not to take the comments of his classmates so seriously. "I told him not to get so upset," the student recounted. "People are just people, you know. Some people are white and some people are black, and if you are going to get bummed out about it, it's pretty dumb. But I could never convince Eddie of that. He was always trying to prove something, always trying to show you he was just as good as you, just as smart as you. At Exeter, you don't have to prove anything to anybody. Everybody is smart. That's a given. But Eddie didn't get it."

In the dorm, life was easier, at least with the students, a number of whom recalled Eddie as being witty, fun to be with, and a standout on

the intramural baseball team. Eddie, however, was having problems
with the white dorm faculty, or so at least he told others. Whatever the
problems were, whether or not they were real, they were pressing
enough for Eddie to talk to Jonah about leaving school and coming
home. His brother, however, urged against it, and not wanting to dis-
appoint his mother, Eddie eventually decided to stay. The one change
he did make was transferring to another hall in the middle of his second
year. Daniels, whom Eddie had not told of his plans to transfer, was
surprised. When he asked Eddie the reason, Eddie was evasive, and
it was not for several weeks that he finally admitted the truth. "He
said that there were faculty members in the dorm who were sneaking
around, waiting for him to do something, because he was black and
from Harlem," Daniels recalled. "He said he couldn't live under those
conditions. McConnell was a smaller dorm. It was also less super-
vised—and Eddie knew that."

Despite the move, Eddie continued to visit his old dorm frequently,
and he and Daniels had a number of long talks. According to Daniels,
the subject that preoccupied Eddie most was being black at a white
institution.

> He said that people at Exeter would not know how to survive
> in Harlem. He claimed he did know how to survive in Harlem,
> even at night, and he thought that was a plus. He also said that
> if he tried to describe to the other kids that he came from a home
> of middle-class values on the other side of Morningside Park,
> it wouldn't make any sense to them, because it wouldn't fit
> their stereotype of what blacks from Harlem were supposed to be
> like. . . .
>
> He was sensitive about race, probably more so than the other
> black students. I never saw any racial hostility, though. Instead,
> there was frustration, exasperation. I remember once, he was vis-
> iting my room, and the two of us were going over his application
> for School Year Abroad. It got to be quite late, and I asked him if
> he wanted me to call the faculty person at McConnell, to let him
> know where he was. Eddie told me not to bother. He'd explain
> when he got back to the dorm. Apparently, the faculty member
> didn't believe him, because later he called me to check out Ed-

die's story. When Eddie found out, he was quite upset. He was convinced that the faculty person thought he was a liar because he was black. You could tell that bothered him. Dealing with whites, trying to figure out their reactions to him, was something that was always on his mind.

10

IN RECONSTRUCTING EDDIE'S FIRST TWO YEARS AT EXETER I HAD relied heavily on the recollections of his black classmates. Though they had been helpful, they had also been guarded, not only in their comments about Eddie, whose guilt or innocence most did not want to discuss, but in their descriptions of their own experiences at Exeter. There was, however, one exception, and a most impressive one he was.

His name was Lamont O'Neil, and over the phone he had seemed exceptionally friendly and open, as if he had a story to tell and was eager to tell it. I was eager to hear it, for while Lamont and Eddie had not been particularly close (Lamont had entered Exeter the year Eddie was in Spain and had thus come to know him only when Eddie was a senior) and in a number of ways differed from each other, there was in Lamont a lot of what had been in Eddie. Both were bright and curious; both had come from similar neighborhoods (in Lamont's case, East New York, a dilapidated pocket of Brooklyn in many respects even bleaker than Harlem); both had strong mothers whom they plainly adored, and both had been placed at Exeter by ABC. Like Eddie, Lamont, who headed up the Exeter gospel singing group, was also very religious, loved sports (he was a star sprinter and high-jumper on the track team), and was intensely proud of his culture and race. Finally, Lamont was a talker, just as Eddie had been, and not at all reluctant to discuss his dead friend, whose guilt or innocence was, to Lamont, a very open question.

As our phone call drew to a close, I asked Lamont if he could meet me for lunch at a trendy waterside café at the edge of Brooklyn Heights. Lamont agreed, and I began laying out the logistics of how he should get there. I had only a vague notion of the whereabouts of East New York, and even less about the intricacies of the subway system, so finally I told him to hop a cab and said that I'd pick up the tab.

Had I known Lamont O'Neil, I would have realized that I was making an impossible request. He may have been at Exeter on scholarship, but he was not about to let anyone pay his taxi fare. Instead, he made the hour-long trek by subway on an August day when temperatures were in the nineties. He arrived looking a little wilted from his travels underground but cheerful nonetheless. We took a table by the window and, while the waiter went off to get us refreshment, stared out across the East River at the skyline of lower Manhattan. Lamont, who had a smooth-skinned handsomeness about him, pointed to one of the buildings, identifying it as the headquarters of a law firm where he had a summer job as a clerk. For a few minutes, we bantered awkwardly about mutual friends at Exeter. Then, shyly at first, but with growing confidence, Lamont began to talk.

I was always interested in learning, right from preschool. Things always came easily to me. Also, I got a lot of attention and recognition because of how I did in school, and I liked that. In the seventh grade, a teacher mentioned prep school in class. Going away sounded interesting and exciting, and I guess I also wanted to get out from under my mother's wing. I had never known anyone who had gone away to school, but one of my friends had a sister who had gotten into St. Paul's and she was supposed to be having a great time. All I knew about Exeter was that there was a lot of competition and that everything was really fast. I like to believe that I can conquer things. I don't like to believe that I can fail at all. So I decided to check it out.

At the interview with Mr. Herney there was one girl and myself. The girl talked and talked. I just sat back, without a chance to say much of anything. When the interview was over, I thought to myself, "Oh, brother, I am never going to get in." But about a week later, I got a letter from Mr. Herney, saying how much he enjoyed speaking to me, and asking me to write him and tell him about myself and what I wanted to do. So I did. I told him a little bit about my family, and I told him that I wanted to be a doctor ever since I was small, because I had a cousin who died of cancer. I've always been scared of that word, cancer. I told him I wanted to kill cancer before it killed me. I also told him I wanted to learn about different people, people from different ethnic backgrounds.

Well, I got in, and everyone was really happy for me. The people in my building said, "You gotta get out of this neighborhood. This neighborhood will take you down the drain with it." The only people who weren't happy were my friends. They all said, "How are you going to deal with all those white people up there?" I told them I'd deal with it, but they wouldn't let it go. They said the only reason I was going was because I was black. Other people may have thought that, but my friends were the only ones who came right out and said it.

My mother told me not to pay any attention to them; they were just jealous. She also gave me a pretty good piece of advice, and that was that I have to respect myself. My mom, you see, grew up in the South, in North Carolina, and the older people coming up there had to go through a lot. The only way they survived was respecting themselves. That's what she was taught, and that's what she taught me. . . .

The first time I met Eddie was at a party Exeter had for all the new students at the Yale Club. He was about to go to Spain, but he came anyway, I guess, just so he could check everybody out. Anyway, I was just standing there when Eddie came over and introduced himself and started talking. He was so confident and sure of himself, it was almost scary. We talked for a while, and then Eddie started telling me some of the underground stuff that goes on at Exeter, the hazing and the drugs. I have to say, I was kind of surprised. Eddie didn't down the school, though; he just said the place could be really bad sometimes. Mostly, it was things piling up on you: the work, problems at home, problems with social life. He said it could pile-drive you into the ground if you didn't watch yourself. But he also said I shouldn't worry too much. If I had any problems, there would always be people there for me, and that when he got back from Spain, he'd be one of them.

Just before he was about to go, I asked Eddie if there was any racism at Exeter. Eddie didn't say anything for a minute. Then he looked me right in the eye, kind of lowered his voice, and said, "There is. You may not be able to see it, you may not be able to smell it, but you'll feel it. It's there. You'll have to deal with it." He told me I should never let it get to me, because that would show the racist people that they had won, and I should never let them see that. He said if I ever had a problem, I should come and see him. He would take care of it.

A few weeks later, I went up to Exeter for the beginning of school. Now I had never really been out of New York, so traveling was kind of new to me. I remember leaving early that morning, looking back at my neighborhood, and thinking about it all the way to the airport. It's like any neighborhood, I guess, except that there isn't any money and a lot of the buildings are abandoned and falling down. But then I get on this airplane and a couple of hours later here I am in this place with nothing but green trees and grass and clean buildings. I kept saying to myself, "Hey, am I here?" Everything seemed so different. I couldn't believe it. This place seemed like heaven. The first night I was there, I kept waking up. I couldn't figure out where I was.

The first few days, I spent a lot of time walking around the campus, looking for another black student. There weren't many of them. The white kids, though, were nice—offered to take me around and all that. That surprised me. You build up these perceptions of whites, that whites are mean and vile, never trust a white person and all that, so in the back of my mind I was sort of afraid. That's why I was shocked that they were so nice.

Then, about a week after I got to school, I went downtown to go to McDonald's. I was walking back when a car came up behind and started following me. Finally it pulled alongside and a window rolled down. There were three teenagers in the car. Local kids. One of them—he had on a sweatshirt and had kind of short blond hair—leaned out the window and yelled at me, "Nigger, go home!"

I had seen racist things on TV, Martin Luther King and civil rights stuff and all that, but this was the first time anyone had ever called me nigger. It shattered it all for me. Here I had been trying so hard to fit in, even though it wasn't mine and didn't belong to me, and it made me realize that this is a different world than my own, that there were some people who didn't want me. Also, it scared me. I kept wondering what these kids would have done to me if they had caught me out there alone at night.

So I ran back to campus and called my mother and told her I

wanted to come home. The first thing she said was, "I told you this would happen." The second thing she said was that I should stick it out for a week, and then see how I felt. I didn't want to—I was dead set on coming home—but I said I would give it a try. I'm glad I did, because I have been there ever since. . . .

It took me a while to get used to the place, maybe two or three months. One of the hardest things was getting used to all this responsibility, and at Exeter you are expected to be responsible from day one. You are responsible for keeping your clothes clean, for keeping your room up, for waking up and getting to class on time, for doing all the work. It's rough, but it's more rough when you make it rough. Eddie was right: if you don't watch it, don't schedule your time, you can pile-drive yourself into the ground.

Being black, of course, makes it that much rougher. You have to understand: in a black family, from the moment you are born, you are told that you are different, that if you go into a white neighborhood, people are going to treat you as if you are differ- ent. That's what you grow up believing: that you are different. In a black neighborhood, you feel secure. You don't stand out. But when you are in a dorm, you *do* stand out. People do notice you, and you get a little paranoid. You are always thinking, "These people are looking at me"—even when they aren't looking at you. You are always aware of the differences, of the fact that they are white and you are black. Whenever there is a conflict, you wonder, "Is it because they don't like me? Or because they don't like blacks?"

Before I came to Exeter, I never thought much about being black. It was just something that was. When I'd be walking down the street and hear these political types ranting about black this and black that, I'd ignore them, like they were crazy, you know? Now I stop and listen, because I've started thinking about my blackness a lot. If you're black and going to a place like Exeter, you have to think about your blackness, because you are being reminded about it all the time. Any time anything ever comes up about blacks, kids always look at you, as if you knew everything there is to know about black people. . . .

I remember once in English class we had a black poet come in, and afterward everyone was talking about what he meant. And of course they were all looking at me. But I was tired that day and just didn't have much to say. Besides, how was I supposed to know what he meant for all black people, quote unquote. But I went out of there very disappointed in myself. I felt I had not only let down the class but the entire black race. I feel that pressure all the time. Everyone who is black at Exeter does. It's a burden we all have to carry. . . .

Once in a while you will hear one of the white kids make a racial remark, but that kind of stuff is rare. Most kids at Exeter aren't racist; they just don't know anything about blacks. One day, for instance, we were out on the field, having track practice, and a guy named Stu Brown, a friend of mine, said, "Can I ask you a question? Do all black people wear undershirts? You're wearing an undershirt, and I notice that Dennis and Dal are wearing undershirts, too. Is it some sort of security blanket or what?" The question stunned me, but obviously Stu was serious. So I told him, "Yes, it's true: we all do wear undershirts. Just like we all like watermelon and fried chicken." All the while I'm telling him this, Stu is listening, soaking it all up. But then I say to him, "And, if you aren't looking, we will steal your car, too."

That caught him on and he was really angry. "Why are you being such an ass, Lamont?" he said to me. "Because you are," I told him. By now there is a little crowd standing around us, wondering, I suppose, whether we are going to fight. Well, I cooled down and said, "Look, Stu, truthfully, all black people do not wear undershirts." Then I apologized for getting mad and we shook hands. He really wasn't being racist. He was just trying to understand. I respected him for asking me that question. If he hadn't, he might have gone through the rest of his life thinking that all black people wear undershirts. *(Laughs)*

The thing is, if I had let Stu walk away, or even worse, if we had had a fight, then he would have formed some opinion about black people. Once white people have a bad experience with a black, it puts all black people in the same silhouette. Eddie understood that. He told me once, "Don't ever do anything bad, because people are always looking for you to do something bad.

You not only have to be good, you have to be perfect. If you do something bad, it's not only a mark against yourself but a mark against the entire black race.'' He really believed that. ''Don't murder or rob,'' he'd say. ''It's a disgrace to the black community.''

I always tried to keep what Eddie said in mind, even when I went home. It's harder at home, though, because the kids aren't like they are at Exeter. They aren't school fanatics, if you know what I mean. Like, I have a friend at home who became righteous. You know what that means? *Righteous?* Well, for him, it meant becoming a real pothead. He said to me, ''You're up there with all those white people. You talk white. You dress white. You even act white.'' Then he took out a joint and asked me if I wanted some. When I told him no, he said, ''You see what I mean? You *are* white.'' A couple of days later, he came by my house and asked me to lend him some money so he could buy marijuana. I told him I wasn't going to give him any. He just kind of smirked and said, ''You are *too* good.'' Well, that upset me, so I said, ''I'll give you some money, but let me come along with you.'' So we went out and he got a little bag and the two of us went up to a roof to smoke it. I only had a couple of puffs, but it nearly made me sick to my stomach. I tried to be loose, though. ''This is good,'' I said. ''It's good.'' The truth was, I was having a hard time not coughing.

When I went home, I told my mom what had happened. I felt so bad. *(Laughs)* I was also out six dollars. But right then I decided something: no one was ever going to pressure me again. I was going to be Mr. Rock.

For a while after that, I didn't even want to walk outside. I'd go through the back door of my building so people wouldn't see me. When I wanted to talk to somebody, it would mostly be relatives and other kids from Exeter. I started hanging out with an older crowd. The kids my own age at home seemed so immature. They're always doing dumb things, hanging out, getting into weed, and I don't want to do any of that. When I see them now, they are simply people to be around. I don't tell them anything I feel. I don't disagree with them. I know it would be confusing to them. So I just go along with what they are saying. . . .

It's lonely, but I can't blame my friends for that. Because in a way they're right: I *am* a different person since I went to Exeter. I don't wear Tango hats anymore, or bebop, or talk slang. I tried to do it for a while—use words like "ain't" and "ya'll" so I'd fit in. But it just wasn't me. I can't pretend anymore, changing back and forth, trying to be two different persons. I'm not two different persons and I can never be. I'm just one person living in two different worlds. You've always got to remember that, remember who you really are, because when you don't, that's when the emergency light goes on. It happened to a girl I knew at Exeter. She had to go home because she forgot who she was.

I think I know who I am. I'm black, and there's no way I'm ever going to forget that, no way I'm ever going to give up my culture and heritage. But I'm also at Exeter. It's my home now. It's where my friends are—*real* friends, friends you can see every day, friends you can talk to, rely on.

I always thought of Eddie as being one of those friends—I do now—but I don't want to exaggerate this situation. I mean, we were never that tight. I don't know anyone who was ever that tight with Eddie. Eddie was his own person; he was not the type to get close to anyone—not the type to even need anyone. I remember, once, I was waiting outside a classroom for my friend Al, and Eddie came along and asked if I wanted to go to lunch. I said, "Sure, but I have to wait here for Al." He said he would wait with me, too. That surprised me, because Eddie was not the sort of person who waited for anyone. Anyway, we just stood there for a long time talking. And for a small instant, it seemed to me that he was really lonely.

Since he died, a lot of people have asked me about him, asked how I would sum him up. I never know quite how to answer that question. Maybe it's because I hate summaries; there's always something you leave out. With Eddie, it's even harder—he was so varied, there were so many parts of him. To be truthful about it, I never really wanted to get all that close to him; I had some friends who did, and they had a lot of conflicts with him. But I respected Eddie, I really did. He was his own person. He believed in himself. His attitude was, if he didn't believe in himself, how could he ask anyone else to believe in him?

I know he rubbed a lot of people the wrong way, but that was because he was so honest. He didn't care what they thought; all he demanded was their respect. We all have our negative views of people, we all take and do things we don't want. We just never say so. But Eddie was different. Things you didn't want to hear, things you try to overlook, he'd come right out and say them. "Hey, man," he'd say. "This is the way it is." I admired that. He was being honest. He was being real.

Last semester, though, I noticed a change in him. He just didn't seem to care as much. A number of times he said to me, "I hate this place. I can't stand it. Exeter has done nothing for me." Sometimes, though, I saw a little regret. I don't know for what, because like I say, it was rare for Eddie to reveal himself to any-one. But it was obvious he was having a hard time. I guess girls were part of it—he used to complain they were "gaming" on him—but there was something else, too. He just didn't want to talk about it. . . .

The last time I saw him was the day before I was going home from school. He called me up and said, "Listen, man, Malcolm [Stephens, Eddie's roommate senior year] and I are coming round to all the brothers. It's going to be you guys who are going to carry on the place after we leave, and we want to be sure you do it right." A little later, he and Malcolm came over to my room. They were really happy; Eddie was joking a lot. He was also giving me a lot of advice: about how to succeed at Exeter, about being black, about how to use my blackness in a positive sense. He also gave me a big lecture about girls, about how to tell when they were bluffing, I guess because he had been having such a bad time with them. Before he left, he signed my yearbook. You want to hear what he said?

I said I did, and Lamont reached into his wallet, pulled out a sheet of paper, and began reading:

"This year was fucked up and I'm sorry that you and the other home boys gotta stay here two more fucking years. . . .

"Remember, man, to get ahead in this world you must control your own destiny. So don't allow someone to trick you into going against your own will. Your feelings will guide you right, and even though you may not be able to explain your feelings to another person, you always understand after a little thinking to yourself. Always know what you feel and who you are.''

Lamont carefully refolded the paper and placed it back into his pocket. ''How I found out what happened to Eddie,'' he said, ''is that André François called my sister.''

I was out when he called, didn't get home until ten-thirty or eleven. My sister was doing her hair. ''Call André back,'' she said. ''Something happened. Eddie got shot and he died.'' She seemed so calm, I didn't believe it. I just said, ''Yeah, man, sure,'' and started talking to my mother, telling her about the day, and the clothes I had bought. Then I turned on the TV, and the man is talking about Edmund Perry and Eddie's graduation picture is behind him. I just broke down. All I could do was holler.

For the first few days after Eddie's death, I kept thinking, ''What's the use? What's the use? No matter how far I go, how far I climb, it can always be taken away from me so fast.'' Look at Eddie: he went through four years at Exeter, four years of tears and pain and struggling, and boom, it's all just taken away. Do you know how long four years is? Do you know how hard four years is at Exeter? It's hard, man, it's hard. Maybe he didn't leave on good terms. Maybe he did think his time at Exeter was a waste. But now he'll never get a chance to see how far those four years would have taken him.

So I thought to myself, ''Why should I bother?'' And for a while I didn't bother about anything. Really, I gave up. I didn't want to succeed anymore. I didn't want to rise and keep struggling. I didn't even want to leave my room. I told my adviser I wanted to withdraw. But then a teacher of mine, Mrs. Piana, wrote me a letter. She said, yes, it was a bad incident, and yes, it could happen to anyone. But I couldn't live my life on the assumption that something bad was going to happen. I couldn't sit around just waiting for it. That letter surprised me. I didn't know she cared for me that much.

I'm glad I changed my mind; I'm glad I'm going back. But

still, I can't stop thinking about Eddie. A friend of his, a white boy, told me that in knowing Eddie, we all had a part of him in us. If we keep that part alive, we keep Eddie alive. That white boy was right. Eddie is still here. You can't tell me he isn't. I can feel him closer now than when he was living. I think about him every day. I go to my job and I'll start thinking about him and all of a sudden I will bust out crying.

At that point, Lamont paused. For several minutes, neither of us spoke. Finally Lamont sucked in his breath and smiled self-consciously.

"You know," he said, "I'm going to be devastated if I don't graduate. It means so much to me. I had a dream once about being kicked out. I was sad for days and days. I don't know what it is about Exeter, whether it's the people or the place, but I think I've found what I am looking for there. Maybe my friends are right. Maybe the only reason I am at Exeter is because I am black. Maybe they needed me as a token. I don't care. All I know is that when I graduate, I am going to walk away with more than they do."

The restaurant was now deserted and the waiters were hovering over us. We got up to go. Outside, we lingered a moment, watching the boats parade up and down the river. "You hang in there," I said as we shook hands. "Don't worry," Lamont grinned back. "Nothing's going to get me down. Remember? I'm Mr. Rock."

With that, he was off, running up a long hill in the direction of the subway. I knew why he was hurrying. He had told me he had to get home to change clothes, then head into Manhattan. There was a gathering he was attending that night, an annual event he had been to before. They were holding it, once again, at the Yale Club.

11

IN TALKING ABOUT EDDIE, LAMONT MADE A GREAT DEAL OF THE year his friend had spent in Spain as an Exeter junior. "Eddie talked about Spain all the time," Lamont recalled. "The girls, the beaches, the weather, all the fun he had—he made it sound like paradise. But the thing he talked about most was the way he had been treated over there. Eddie said it was the only place where he had not been seen as black. In Harlem, at Exeter, he was always being judged as a black person. In Spain, he was just Eddie."

Others of Eddie's friends had made similar comments, and however rapturous the language—"Whoever you had been," said one, who had been to Barcelona, "in Spain you got a clean start"—I had not made much of them. Young people who studied abroad invariably came back proclaiming how life-changing the experience had been, as well it might be, since for most of them (including Eddie), it was their first extended contact with a foreign culture, as well as the first time they had been out from under adult supervision. Nor was I surprised that Eddie should have such a particularly high regard for Spain. It was a charming country, and Barcelona, where Eddie lived for the 1984–1985 school year, perhaps its most charming city. Similarly, Eddie's statement that Spain had been the only place where he had not been judged as black had not seemed unusual either. There was a long tradition of talented blacks finding refuge in Europe (as, for a time, had Eddie's mentor at Wadleigh, Edouard Plummer) and, on their return, calling life there far more accommodating than that here. Small wonder, then, that Eddie would be infatuated by Spain, and that the memory of what he habitually called "the most important year in my life" would loom large once he had returned to the shivering climes of New Hampshire.

This, at any rate, had been my assumption during that pleasant lunch with Lamont O'Neil. But as the days passed and I learned more about Eddie's time in Spain, my opinion began to change. Spain, it became increasingly clear, had been something more to Eddie than nine months of late-night carousing. It was a year of conflicts, change, and contradictions. It was also the year he fell in love and though he would ever deny it, encountered racism at its ugliest.

That Eddie went to Spain at all had required some doing. School Year Abroad, which was sponsored by Exeter, Andover, and St. Paul's, in association with nineteen other prep schools across the country, was an expensive undertaking, usually beyond the reach of scholarship students. Eddie, however, had been eager to go, and since he spoke grammatically excellent if torturously accented Spanish (a skill he picked up in his prep year at Exeter), special allowances had been made. ABC paid some of his additional costs, and more money was provided by his Baptist church, which took up a collection for him. Ed Plummer also lent a hand, paying for his airfare out of his own pocket. Additional spending money was earned by Eddie himself, who worked all through the summer of 1984 painting benches and clearing brush in Morningside Park. The work was hard, but Eddie told people he didn't mind. It was worth it, he said, if it would take him to Spain, away from Exeter, Harlem, and home.

On arrival in Barcelona, Eddie and his classmates—forty-six of them altogether, all of whom but Eddie were white—were assigned housing with "foster parents" throughout the city. The household Eddie drew consisted of three Spanish spinsters in their late fifties. They and their black American charge did not get along well.

"Eddie used to complain all the time that he never knew what was expected of him," one of his Barcelona classmates remembered. "They were always leading him to believe that he could do whatever he wanted—stay out all night, if he wanted—and Eddie did stay out late a lot. But when he'd come home, they'd be mad at him. Eddie thought they were playing games with him, and he didn't like it. He wanted to know where he stood with people."

Another classmate, one of the half dozen or so who had gone to Barcelona from Exeter, had a different explanation. "It was a race thing," she said. "To them, he was big and black and scary, and that caused a lot of tension. Eddie knew what was going on in their heads. He said to me once, 'I'm black and it worries the hell out of them.' He didn't seem that upset about it, though. He knew the kind of people they were, and he knew the person he was. He didn't dwell on it a whole lot."

Whatever the explanation—and it was becoming apparent that Eddie had a propensity for telling different stories to different people—the ill-feeling was sufficient for Eddie to transfer to the home of a young mother and her two-year-old daughter. Here, Eddie told his classmates, the atmosphere was much warmer, and there were no complaints about his late-night partying.

Adjusting to the classroom, where nearly all the courses were taught in Spanish, was not as easy. The trouble was not with the language but with his teachers, in particular a mathematics instructor who had recently given him a D on a test. "The teacher does *nothing*," he reported in a Christmas card to his mother. "He is a little, short Spaniard that is so insecure of himself that he attempts to assert his authority too much. He thinks he's always right, just because he's older and supposedly wiser. . . . Simply said, I detest him and all he stands for. Don't worry. There'll be no more D's."

There were, in fact, no more D's, and Eddie went on to establish himself as one of the top students in the group. Alexandra Wolf, who had gone to Spain with Eddie and was a year ahead of him at Exeter, recalled that he was especially good at Spanish, and that whatever the subject, Eddie was invariably the sparkplug of the class.

Eddie spoke perfect Spanish, better, I'd say, than any of us, and that told me something about him. Because there is an art to learning a language, and half of it is leaving your pride at home. You gotta be willing to go out and make mistakes and look like an idiot. You gotta lose yourself and find yourself again. It takes a lot of guts and self-assurance to realize that even if you make a mistake, you are not a loser. Most of the other kids couldn't do it. They were afraid to be spontaneous. In class, they'd simply sit there, waiting for something to happen. Not Eddie, though. He'd always jump right in. If no one else would talk, he'd talk. He was never afraid of speaking his mind.

That didn't sit well with everybody. There were a lot of kids who thought he was too aggressive, and up to a point they were right. Eddie *was* aggressive. He'd always see how far he could go

with you, how far he could push you. It was like he always
wanted to stretch everything, to test the validity of it, just to see
how real it was. Sometimes he'd go too far, say things that were
really absurd, and that's when the kids would react negatively.
But Eddie knew what he was doing. He was going too far just so
he could be sure that he had covered everything. Once he knew he
had, once he knew he couldn't push any further, he pulled back
and got himself together. I thought he was an extraordinary kid,
really playful intellectually.

Some of Eddie's classmates, like Sarah Wood, an Exeter junior,
took a dimmer view of Eddie's performance. Where Wolf saw intellectual playfulness, Wood saw hostility, much of it racially motivated.

Eddie had a chip on his shoulder. You could tell it just by the way
he sat in class: all spread out, bored-looking, like everyone was
wasting his time. He was all the time very arrogant, all the time
very sarcastic. I never knew why—and Eddie was never the kind
of kid who would tell you why—but I always supposed it had
something to do with Harlem. In a way, it was like he was trying
to be as tough as the place he came from. The funny thing is, I
always had the impression that Eddie didn't really like the toughness of a place like that—in fact, was really kind of scared of it.
But I also had the feeling that he had to take on that toughness as
his image. Anyway, that's certainly how he came across: all the
time very tough and very sarcastic—about the authority at the
school, and especially about Americans and people from Exeter.
Eddie's interest was in the Spanish, in getting to know the people.
The rest of us he really disdained.

Eddie's chip-on-the-shoulder attitude and his occasional non-
chalance about attending class and turning in assignments were also a
source of concern for Edward Sainatti, the SYA program director and a
stickler for academic performance. Several times Sainatti called Eddie
in for long talks, and though the conversations failed to produce any
noticeable results—in the classroom Eddie remained as caustic as
ever—Sainatti came away from the conversations liking Eddie and,

like so many other adults, being impressed by him as well. "He was mature for a student his age," Sainatti remembered, "very sure of his goals, very ambitious academically, and very, very realistic. He knew what had been given to him, and he knew, too, how far it would take him on the road to success. You never had the sense that anything was going to deter Eddie. He was quite intent about everything."

Nonetheless, Sainatti was worried. Something about Eddie didn't sit quite right. There was nothing major he could point to, nothing, certainly, like using drugs—"I've been around for a while," he said, "and I can spot kids who are doing that"—and though, in Sainatti's words, "Eddie's comments could border on the offensive," it was not that, either. Words, after all, were just words. As for the petty trouble Eddie got himself into—the missed classes and late assignments— that, too did not seem out of the ordinary. "Eddie was trying to be a wise guy," Sainatti said, "trying to get his peers to look up to him." In any case, Sainatti never had any trouble getting Eddie back into line. "If you speak with him firmly and show him that you care," he wrote in a confidential evaluation for Exeter, "he will respect you in any situation." Sainatti followed that prescription, and it always worked. "In a way," he said, "Eddie wanted you to be firm with him."

What concerned Sainatti, what, for all his efforts, he could not get at, was an attitude Eddie had, "a coldness," as Sainatti put it, "almost a hostility. . . . There was nothing evil or malicious about Eddie," Sainatti explained.

There was just, well, a kind of calculation about him. He never professed any great love of learning, for instance. Instead, it was what learning could bring for him—what he could acquire from it. That's why he wanted to get the best grades possible. Not because he loved the subject, but because getting the best grades would get him into one of the Ivy colleges, which in turn would help him realize his ambitions. He viewed Exeter the same way. He didn't love it and he didn't hate it. For him it was simply a means to an end. He was very clear about that, very intent about it, and also clear what that end was going to be. I read now that he told other people he was going to do something to help blacks, but he never said anything like that to me. We talked several times about his ambitions and his goals, and it was always how he was going to make a lot of money.

I tried to talk to Eddie about his life, tried to let him know that there was no reason for hostility. I said to him that if he looked at everything, he would realize that people had actually been pretty good to him. He acknowledged that was true, but he also said he had to maintain this stance, this attitude of not giving any ground. He didn't explain why; he just said it was very important to him.

Away from Sainatti and the classroom, Eddie seemed a different person entirely—"much looser," as one of his schoolmates put it, "much more laid back, like he was completely out of his shell." He joined a Spanish basketball team and, not having to compete with his Harlem friends, quickly became a popular star. He toured Barcelona, vacationed in southern France, sunned and swam on the beaches at Sitges. By night he did the bars, and when the bars closed, did the discos. According to Dave Nance, an easygoing Texan who was his running partner on these expeditions, Eddie was the ultimate free spirit, curious, interested, in love with life. He was also, said Nance, very much aware of who he was. "He wasn't one of these people who try to hide from their blackness," as Nance put it. "He was very proud of it—and yet he was still able to cope."

Coping, however, was always a struggle, especially in the beginning, and especially with the local girls. "I don't know what you know about Spanish girls," drawled Nance, "but I can tell you, they are the best, the absolute *best*."

Eddie's trouble was that he couldn't figure out how to get to them. It was a racial thing, and for a while it really bothered Eddie, really got him frustrated and upset. We'd spend hours together, talking about it, plotting out all these little things having to do with girls. He really wanted to understand them, figure out how they thought. He'd even go out on the streets just to watch them, trying to pick up on how they related to guys. All the time he was trying to understand what it took to get close to them.

I guess he must have finally figured it out, because after a couple of months, Eddie had all kinds of girlfriends. I mean, *all kinds* of girls. You'd go down to the McDonald's, a couple of blocks from school, and you'd see him with a new girlfriend every week. I had to hand it to him. I knew how Spanish girls thought, how reluctant they were to go out with a black guy, and he just broke right through it. To me, that was a hell of an accomplishment.

Eddie's success at romance did not bring his racial troubles to an end. According to Nance, he would "get static" about his blackness all the time he was in Spain. "The Spanish people would call him a nigger and a big Negro and things like that," said Nance.

Eddie couldn't understand it. He said it just didn't make any sense for people to treat him this way. I tried to tell him it wasn't anything personal, that this was just the way these people had been brought up. They were ignorant; the only blacks they knew about were these poor Africans who would come up to Spain to work. I said to him that he had two choices: he could try to educate them, to change their opinion, or he could blow them off. Whatever he did, it just wasn't worth getting upset about.

I guess that made an impression on him. At least after that we didn't talk about it so much. The attitude he began to take was that if they didn't want to get to know him, if they wanted to judge him just by the color of his skin, that was their problem, not his. They were the ones who were missing out. You could tell, though, that he still felt pretty emotional about it.

Nance, too, was "pretty emotional about it," and one night, when he and Eddie were in a bar, wound up punching a Spaniard who called his friend a nigger. "Eddie was really happy about that," remembered Nance. "He said what I did was cool."

Another night, in another bar ("It seemed like we were always in bars," said Nance), this one in the resort town of Sitges, it was Eddie who did the belting. "We were with a friend of ours from the Caribbean," recounted Nance.

He was studying to be a doctor, and is also kinda dark, and at one point during the evening somebody came up behind him and hit him—I guess it was over a girl. Well, Eddie just jumped on the guy, knocked him down and all that. To me, that was a good example of the kind of person he was. He was close to his friends and he would do a lot for them. Plus he really knew how to handle himself. He was taller than the average Spanish person, you know, and a lot tougher. The fact that he was black also scared a lot of people, which was great for Eddie because it gave him power for defensive purposes. Fights like the ones we got into, though, were pretty rare. Eddie was smarter than he was tough. He had to be smart, growing up in a place like Harlem and getting as far as he did. He said to me once that if you weren't smart, Harlem could be a very dangerous place. You had to be confident and chilled out, Eddie said, or else you would get into trouble. He also said you had to stay off drugs, or you could die very quickly.

Eddie used to talk about stuff like that all the time. One thing he said to me, though, I'll never forget. "The only way you can make it in Harlem," he said, "is to have enough pride to be your own person." Eddie had that pride. No doubt about it. He could take care of himself better than anyone I ever knew.

Nance was not the only classmate in Spain who was close to Eddie. There was also a girl, a very special one named Arielle Natelson.

A year older than Eddie, Arielle had been raised in a tight-knit, conservative Jewish family in suburban Los Angeles. Her ambition was to become an artist after Spain and college. In appearance, however, she seemed more like a model—and a stunning one at that. Olive-skinned, dark-eyed, and curly-haired, she was the acknowledged beauty in the group and, according to many, the one with the sunniest disposition as well. "She was so perfect—so sweet, so kind, so loving, so goddam gorgeous that you almost didn't believe it," said one of her female classmates. "The first time you saw her and she batted those big eyes at you in that coy way of hers, you thought to yourself, This can't be real. This must be an act. But it was no act. Arielle was the genuine article, a real live virgin goddess."

Arielle's charms were not lost on Eddie, who maneuvered himself into the seat next to hers on the long flight across the Atlantic. By the time they'd touched down in Madrid, Eddie was smitten and on his way to the only serious romance in his life.

It was, to most who saw it, a tender, touching relationship, almost childlike in its innocence. "What was going on between them went beyond sex," said one classmate. "In fact, I don't think Eddie ever touched her. She was so precious to him, it was like he was putting her in this special place, guarding her, almost. Eddie had lots of girls— even when he was seeing Arielle. But Arielle was always the one who was different."

She was different. That was obvious, even over the phone to California. And the way she talked of Eddie, shyly, almost reverentially, with frequent references to Eddie's "warmth," "understanding," and "openness," was different as well. "I don't know if I've ever met anyone so full of life as Eddie was," she began.

He was always living for the moment, trying to cram as much into it as possible. Every new experience there was, Eddie wanted it. He wanted to taste it all.

I knew that from the moment I met him on the airplane. Here we all were, going over to live in a foreign country for a year, and a lot of us were pretty nervous. I know I was. I had never been away that long by myself ever. But Eddie didn't seem threatened at all. He seemed so confident and knowing, like getting on an airplane and going to Spain was no big deal for him. Just being around him made you think that everything was going to be all right. And funny? I thought he was hysterical. Really, he was cracking everyone up.

There was something about Eddie, something I really can't describe, that made me trust him immediately. It was like he knew what I was feeling, even before I knew it myself. I remember when we were being assigned to our families, a couple of days after we got to Spain. I was feeling pretty apprehensive about it, and all of the sudden, there was Eddie in front of me, giving me a rose, telling me everything was going to be cool. I hadn't told him how I was feeling; he just sensed it. He was like that all the time. Whenever I'd be upset, he would sing me a little Bob Marley song. One of the lyrics went, "Don't worry about a thing. Every-thing is going to be all right." Hearing it from Eddie, I always believed it. He didn't lie to me about anything.

As Arielle described it, her relationship with Eddie was like that of close friends or brother and sister. They would spend hours together simply talking: about Spain, about home, about anything that was trou-bling her, including her romantic involvements with other boys. One thing they did not talk about was race. "Race was never important to us," she said.

> We never even discussed it. Eddie was getting along so well, fitting in with everything so beautifully, there didn't seem to be any need to. I know that some people think he was hung up about race, but I never saw it. When he was with me, he never seemed bitter about black/white things. The closest he came was when he said once that he resented the fact that there were a lot of cool people in Harlem who could not get all the benefits that people at Exeter got who were not cool at all and only got them because they were rich. He didn't think that was right. He didn't think that was fair. But he was only stating a fact, and as far as I was con-cerned, it was a true fact.

In Arielle's gentle retelling, everything about Eddie and their rela-tionship was nearly idyllic. He was not bothered by race, not troubled by his conflicts with classmates, and most assuredly not upset that she was keeping him at arm's length, even while she was dating other boys. "It's hard to explain," she said. "You had to be there to under-stand it."

There were friends of Eddie, in New York particularly, who told a different story. According to them, the relationship was not so simple or so placid, especially for Eddie. "Emotionally, racially, sexually, he was quite confused about her," said an adult Eddie later confided in at home. "He couldn't figure out what his feelings were, or what they should be. Sometimes he talked about possessing her, almost as if he had a right to her. Other times he spoke of her almost in a kind of awe, as if she was above him, better than him. It was clear he was very tormented."

While in Spain, though, Eddie hid those torments well. Neither his classmates nor Arielle herself was aware of the conflicts he was going through, and Eddie did nothing to enlighten them. Instead, as the school year wore down, he talked increasingly of his plans for the future. He had made his mind up, he said, about a lot of things, including where to go to college. After toying with the notion of attending Berkeley, where Arielle would enroll in the fall as a freshman, he had decided, firmly, on going to Stanford. His choice was part calculation—a Stanford diploma, he decided, would be more prestigious than a Berkeley one—and in part the result of a football game he had seen on television the previous fall. Stanford and Cal had been playing, and Stanford had come back from a forty-point halftime deficit to win by a point. A school that could overcome such adversity, Eddie jokingly told friends, was obviously for him.

What he would do after college was less certain, but one way or another, according to Eddie, it would involve Spain. Already he was talking of returning to Barcelona the following summer and working as a rhythm-and-blues disc jockey at a local discotheque. Once college was completed, he said, he'd come back for good, take up a career in business, perhaps manage a string of hotels. He loved the Spanish, he told Arielle. They were "generous" and "real," not at all like "the phonies" he knew at Exeter.

He continued to hold to that view, despite being accosted one spring night by two submachine-gun-toting members of the Guardia Civil. They had been suspicious of a black boy's presence in a white neighborhood after dark, and they remained suspicious, even after Eddie informed them he was an American prep school student, studying at SYA. As Eddie later told the story, they would have jailed him but for his insistence that they go to the home of his Spanish "mother." Grudgingly, the police agreed, and they released Eddie only after his "mother" had testified to his bona fides. In many respects the incident was not unlike the night the faculty member at McConnell had confirmed his whereabouts by calling David Daniels. On that occasion Eddie had been highly upset and accused the faculty member of racism. About the Spanish cops, however, Eddie could only laugh.

The rest of the school year passed uneventfully, and in early June classes were dismissed. On what was to be the group's last night in Spain together, Arielle, stricken at the realization that she would not be seeing many of her friends again, went to Eddie seeking solace. They spent seven hours together, Eddie talking to her and soothing her. By the time he had finished, dawn was breaking. "I need to kiss you," Arielle said. Eddie leaned forward and they embraced. As he pulled away, he could see that Arielle was crying. "Don't worry," he sang to her, "everything's going to be all right."

12

ON A SUNNY SUNDAY AFTERNOON IN EARLY SEPTEMBER, THREE
months after Eddie's return from Spain, and a few days before the start
of classes for what would be his final year at Exeter, there was an
unexpected knock on the door of the Perry family apartment. Eddie,
who was spending the day alternately packing his things, baby-sitting
his sister, and writing a long letter to Arielle, opened it and immediately burst into a smile. It was his old friend from Cilley Hall, David
Daniels.

More than a year had passed since the two had seen each other, and
Daniels, who had come to New York to take up graduate studies in
theology, was startled by how much Eddie had changed. The boy who
had gone off to Spain had grown into a young man, tall, confident,
mature. Daniels barely had time to register his surprise before Eddie
began pouring out all the wondrous things that had happened to him in
Spain.

On and on he talked, describing his good times and adventures, until
Nichol, who had been confined to the apartment for failure to attend
church that morning, burst into the living room, begging to be let out.
Eddie was adamant: rules were rules, and Nichol had broken them.
She was staying in.

Nichol, however, was not easily deterred, and after more minutes of
whining pressure, Eddie finally negotiated a compromise: Nichol
could go out, but only after she had written a book report. When she
did go out, there would be very precise limits on how far she could go,
what she could do, what time she had to be home.

Listening to Eddie's prep school legalisms, laid out exactly as they
were at Exeter, Daniels was tempted to laugh. Without any sense of
irony or contradiction, Eddie was visiting on his sister the very stric-
tures that so infuriated him.

"I was going to call him on it," Daniels recalled nearly a year after
the visit, "but I didn't have the heart. Eddie was in such a good mood

that day. In fact, I'd never seen him so excited, so completely happy. It was Spain that had done it to him. He was so positive about everything that had happened to him over there. Even the racial incidents he'd run into, some of them a lot worse than had ever happened to him at Exeter, didn't seem to bother him. He was still in the afterglow of that experience.''

So, according to many people, Eddie seemed that final year—at least at first. Coming back to Exeter, he appeared not only ready but eager to reinvolve himself in campus life. He tried out for the football team, something he had never done before, and though he barely made the squad and seldom played (as a defensive back), he impressed his coaches as an uncomplaining hard worker, unafraid, as one of them put it, ''of sticking his nose in and taking some licks.'' His classmates were taken with him, too, particularly after Eddie delivered a joke-filled speech in daily assembly on his experiences overseas—not the racial conflicts he had encountered but the señoritas. He also seemed in excellent spirits in mid-October, during the on-campus appearance of a State Department official who had come to Exeter to defend U.S. policy toward South Africa. Eddie was one of the few students to challenge the official, but his questions were respectful, and afterward the official sought him out to congratulate him for the thoughtfulness of his views.

But as the year wore on, Eddie's good humor and civility began to wane. ''Something happened to him,'' said one of his classmates. ''He wasn't the same old Eddie anymore.''

The change showed up first in his academic performance. Though still capable of doing excellent work, such as a paper on *King Lear* that fairly dazzled one teacher for the originality of its insights,* Eddie increasingly began coasting through assignments, doing only the minimum required to get by. ''I always had the impression that Eddie was winging it,'' said Donald Schultz, who taught a course in business theory.

---

*In his *Lear* paper, written for English teacher David Weber, Eddie took the famous line from Edgar's concluding speech—''[We must] speak what we feel, not what we ought to say''—and stood it on its head. Lear's daughter Cordelia, he pointed out, had done just that, and as a result, Lear's world had gone to hell. ''It was, I thought, a very subtle and sophisticated argument,'' recalled Weber. ''It showed me that Eddie intuitively knew what irony and ambiguity mean. He thought in those terms. There was a formidable mind there, which was not seeking easy answers. He was trying to analyze and break down situations, and once he had, he knew they could not be put back together in any sort of easy or convenient fashion.''

He had a lot of theories, a lot of things he believed in, but nothing to back them up. I suppose he thought he could just out-argue everybody. But the other kids were ready for him. They were all seniors and they had been dishing it out around the Harkness Table for four years. Eddie would start defending something like government social programs or black enterprise and these sophisticated suburban kids would just tear him to pieces. I told him several times, "You've got to do the reading. If you don't prepare, you're going to wind up getting beat every time." It seemed to have an effect for a few days, but then he'd slip back into the same old pattern and wind up getting devoured all over again. It was frustrating to me, because I knew he was bright—he was bright as hell. I just couldn't get him to do the stuff.

Other teachers noted the difference in Eddie as well, not only the drop-off in his effort, but also the growing ferocity he was bringing to class discussions. He startled one class, which was examining the history of the civil rights movement, by endorsing the Black Power militancy of Stokely Carmichael, and denouncing the nonviolent coalition-building methods of Martin Luther King as "accommodating white racism." In another course Eddie interrupted a discussion of apartheid by calling for the violent overthrow of the South African government. "He'd make statements with such strength," recalled Rick Schubart, who taught Eddie history in the first semester of his senior year.

It wasn't so much his words as the way he said them. There'd be such a feeling of hostility and tension. He'd be sitting back with a look on his face that said, Well, I'm sitting here listening, just to be polite, but here is what the real situation is. If you disagreed with him, he gave you a look like you were either a racist or an idiot. Instead of stimulating discussion, it had the effect of ending it.

I'd never had this kind of trouble with another student. Oh, I've had students who were as radical as Ed, in some cases, more radical. But he wasn't radical in the political or intellectual sense. Ed lacked the intellectual depth to be a true radical. Instead it came across as this pervasive personal angst.

It got to the point where I began having a nervous anticipation about going to class, wondering what he was going to do. Because with Eddie, you never knew what would set him off. Some days he could be very pleasant to be with, very kind, very supportive, very loving. But just when you got to the point where you thought everything was fine, he would say something that would throw the whole class out of whack.

By the middle of the term I had really had it with him. I was sick of all this nastiness and obnoxiousness, and I was thinking seriously of asking him to leave the class. But after thinking it over, I decided to give him one last chance. So I took him aside one day and tried to explain to him what his attitude was doing to the rest of the class. His reaction really stunned me. He told me I was overreacting and didn't understand him. He said I was the one off base, not him. I said to him, "Look, Eddie, if you want to reject any attempt at dialogue, that's your decision." He said "Fine" and walked off. I like to think that somehow, at some point, I can reach anybody. But I couldn't reach Ed. He had—and there's only one way to describe it—this almost scary contempt for people.

Outside of class Eddie was being difficult as well, especially, it seemed, with anyone who was white. Mike Drummey, who had been his football coach, spotted him walking across campus after the season was over and called out to him, "Eddie, how ya doing?" "He just laughed," said Drummey, "as if to imply, You don't care how I am doing." On another occasion, Werner Brandes, a German teacher who had taken a special interest in black students since the early sixties, went to Eddie's dorm to ask him to appear on a special panel for a visiting group of educators. Eddie snapped at him, "What do I get in return?" Still another teacher told of seeing Eddie atop an expensive new ten-speed bicycle, and suggesting to him that he ride out to the edge of town, where a group of poor whites lived in a trailer camp. "I thought he'd like that, being able to see for himself that there were poor whites as well," the teacher recalled. "But Eddie wasn't interested. He said—a little flippantly, I thought—that he was really a city kid, that he didn't care how people lived around here."

By the end of the first semester, Eddie's behavior, so un-Exonian in its rudeness, had become the source of some chitchat in the faculty lounge. Most teachers tended not to make much of it. Eddie had a reputation for being argumentative, and this was only more of the same. Others felt that he was acting out his racial identity, expressing, as one of them later put it, "legitimate black rage." The few, like English teacher Alan Levy, who approached Eddie, trying to find out what was wrong, were invariably rebuffed. "There was always a don't-bother-me-I-don't-have-time-for-you look on Eddie's face," said Levy. "Without ever coming right out and explaining it, he always gave you the sense that Harlem was his world and that somehow Exeter was cheating him out of it."

The one faculty member Eddie did open up to, if only a little, was Anja Greer, who had taught him freshman math, and to whom he came for a college recommendation just before Christmas. To Greer, who had grown up herself in Harlem, in a small Finnish ghetto on 125th Street, it was apparent that Eddie was troubled, and that race was troubling him most. "He said he was finding it very difficult at school," she remembered.

Everything was so different at Exeter: the values, the experiences, just the way people were as human beings. Even after four years, it was still confusing to him. He said he felt, in a way, like a hypocrite. Here he was, coming on like a kid from Exeter, and his true self, the person he really was, was the boy on 114th Street. He didn't know which were going to be his values: Harlem's or Exeter's. It was apparent he was very upset by it—upset to the point where he should have had counseling. I told him he needed it and asked him why he didn't seek it. He said there wasn't anyone on campus he could talk to, that the only people he could talk to were black. Any time he tried to open up to whites and be honest, he always wound up hurting someone's feelings. I asked him why he was talking to me. He smiled and said, "Well, Mrs. Greer, you *are* black."

It would be some weeks, however, before all of Exeter knew just how upset Eddie was. The means that would reveal it was a schoolwide symposium called, ironically, to ease racial tensions. For Eddie, it was to be a decisive event.

I had known, dimly, of the symposium, as well as the fact that Eddie had played a leading role in it. But further information about it had been hard to come by. Racial friction was a sensitive topic at Exeter, more than it was at most prep schools—"You're touching a raw nerve here," one faculty member said. "No one at Exeter wants to believe they're prejudiced; we're better than that"—and repeatedly I had trouble drawing faculty and administrators out on the subject. Instead, they preferred to dwell on Exeter's long history of bringing blacks to the Academy (the first black student entered Exeter in the 1870s) or on the faculty's involvement in the civil rights movement, or on such distinguished black graduates as Joel Motley, '68, who had been student body president at Exeter, had gone on to Harvard, and was now a successful investment banker in New York. When pressed, a few would admit minor problems—"The local redneck population is an occasional annoyance" was a typical comment—and concede that some blacks had "adjustment problems," but claim that, by and large, race relations at Exeter were excellent, particularly in comparison with those in the outside world. "On a scale of one to ten," as one dean put it, "I'd say they were a nine."

Students, I found, had a somewhat different view of things. According to them, there were racial problems at Exeter all right, and who was to blame for them depended largely on the race of the student doing the accusing. White students, like my son and his friends, tended to put the onus on blacks. Some of their complaints—such as the charge that blacks ridiculed "white" music and refused to attend "white" dances—seemed petty, while others—such as the gripes that blacks received preferential treatment in grading and college admissions—appeared to be more legitimate.* What seemed to bother them

---

*Like quotas and affirmative action elsewhere, the racial "leveraging of grades"—giving a marginal black student, say, a C minus for work that would have merited a white student an F—was a controversial subject at Exeter, "a taboo topic," one faculty member called it. Quietly, however, grade leveraging for racial reasons did go on, especially in such courses as history and English, and white students were well aware of that fact, and were nettled by it. "My position is very simple," explained one teacher who habitually leveraged grades. "We brought them here, and we have an obligation to get them through here." As far as I was able to determine, however, Eddie was never the beneficiary of such leveraging. Clearly, though, his race assisted him in winning admittance to colleges like Stanford and Yale. Several Exeter faculty members admitted

most, however, was the sense that blacks had become so suspicious of white motives that any meaningful contact between the races was impossible. "Most of them don't want to have anything to do with us," said one white student. "They aren't interested in talking to you, eating with you, being with you. You try to be nice, and they say you're only trying to cover up being a racist. You don't like them, you're a racist, too. It's always racist this and racist that, as if there is some kind of war going on. I don't know who they are fighting against, because there isn't any enemy."

Black students, not surprisingly, denied any such thing. There was no war, they insisted, but there was a lot of racism, and it was entirely the fault of whites. "You're not going to find people on street corners in white sheets calling you nigger," said Kevin Prager, a classmate of Eddie's from Riverdale, New York, "but there's racism at Exeter, just like there is anywhere else. It's just more subtle."

The incidents Kevin and his classmates cited—the "stupid questions," the racial jokes, the slights, real and imagined—sounded very much like those I had heard about from Lamont O'Neil and Carolyn Jones. There was little that was overt, almost nothing any of them could point a finger at much less do anything about. It was, rather, white ignorance and insensitivity that was so maddening. "They just don't know anything," as Maureen Brown, an ABC student from Cleveland, put it. "Basically, their feeling is that blacks don't have any problems. They were in slavery way back when, but now everything is all right. I guess if you are brought up in an all-white neighborhood, you don't see any problems. You think the whole world is okay." Tamara Horne, who led the black Exeter student association, the Afro-Exonian Society, during Eddie's senior year, stated it more succinctly. "It's their world," she said. "They don't have to adjust to you. You have to adjust to them."

That adjustment was particularly hard for black students with backgrounds like Eddie's. Nearly all of them had attended inner-city schools where, usually, little was expected, only to suddenly find themselves in an environment where even the best students had to

---

as much, pointing to the experience of the Exeter valedictorian in Eddie's senior year. The valedictorian, who possessed an academic and extracurricular record far more distinguished than Eddie's, also applied to Stanford. The valedictorian, who was white, was not admitted.

struggle merely to get a B. For many, the change could be a jolt. "I wonder if we are actually doing them any favors," said one faculty member. "We're taking kids out of a setting where they are comfortable, where, usually, they are the top of their class and the best in the school. We then bring them here, where they are not comfortable at all, where, in fact, they are having a helluva time. The way we rationalize it, the way we make ourselves feel better, is by saying to them, 'Go ahead, it's up to you; work hard and you can make it. This is your passport to the upper middle class.' But I wonder about the damage we are doing to them in the process. We bring them here for good reasons, but we don't very often ask ourselves what we are doing by bringing them here."

Difficult as the academic regimen was at Exeter, an even larger problem for black students, according to a number of faculty members, was the sheer difference in culture. "There are things they go through you and I can never imagine," said one teacher, a longtime proponent of bringing blacks to Exeter. "Most of them have never dealt with whites before, or been so isolated. We had one kid who came here who almost panicked. He was having nightmares every night. And the reason was he had never slept in a room before by himself."

Eventually, most black students overcame such fears, only to face an even larger dilemma: how to fit in back at home. "It's hard for these kids," said poet Dolores Kendrick, one of three blacks on the Exeter faculty. "It's not that they are running into gross racism all the time, because they aren't. And it's not that the faculty isn't genuinely concerned about integration and Exeter's not becoming a school for rich kids. They are—they really do want to make this a place for everyone; the intentions are the very best. It's just that these kids know that they will be different when they leave here. They will never again be a part of the world from which they came. You hear them talking about it all the time—and they are right. Everyone who comes to Exeter loses their homes. It goes with the territory. You might say it's part of the Exeter experience."

Other prep schools presented the same sort of difficulties for their black students. Where Exeter differed was in its attitude about them. More than most schools, it prided itself on tradition, on "the Exeter way of doing things." Thus, while other schools were busily stocking up on black faculty and minority counselors (and, in some cases, bending academic standards to do so) and instituting measures like special orientation and remedial programs, Exeter resisted doing anything that would treat black students as separate and distinct. Even so mild a proposal as creating a black student organization had initially been opposed (when the idea was put forward, in 1968, the then principal said it could come into being "only over my dead body"); it was finally allowed only with the proviso that whites would be admitted. "You go into a faculty meeting and say that Andover or St. Paul's is doing such and such to help blacks and maybe we ought to do the same, you've lost fifty votes already," said one administrator. "This is a place that prides itself on being different, that goes out of its way to find things that will make it different."

The resistance to change was still evident in 1982, when several faculty members conducted a study on black Exeter dropouts. The study revealed that of the black students who had come to Exeter in the previous seven years, 30 percent had withdrawn before graduation—a rate six times that of whites—and that the vast majority had done so not for academic or disciplinary reasons, but because, as one of the study's authors put it, "they had been psychologically crushed."* But when the study was presented to the Academy's authorities, along with a number of recommendations for changes, the reaction was indifference. "Most people didn't seem to think that the data was all that shocking," recalled one faculty member. "'What do you expect with kids from this background?' they said. 'We shouldn't really expect a higher level of success and we shouldn't make any exceptions for black kids. It's sink or swim. If they make it, fine. If they don't, so be it.' Even the most ardent believers in admitting black students weren't

---

*Among the study's other findings was that black students who enjoyed the greatest success at Exeter were those who had come to the Academy with some special talent, either academic or extracurricular. "Self-esteem is the key ingredient," said one of the study's authors. "If a kid comes in with something he knows he's good at, he's got a lot better chance of standing up to the pressures of the place." Self-esteem, however, could easily be damaged. A black girl who had been a close friend of Eddie's had entered Exeter with a standout extracurricular and academic record, seemingly everything needed for a successful prep school career. On her first day of school, however, the father of a white girl who was scheduled to be her roommate attempted to bribe another student to take his daughter's place. Though the authorities put a stop to it (the father withdrew his daughter from school), they could not prevent the black student from discovering what had occurred, and as a result, said one dean, "it was all downhill from there." After repeated academic and discipline troubles, the student was expelled, three weeks short of graduation.

so alarmed. They looked at the figures and said, 'So what? Seventy percent are getting through. That's good.' No one was shocked. No one was even particularly surprised. The feeling seemed to be that minority kids were taking care of themselves. There were other problems at the Academy that were more important.''

The black students, however, were becoming increasingly restless and in the fall of Eddie's senior year, leadership of the Afro-Exonian Society passed into tougher, more militant hands. ''There was a sullenness about them,'' said one administrator, ''a real sense of hostility and confrontation. You had the feeling that blacks and whites were living in two different worlds. It made the place damn uncomfortable.'' After several months of growing tension, Exeter devised a solution befitting Academy tradition. It called a symposium.

Titled ''The American Dream Deferred,'' the symposium ran through January and February and featured speeches, seminars, films, and sensitivity sessions, all devoted to raising racial consciousness. Eddie was a key player throughout.

His decision to become involved surprised many because, until then, he had played only a minor role in the activities of the Afro-Exonian Society, utilizing it more as a social center than as a platform to express his political beliefs. ''He was not a leader,'' as one of his teachers put it. ''Not a demonstrating type.''

The symposium itself was a rather haphazard affair—at one point, a schoolwide sing of ''We Shall Overcome'' was aborted when it became apparent that few students knew the words—and after satisfying their initial curiosity, the majority of white students found other things to do. Attendance was even lower at the racial workshops, where mixed groups of ten or twelve students were supposed to talk about their concerns while monitored by a faculty member. Eddie, who had helped organize the workshops and attended all of them, was clearly disappointed by the response. He was also confrontational with the white students who showed up. ''He was always going after people, always challenging them to say things,'' said David Weber, who taught Eddie English senior year and organized the workshops with him. ''The problem with the workshops wasn't Eddie, though. The trouble was everyone else. Every discussion group we had, the questions from the white kids were always the same: 'Why do black kids eat together in the dining hall? Why don't they like our music?' All the usual stuff. Finally, the whole thing just ran out of gas.''

By the first of February, the symposium was already showing signs of sputtering. Nonetheless, scheduled speakers continued to arrive, including a black professor of German literature from Yale named Jamie Snead. His address, delivered at an attendance-required morning assembly, was on racism at Exeter, a subject with which Snead, a highest-honors graduate of the class of 1971, had more than passing familiarity. Raised in a middle-class black section of Queens, New York, he had enrolled at Exeter with eight other blacks, only two of whom were destined to graduate. Some dropped out for academic reasons, others because of problems at home. All, however, experienced racism, including Snead, who went on to Yale and later studied as a Fulbright Scholar at Oxford University. As a packed house in the Academy Building listened, Snead told them of the indignities he had suffered, the questions he had gotten in the locker room about his "funny smell" and penis size and "how blacks did it." He remembered one white boy who, on learning that he was going out for track, advised him to try the javelin "because everyone knew how good black people were at throwing spears" and another who informed him that there would never be any blacks on the swimming team "because of the physiological imbalance between races in the ratio of lung capacity to body weight." He told how he felt, sitting in a classroom, knowing that whenever a question arose about race, the teacher would turn to him and say, "Jamie, why don't you give us the black perspective on this?" He described the loneliness of being in a small New England town with no black girls, no black music, no blacks at all save the apple-pickers from Jamaica who arrived every fall. He described, finally, sitting in his room in April 1968, reflecting on what his mother had told him—"You won't have trouble with racists at Exeter; those people up there have class; they're secure. Racists are people who are afraid"—and having the reverie broken by the harsh announcement from a white boy, "Hey, Snead, someone just shot Martin Luther King's head off."

And yet Snead had treasured his time at Exeter. It was at Exeter, Snead recalled, that he had learned to say "Why not?" "Not only why not go to Exeter," Snead told his audience, "and why not sit at white tables, but also why not think America can fulfill its pledge of justice, democracy, and compassion, and why not a society that will make America the ethical, and not just the nuclear, capital of the world. Why not?'' he repeated. ''To me, these are the two most important words in the world.''

It was a personal, deeply affecting speech. The reaction to it, however, was curiously flat. ''To look out on those blank faces,'' Snead said later, ''I might as well have been talking to them about child abuse.'' At least one person in the audience, however, seemed quite taken with what Snead had had to say and came up to him afterward to say so. It was Eddie.

Eddie was also on hand that evening at a workshop called to discuss the meaning of Snead's speech. To Snead, who made a special note about him, he seemed loquacious, charming, and also a bit of a hustler.

He talked and talked, took over the whole group, really led the discussion. I liked him though, maybe because he was interested in the speech, which no one else was, but I think really because he reminded me so much of what I had been like at that age. Back then, I was caught up in all these black-white issues, like is it okay to have white friends, do we sit with white students in the dining hall, should we make an effort to excel at so-called white areas of scholarship, the whole routine. And those were precisely the sorts of concerns Eddie was talking about. It was like nothing had changed, like ten years hadn't passed.

I tried to steer the discussion back to the point, which was what is racism like today, and how do we all deal with it, but it wasn't much good. When I asked the white students if they had any ancestors who had been discriminated against, who had had to give up part of their cultural background to become part of the American dream, no one seemed to know what I was talking about, which sort of shocked me. I don't think the black students knew what I was talking about either. One girl did say, ''Oh, yeah, I want the American dream, I want to make as much money as I can, and I know I will have to act in a certain way to do it,'' but that was as close as any of them came. Everyone thought I was talking about money. I wasn't talking about money at all.

What I was talking about, what I was trying to get across, was the importance for blacks of learning to be able to shuttle between cultures, while being critical of each.

Eddie didn't buy that argument at all. He was saying, "Why should I have to pretend? Why should I have to take on another culture? I have my own." You could tell he was hostile to white culture, and you could also tell he was very resistant to the notion of making any compromise. In a way it was hard to argue with him, because, let's face it, what I was asking him to do was to give up everything, or at least much, of what he knew. Quite clearly he wasn't willing to do that. He wasn't going to give up those cultural coordinates or reference points, even if that was what it took to make it in the real world. He didn't see why he should have to. Sooner or later he might have come to the point where he could say, "I can give up this, but I can't give up that." But he wasn't at that point yet. That night, he couldn't articulate what he would have to give up. In fact he couldn't articulate what his culture was. It was just his way of behaving. . . .

You got the feeling, listening to Eddie, that he could have been extremely good academically if he wanted to be. But you also got the feeling that he didn't want to be, that he wasn't at Exeter for academic reasons but for practical ones. Exeter was going to teach him things, yes, but more important, it was going to open doors for him. That's what he was centered on: dealing with people, not abstract concepts.

I also came away with the very distinct impression that he was, in a way, putting on an act for me and everyone else in the room. He was coming on as a slick, fast-talking, uncompromising ghetto resident, a real hustler. He talked like a hustler talks: very, very glib. But there was also something playful about it, too, as if he were trying to engage people by being devil's advocate. The more he talked, the more I wondered whether he really believed everything he was saying. It was like he was testing out his opinions on people to see how they would react to them. He was almost kind of bargaining with you about the levels on which you would take him, as if he was trying to see how much he could get away with in convincing you he was this or that person. It was like a negotiation, like bargaining in a store over the price of an

article. If you didn't like one personality, he would give you another, and if you didn't like that one, he'd give you still another.
He'd play any role you wanted him to play. He had a whole reper-
toire of personalities, five or six of them, and you had the feeling
that he could put one on to fit any person or situation.

There was something very endearing about that, something
very charming, but also something very unsettling. I remember
thinking afterward that I wanted to talk to this kid more. I thought
it would be nice if I could steer this guy in the right direction, give
him some sense that if he made some token compromises, everything would be fine and he'd come out ahead. At that point,
though, it wouldn't have worked. He was really resistant. He was
really clinging to something he didn't want to let go of.

Twelve days later, the full depth of Eddie's feelings were revealed
to the entire Exeter student body. The occasion was a schoolwide assembly to mark the birthday of Martin Luther King, and Eddie was the
featured speaker. He chose for his text an address that had been written
immediately after Dr. King's assassination by a former Exeter student
named Thee Smith. Smith had been one of the founders of the Afro-
Exonian Society and his speech had been tough and angry. In the context of the times, however, it had made jarring sense. But the times had
changed, and several of Eddie's friends urged him to tone down the
rhetoric. "I was worried for him," one said. "I didn't know how it
would go down. Exeter is a very white place, and when you start
talking about race relations, people feel uncomfortable. But Eddie
wouldn't soften it. 'No,' he said. 'This is important. They've got to
hear all of it. All of it.'"

There was an expectant buzz when Eddie mounted the Academy
Building stage the morning of February 13. Word had already spread
that Eddie was going to say something unusual, something provocative. Few people in the hall, however, knew just how provocative it
would be. Eddie himself seemed calm. As he began to speak, his voice
was clear and firm. "I am the new black," he proclaimed.

I will neither babble about how much I love Jesus nor entertain
you with sparkling racial comedy. I will not eat with my fingers

nor go out of my way to sit down at a dining-hall table with you. I will not flunk out of this place, but neither will I participate in the childish fanaticism of raving with you about your math test, or your Phy Sci lab, or your grade in English. I want neither to be your enemy nor your friend. I don't want your love, or your pity, or your guilt, or your fear. I demand only that you respect me. . . .

The fact that I once accepted your definition of my role as a black nauseates me. I see in your definition . . . a continuation of the efforts to teach blacks how to act "white," and at the same time teach them to deny the legitimacy of their own culture.

As the new black, I shall not tolerate the teaching of other blacks to be industrious, puritanical, and relatively unemotional—as you are; for I feel that we, as human beings, have much more to lose by becoming white than by remaining true to ourselves, true to our culture, and true to our blackness. . . .

I, the new black, acknowledge my blackness, and the improbability of ever becoming respected in your society by getting white. . . . I am a black first, and an American when I can afford to be.

I am at Exeter not to be like you, nor to prepare myself to enter your society. . . . This school's efforts to prepare me for that type of role in tomorrow's world are futile. . . . Assimilation is no longer the solution. . . . My most effective role in tomorrow's society will be to lead the achievement of Black Power; and I, the new black, dedicate my life to that role. . . .

We are at Exeter to obtain knowledge of ourselves, and when we become leaders, we will derive strength not from your friendship, or your brains, or your money, but from ourselves.

As he finished, Eddie looked out at his audience and in a low voice announced that the speech he had just read had been written seventeen years before. He added, "Nothing has changed."

The white students in the auditorium appeared stunned and shocked. It was weird, many of them whispered to each other as they filed out; it wasn't what Exeter was about. There could be only one explanation for so blistering, so unwarranted an assault: Eddie Perry was a racist.

13

OF THOSE WHO HEARD EDDIE'S SPEECH IN ASSEMBLY THAT DAY, there was at least one student who was not troubled by it, who thought that Eddie was merely telling an important truth as it needed to be told. He knew Eddie wasn't a racist because he knew Eddie. Eddie was his closest friend.

The student's name was Kennet Marshall, and, since the shooting, no one from Exeter had been more outspoken in proclaiming Eddie's innocence. "Eddie never steals from anyone. No way. No way," he told one of the reporters who interviewed him. "He's a very religious and moral guy. He doesn't do things unless they are right. I *know* he didn't mug him."

There was an earnestness about Kennet's testimony (according to the reporter, there were tears in his eyes when he spoke) that, whether it was true or not, struck me as impressive. I was further impressed by the fact that unlike so many who had taken up the banner of Eddie's innocence, Kennet, who had come to Exeter as a postgraduate transfer student from Washington's exclusive Morat School, did not appear to have an ideological ax to grind. He was simply the best friend of a boy who had been killed, or as Kennet himself insisted on putting it, "murdered." Striking, too, was Kennet's behavior since Eddie's death. He'd actively involved himself both with Eddie's family, to whom he had given a thousand dollars he'd received as a graduation gift, to help cover burial expenses, and with his classmates, several of whom were able to fly in for the funeral thanks to Kennet's generosity. Afterward, he'd been in the lead of the demonstration that marched on Van Houten's police precinct, and later still he expressed even more intimate solidarity by having himself baptized as a member of Eddie's church. Even now, months after the killing, he continued to refer to Eddie in the present tense, as if he were still living, as in Kennet's memory he clearly was.

All this made me want to talk to Kennet Marshall and test on him the various things I had been hearing from Eddie's classmates and teachers. But there was one other reason as well, one other item that made his relationship with Eddie seem so intriguing. Kennet Marshall was white.

After several false starts—Kennet was shuttling between the New York apartment of his father and stepmother and the Washington home of his mother and stepfather—I finally got hold of him in New York, where he was working a summer job, prior to enrolling at Occidental College in California. Over the phone Kennet said he was quite anxious to do everything possible to help clear his friend's name, including, if necessary, granting another interview. We made arrangements to meet the next afternoon, and then, disconnectedly, Kennet started talking about Eddie. He told of seeing his body at the funeral home ("His face was all bloated up; it just didn't seem like Eddie"), and of the march on the police station ("I thought that everyone in Harlem would walk along with us, that they would stop what they were doing, which was nothing, and come along. But that didn't happen. No one seemed to care that much. On the streets, Ed's death was no big deal"), and finally, of what it had been like for him to carry Eddie's memory all these weeks. "I try to forget what happened," he said, "but then something comes along and I remember and I feel like shit and get mad at the world. It's hard not to feel that way, hard not to remember. He was my best friend, you know."

In person, the next afternoon, Kennet turned out to the picture-book prep: fresh, open-faced, blue-eyed, and eager—the sort of student an admissions officer likes to have on the cover of his catalog. Kennet's portrayal of Exeter, however, was far from idyllic.

"The intellectual atmosphere was amazing," he said, "but basically, it was like a jail. Every day I woke up hating it, and every day something else would happen that would piss me off even more. I couldn't stand being in this tiny little town, having everyone tell me where to put each step. The kids always bitch about it, but deep down, they really like it. They really think of it as their home. I think that was more disturbing to me than anything else, knowing that there were a lot of people my age who actually felt comfortable there."

As Kennet proceeded to tell his story, however, it was clear that he had found at least one comfort: the friendship of a boy from Harlem named Eddie Perry.

The first time I met Ed was one night in late October. I was in my room in Ewald Hall and a PG named Dave Smith came over with some of his friends, one of whom was Ed. There must have been seven or eight of us and we were sitting around having the usual Exeter conversation, telling each other how terrible it was and how we couldn't wait to get out. Everyone was talking and joking and having a pretty good time. Everyone, that is, except Ed. He wasn't saying anything. He was just standing off in a corner, arms folded across his chest, looking cold and serious and kind of scary. It was like he was checking us out, trying to make his mind up whether we were worth his attention and energy.

This went on for about twenty minutes, all the time Ed standing there, this big scowl on his face, not saying anything, like he was in some kind of trance. And then, click, he just came out of it, sat down and started talking and laughing with everybody else. The only difference is that Ed was sharper than anyone in the room. Whatever we were talking about, he'd get to the point of it, sum it up, and make some really hilarious comment. I saw right then that he was incredibly smart and perceptive and insightful and cool. He was a ''bad dude'' in the good sense of the word.

After that, Ed and I hung out together all the time. Since most of his friends were black, mine ended up being black, too, and for a while I went out with a black girl. It wasn't any big deal for me—my stepmother is black and I have a lot of black friends in Washington—but it was a big deal for some people at Exeter. I didn't get any static from the white kids—they were too smart to be prejudiced—but I did get some looks. There were plenty of people wrinkling up their noses and making jokes. As for the black kids, I never had any trouble from them. Ed was a big man in that community, and right from the beginning, he made it plain that they had no choice: they had to accept me. So they did.

Ed himself wasn't hung up about race at all. Yeah, he was sensitive—more, I guess, than most of the other black kids—and yeah, he spent most of his time with other black people. But at Exeter that's not unusual at all. The whole cultural and social atmosphere there is different. The jokes you make, the way you talk to each other, it's just *different*. So of course he spent most of his time with other black people. But he could be with white people just as easily. I'm white, and I was his best friend. The kid who was his best friend in Spain was white, too, and so was the girl he was going out with. Eddie didn't let any group or clique tie him down, which is kind of amazing, since cliques is what Exeter is all about. He could be with black people and he could be with white people and he could be with himself.

That's the way it was with our friendship. Race had nothing to do with it. It was beyond race; it was above it. We were best friends because we were better, stronger, and happier together than we were when we were alone. That's how we dealt with the freezing cold, the long work hours, and all the restrictions that make Exeter seem like such a prison. We were both city boys and we both wanted to be back home. . . .

I know he was having problems with a lot of other kids at school. But it wasn't a black/white thing—Eddie hardly ever put things in racial terms—it was personal. He thought, and he was absolutely right, that most of the kids were incredibly closed-minded, and it was really getting to him. Everything up there is so homogeneous: the kids, the administration, the faculty, the little town. For a kid like Eddie, who was such a worldly guy, who had this total confidence in himself, who had this vision that ninety-nine percent of the world doesn't have, it was hard to deal with. Exeter was holding him back. It was restricting him. He was so much more on the mark than anybody at that school, and here he had to follow all their petty rules and regulations. He had that place by the balls, basically, and he couldn't do anything about it. All he wanted to do was get out of there. That's what he talked about all the time: getting out, moving on, going home. . . .

Home was important to Ed; it was on his mind a lot. When I'd go to his room, I'd notice that he'd have the shades all the way down and the window closed, even if it was hot and sunny or if it was snowy and beautiful. One day I said to him, "Ed, don't you want to have some fresh air and see the sun?" He said, "Look, Kennet, I'm not really here. I'm dreaming I'm in New York now . . . I'm anywhere but here. I don't want to be looking out at those people with their books."

At first, I didn't know what Ed was talking about. I couldn't understand why he was so in love with a place like Harlem. I thought to myself, Isn't he ashamed of the place? But then, at Christmas, he invited me home with him. After I got on the block and saw all the kids jumping rope and running across the street in the daytime and the lights and the old people who stayed outside late at night, my eyes lit up. I knew why Ed liked it so much. It was as if the place was on fire with people. . . .

I liked the people on that block. They weren't doing anything scary. They were just poor, poor black people who weren't doing much except hanging out. They never came downtown. Their whole life was there in that neighborhood. But, I can tell you, they are good people, really open and friendly, the kind who will just come up to you and say, "Hi, how are you doing?" Even now when I go up there, kids call out to me, "Hey, white boy. What's up?" They know I'm friends with the Perrys and every-thing's fine.

Anyway, that Christmas Ed showed me all around. He knew everyone and everyone knew him. Everyone respected him. They knew he was the only guy on that block who was very smart and going away to school; they knew he had gone to Spain; they thought he was amazing.

Ed didn't say anything negative about the people on his block who weren't making it. He just felt sorry that they didn't have a mother like he did. Whenever he'd talk about his mom, he'd al-ways mention how strong she was, how determined, what a great love of learning she had, how incredible it was that she had kept the family together. Ed used to say that if it hadn't been for his mother, he would have ended up on the streets. She devoted her whole life to those kids and Ed knew it. He told me once that all the work he had done at Exeter was for her.

It was on that note that my first conversation with Kennet ended. Nearly all of what he had said about Eddie was interesting, and much of it I thought rather poignant. But Kennet had said some jarring things as well. The comments that everyone on 114th Street was "really open and friendly" and that Eddie was acknowledged by the block as the only one who was "very smart," not to mention Kennet's insistence that Eddie was "not hung up about race at all"—these were all matters on which I had considerable information and knew, simply, not to be true. It made me wonder about Kennet—not about his honesty, but about the way he seemed to be almost living through Eddie, seeing in him the things he wanted to see.

At least to an extent, that also turned out to be the case with Kennet's father, Pitkin Marshall, a self-consciously hip Manhattan attorney, and his stepmother, Vivione, a strikingly attractive young black woman who had once worked as a model. Kennet had told me that during the vacation when he had accompanied Eddie to Harlem, he had taken Eddie to meet them at their downtown loft. The visit, according to Kennet, had gone well. According to the Marshalls, it had also made a deep impression.

PITKIN MARSHALL:

We were having a dinner party and there were ten people around the table, some black and some white, when Kennet walks in with this guy. He was not like anyone Kennet had ever brought home before. He was different—and not just because of his intelligence. In fact, his intelligence wasn't all that remarkable. What was remarkable was the contact he had with reality. He was the kind of kid who, very early on, let you know that if you were going to deal with him, it would have to be on as straight a basis as possible.

The boys sat down and everyone began to talk. We talked about a lot of things: about Exeter, about his year in Spain, about black/white things, about whatever people talk about at a New York dinner party. It was a pretty high-powered social gathering, and that kid turned out to be the star, the absolute star. Wherever the conversation went, he would be there. Without in any way coming on as obnoxious, he would get in front of the talk, dominate and lead it. This guy was strong, he was polite, he was witty, he was sensitive.

I have to tell you, I was impressed. He wasn't like most kids his age. He knew what was important. He was right where it was real. Here he was, at Exeter, in the midst of a world very alien from the one he had grown up in, a highly structured, privileged world, and he had managed both to succeed in it and be objective about it. He had it under control. He had a real understanding of nineteen-eighties racism, and because he understood it so well, he wasn't going to come close to approving anything that kept him down, that controlled him, that made him toe the line. There was an awful lot of bullshit he had to put up with at Exeter, but he was capable of dealing with it. He wasn't struggling against it. He had put it in its rightful place. . . .

And, my God, was that kid smooth. He was so smooth and sophisticated, I assumed he was an upper-middle-class, privileged black kid—some banker's son, helping to gentrify Harlem. In fact, we were talking about Harlem at one point, the effect of the Reagan budget cuts and everything, and I asked him, "How come you know so much? What do you know about Harlem?" You're some Scarsdale black." Eddie didn't say anything. He just smiled. I only found out where he was from when my son began taking the subway uptown.

VIVIONE MARSHALL:

Kennet had been having a bad time at Exeter. He wasn't used to such a closed, strict school. He had been brought up to be a person, to believe that the kind of person you are is just as important as what you read in a book. At Exeter, that is not what they are looking for. They believe books are more valuable than people. Kennet didn't have that rigidity. He was just a very friendly, open, good kid. Also, he is interested in people different from himself. A lot of people don't even see black people. Kennet could see them. So I was impressed with Kennet and proud of him when he said he had a new black friend. But when Kennet told me his friend was from Harlem, I was skeptical. I said, "Jesus, I don't know." I mean, I'm black, but even I am afraid to go to Harlem.

But when he brought Eddie home, I couldn't believe it. He was not what I thought he would be at all. At that dinner he got into a very heavy conversation with Pit, who is a lawyer and so is always interrogating people. But Eddie handled it beautifully. He didn't revert to any clichés. He was calm. He didn't show any hostility at all. In fact, he had less hostility than I do, and I don't have very much. But the most impressive thing about him was his sense of being black. A lot of kids like Eddie who go off to these schools talk like they are white, dress like they are white, act like they are white. Eddie wasn't like that. He knew who he was. he knew he was black. . . .

Afterward, I asked him what he was going to do when he got out of school. He said, "I want to go back to Harlem and do something for my people." The answer surprised me. Maybe he said it because he was seventeen, young and idealistic. But I don't think so. I think that Eddie really meant it. I think he really did want to go back and help his people. He made me feel guilty. I said to myself, "My God, here I am thirty-three years old with a lot of advantages and I am not doing anything for black people and here is this kid who is half my age and he is already committed." It made me reflect on my life. That's what Eddie made me do: reflect on my life and what I was doing for black people.

The visits continued at Easter vacation. Once again Eddie brought Kennet home to Harlem, and once again Kennet took Eddie to meet his parents, this time, though, to Washington and the home of his mother, Julie, and her husband, Dick Clark, former Democratic senator from Iowa. The boys stayed several days in the capital, which Eddie had never seen before, and Eddie had a number of long talks with the Clarks. Julie pronounced herself quite taken with Eddie, particularly his seeming ease. "He treated us in just the most natural, low-key way," she remembered, "as if it was nothing special for him to be in the home of a former senator. He seemed tremendously comfortable with us and that made us feel comfortable, too." The former senator took a somewhat more guarded view.

DICK CLARK:

Frankly, I was kind of surprised that Kennet was attracted to Eddie. It wasn't amazing, just interesting. Apart from the fact that neither one of them liked Exeter very much, they are not really similar kids. Kennet is a lot softer than Eddie, more optimistic. He just has a completely different approach to things. Eddie's a lot tougher. I could tell that right away. There wasn't anything specific—I mean, he was polite, not overly polite, but perfectly fine—and there certainly wasn't anything that was hostile. A little defensive, maybe, but hostile, no. Still, I had the feeling from the moment I shook his hand that I was meeting a fairly tough kid. I can't really describe it. It was just his general demeanor and attitude. He looked like a kid and sounded like a kid who had been around a lot. He wasn't going to take shit from anybody—I could tell that right off. . . .

On the other hand, he was obviously anxious to learn about things. I remember one night we were playing Trivial Pursuit and Eddie didn't do that well. He would make mistakes on small things, like the pronunciation of the names of some American cities. It was surprising. Here he was so smart—and it was apparent he was damn bright—and he was making mistakes on things the rest of us take for granted. After you thought about it, you realized that these were things that kids learned at home. He was much better on the things you learn at school. What was even more interesting to me, though, was Eddie's attitude about his mistakes. He wasn't frustrated or embarrassed, he just wanted to know what was the right answer. He was enthusiastic about learning; he wanted to know everything he didn't know. I have to say also that he had some pretty strong opinions.

That came out one night at the dinner table. We were talking about the Senate and I remember he asked whether people voted for what they thought was right or what they thought politically smart. I said, ''Well, it's a little difficult to separate because this is representative government and to some degree you have to be concerned with what your constituents want. They, after all, are the people who elected you. So you make compromises, and sometimes when you look back, those weren't the right compromises to make.'' What I was telling him, basically, is that people in politics are like everybody else, not any better and not any worse. Which is to say that some of them are pretty damn honest and some of them are pretty damn dishonest.

Eddie was rather upset by that. It was his feeling that people in politics held a public trust and ought to be better than other people. I remember he said that if he was ever elected to office, he wouldn't be the kind of person who did what it took to be re-elected. He would just do what was right.

I suppose you could say that was a naïve view. But I don't think you can say that Eddie was naïve. He knew how the world worked. He just didn't like the way it worked. And considering the background he came from, who can blame him? If I had come from that background, I would probably feel a helluva lot more strongly than he did.

Nothing more came of the conversation and the rest of the vacation passed quietly. When it came time to return to Exeter, however, Julie noticed a decided shift in Eddie's mood. "He was very quiet the last day he was with us," she said. "I don't know what it was, but it was obvious he was down. He had this almost ominous look."

Whatever was troubling Eddie disappeared a few days later, when the college acceptance letters arrived at Exeter. He'd been offered a scholarship to all the schools to which he had applied, including his first choice, Stanford. Delighted, and not above rubbing it in with his classmates, most of whom had not been accepted by their first choices, Eddie tacked the acceptance letter on his dorm-room door. Then he and Kennet set about laying plans.

"We were going to have such a great summer," Kennet said when I talked to him again. "That's all Ed and I talked about: the future and how great it was going to be. We were going to line up jobs together and spend a lot of time with each other's families. He and Jonah and I were going to hang out and go everywhere and do everything."

Graduation at Exeter was on June 2. The Clarks, who came up a few days earlier to help Kennet pack up his belongings, found Eddie in high spirits, partly at the thought of going home and partly, too, because Arielle was flying in from Berkeley to attend the prom. She arrived the next day, bringing with her Eddie's graduation present. To Julie, the gift seemed to sum up the innocence of their relationship. It was a stuffed teddy bear.

That night, the Clarks, Kennet, Eddie, and Arielle went out to dinner. As they ate, the boys talked about Exeter. "They were bitching about it a little," Dick Clark recalled. "Kennet was doing most of the talking, describing how they were able to sneak out of their dorm rooms at night by climbing out a window. It was apparent that both kids were trying to figure out how to beat the system. Eddie, who wasn't doing much more than grunting every now and then over what Kennet was saying, didn't seem to have any deep-seated dislike or hatred for Exeter. He just wanted to get around it. When we dropped him off at his dorm, Eddie turned to my wife and said, 'This is the nicest day I've ever had.' The funny thing is, it wasn't that remarkable an evening."

Following graduation, Eddie, Arielle, and Kennet flew to New York. They spent three days together, summer-job-hunting, touring the city, and taking in all the tourist spots. On June 6, Kennet went to Washington for a planned outing with some friends at Bethany Beach in Maryland. The next day, Arielle returned to California. It was the last time either saw Eddie alive.

JULIE CLARK:

We got the call on Thursday, the thirteenth. My mother was visiting and Dick and I were out playing tennis. When we came back, my mother said that Kennet had gotten a phone call saying that one of his very close friends had been killed. She didn't know who it was or who had called. About an hour later, my aunt, the wife of the Exeter treasurer, called and told us it was Eddie. I just reacted with absolute horror and disbelief. I couldn't understand how this could have happened to Eddie.

DICK CLARK:

I started making calls to find out what happened. I called the Associated Press in New York, but they didn't know much more than we had found out from Exeter. Then I called Eddie's mother in New York, but she was still in a state of shock. We didn't know how to get hold of Kennet. Finally, the next day, his father tracked down a number for him and told him to get home as soon as possible. He didn't tell him what had happened. He just said there had been an emergency and that it was important for Kennet to get home as soon as possible.

KENNET MARSHALL:

When I drove up to the house, everyone was standing on the porch. They all turned around and looked at me. My stepfather was shaking and white. He took me by the arm and pulled me into a room. "What's the matter?" I said. All he would say was "We have to talk." I knew right then that someone was dead. Then he told me: "A good friend of yours has been killed."

DICK CLARK:

I thought when I told Kennet it would just knock him over and he would start crying. But he just sat there. I've never seen anyone so uncertain what to do. He was so shocked by what had happened that it just didn't register. Then he had this strange reaction: he went outside and started shooting baskets. He must have been out there for an hour, just shooting baskets.

14

IN KENNET'S DEPICTION, EDDIE'S SENIOR YEAR HAD BEEN PLACID AS a pond, unmarked, unruffled, disturbed only by the gentle breeze of wanting to graduate and move on. I could understand why Kennet wanted to believe that, since if there had been no problems, no hint of anything about to go wrong, then the case for Eddie's innocence was that much bolstered. The only trouble was I didn't think it was true.

My conclusion was based partly on deduction—it made no sense that Eddie would indulge in anything as reckless as criminality if the months leading up to his shooting had gone as smoothly as Kennet claimed—and partly, too, on the stories I had heard from Eddie's teachers, who repeatedly used words like "hostile," "belligerent," and "angry" to describe Eddie's mood in his senior year. Anja Greer, for one, had been sufficiently unsettled by Eddie's agitation to recommend that he seek psychiatric counseling, but the closest Eddie had come to the Exeter psychologist, Mike Diamonti, was playing basketball with him one afternoon in the gym. Even in that setting, Diamonti could sense that something was not quite right. "The rest of us were out there on the court smiling, goofing around, having fun," Diamonti recalled. "But not Eddie. The look on his face was just a few degrees away from hostility. He was working harder, trying to win. It was almost as if he was trying to prove something."*

What swayed me most, though, was what I had been hearing from Eddie's black classmates.

Originally they had been reluctant to say anything critical about Ed-

*The counseling recommended for Eddie was a relatively new feature at Exeter, which was one of the last major prep schools to hire a psychologist, and then only after one successful suicide and a rash of other attempts. Among a good many faculty members, however, the need for counseling continued to be disputed, and partially as a result, Exeter had seen five counselors come and go in the last ten years. "There are still a lot of people on the faculty who don't buy it," said one teacher, who did a considerable amount of informal counseling on his own. "We're dealing with bright and sophisticated kids, so we assume that they are grown-up as well. Nobody comes right out and says it, but the attitude is we're dealing with the best, the brightest, the most emotionally stable. Many times, though, it's the brightest kids who get into the most trouble. The very fact of their brightness makes it harder for them to fit in with their peers back home. Emotionally, they tend to be a lot younger than kids their age. They and their parents spend a lot

die, but after talking to Kennet, I went back to several of them and pressed harder. Though still wary, a few began to open up, confirming that during senior year something had indeed changed about Eddie, and that the change was for the worse. "He just wasn't himself the second part of the year," one of them put it. "He didn't connect with people the way he used to. He was moody and angry. He wasn't the same old Eddie anymore."

One incident they cited was Eddie's dealings with younger blacks. As an underclassman, said his friends, Eddie had gone out of his way to take new black students under his wing, counseling them about the difficulties at Exeter, assuring them that feeling homesick was all right, adding that he was homesick, too. The important thing, he would always say, was hanging in, sticking it out. As a senior, though, the counsel he provided was radically different. Twice, young black students who were thinking of withdrawing came to him for counsel, and in each instance Eddie advised the student to go home. Both ended up doing so. One was Lori Crozier, a third-year ABC student from Gary, Indiana.

"I was trying to decide whether to stay or leave for the second semester," she recalled. "I was thinking I should stay, to get into this or that college. But then I went to Eddie, and he kind of changed my mind about that. He made me feel that Exeter wasn't the greatest place in the world. He said, 'You go to Exeter and you get presented with a whole lot of ideas that aren't your own. Reagan-type ideas. You gradually begin to believe them and then accept them. You gotta take a break,' he said. 'Go home and talk to the brothers and the sisters.' He said that Exeter wasn't the place for us."*

---

of time developing their intelligence but not their social skills. And the hell of it is, it's hard to reach them. These are kids who regard adult culture as the enemy."

Black students, according to a number of teachers, were particularly hard to reach. "The black kids are less open about their troubles," said a faculty member. "I'm pretty good about picking up when a kid is having difficulty, but the black kids send off different signals, different cultural vibes, and I miss them." The few blacks who did seek counseling invariably did so for personal reasons ("Boyfriends, girlfriends, school work, the usual," one counselor described it), not for help with racial problems. "They're obviously under a great deal of pressure," said an Exeter counselor. "Mostly, though, they don't talk about it. And the problems of being black and being at Exeter—that's something they never talk about. What support they get is from each other, and it usually isn't much."

*After returning home and getting a taste of life in an inner-city high school, Lori changed her mind and applied for readmission to Exeter. Her application was denied.

More alarming than Eddie's rhetoric was his behavior. According to his black classmates, he was doing uncharacteristically risky things, such as sneaking out of his dorm at night, sassing teachers back in the dining hall, traveling into Boston, without permission, to meet a girl-friend from Milton. "Don't worry about me," Eddie informed one friend as he prepared to slip into a female dormitory after dark, an offense that could have led to his expulsion. "I never get caught."

Eddie never did get caught, but that did not stop his friends' concern for him. "I worried about him sometimes," said Maureen Brown, an ABC student from Cleveland who had known Eddie since they had been preps together.

He was always saying the rules were bullshit. Why couldn't he go where he wanted to? Why could he do this? Why couldn't he do that? He thought it was white people's way of controlling him. "That's what these white people are into," he said. "Control. You have to hold back all your feelings, control all your emotions. They don't want you to know about life. They want you to be perfect."

It was really getting to Eddie. He felt cramped, boxed-in. Exeter was not the kind of life he was used to having. He said to me once, "Here I am in this Puritan situation. I feel out of place. These people don't want to be real. They want to live in the sixteenth century."

Eddie was right: there are a lot of kids at Exeter afraid of life, afraid of being real. But I had been with these superrich white people before, and it didn't bother me the way it bothered him. I tried to talk to him about it, explain it to him, but Eddie wouldn't let it ride. He was very, very angry.

Neither Maureen nor anyone else I talked to knew the reason for Eddie's anger. Instead, they had only guesses and theories, one of the most popular being a phenomenon known at Exeter as "senior slide." "After four years here most kids have had it with the place," one administrator explained. "They don't want to work anymore. They don't care. It's especially true of kids, like Eddie, who come back from overseas. They've grown up over there, been on their own, seen the real world. They're ready to move on. But they can't, so it makes them resentful.''

It was an interesting observation, and if true, it accounted for the fall-off in Eddie's academic performance and at least part of his resentment. What fourth-year lethargy didn't explain, however, was why so much of Eddie's anger had a racial bent. As it happened, there was a theory for that, too. "It happens to a lot of black kids that age," said Victor Young, a black admissions officer at Andover. "The older they get, the tougher they get. The more they are around whites, the more they are aware of racial differences. By the time they get to be seniors, most of them are angry as hell.''*

Again, the hypothesis was intriguing, but again, it failed to account for everything. How was it, for instance, that Eddie could have been so relaxed in Spain, so seemingly oblivious to racial insults, and then, in the space of a few short months, have become so profoundly upset? And why was it that so many of Eddie's classmates and teachers had seen such a distinct change come over him at the close of the first semester? Had something happened to him? Had there been an incident? And if so, what?

The mystery remained, and I was beginning to doubt whether I would solve it. Moreover, I was rapidly running out of places to look. There was, in fact, only one spot left: Eddie's dormitory, McConnell Hall.

Among Exonians, McConnell, which was located on the campus's

---

*Young, who had come from a neighborhood similar to Eddie's—the west side of Philadelphia—and like him had gone to prep school (St. Paul's) on a scholarship, also knew Eddie, albeit briefly. Their acquaintance had stemmed from an encounter in the Andover gym a few days after Eddie's graduation. At the time, Andover was playing host to a meeting of the New England Afro-Latino Students Association, and Eddie, who was attending the conference, was taking a break by shooting some baskets. Young, a prep school and college basketball star, was not impressed. "He was the kind of kid," he remembered, "who, if you were choosing up sides for a game of Horse, no one would choose him. I was kidding him about it, giving him a lot of grief about the tough game he was trying to play. 'You can't play.' I told him. 'You can't play at all.' Eddie's reaction was to try to play even tougher. He struck me as a kid who had to play tough— not just on the basketball court but all the time. I tried to let him know that he didn't have to seem like such a tough guy—so *urbane*, as we'd call it in the black community—that there were other options out there for him. But Eddie wouldn't listen. He gave you the sense that toughness was his image, his identity at Exeter. If he wasn't that way, then people wouldn't think that Edmund Perry was black.''

southern quadrant, next door to the Academy library, enjoyed a certain notoriety. "A cesspool," one faculty member called it. "You get a bad reputation just walking by it," a female student agreed. "That place is the black hole of the campus."

According to informal campus historians, McConnell had been *the* place to party at Exeter ever since it opened its doors in 1963. The goings-on that occurred there, which reportedly included the nightly running of a cash bar, were part of Academy legend, passed down from one class to the next, along with instructions on where to hide the beer. In McConnell, that was in a crawl space behind the wall of one of the upper rooms. It was also Exeter lore that McConnell's faculty houseparents never found it, because the houseparents never looked.

It was partly because of McConnell's good-time, laissez-faire reputation that Eddie had transferred into it in the middle of his lower year. Apart from studying and sleeping, he'd barely been in the dorm the next semester, preferring to socialize with his old friends in Cilley. Upper year, Eddie hadn't been in McConnell at all; he'd been studying in Spain. Despite his absence, he was entitled to certain privileges as a returning senior, and one was being among the first to choose his room. The one he selected was a ground-floor double that, though sterile in design, possessed a handy feature: it was easy to slip out the window at night.

There were rules against such activity, of course, as, at Exeter, there were rules against a great number of activities, including drinking, taking drugs, and having women in the room. Needless to say, the existence of such regulations—even the threat of expulsion that went with them—did not prevent their circumvention, and at McConnell, Exonians agreed, there was more circumventing than anywhere else.

The authorities charged with stopping it, at McConnell as at other dorms, were the faculty houseparents, and their lot was not an easy one. Most were underpaid (the starting faculty salary at Exeter was $17,000), all were overworked (in addition to teaching and running a dorm—a ten-year prerequisite to qualify for off-campus, housing—faculty members were required to coach two sports), and many had families of their own. In addition to these demands, they were also expected to provide academic counseling, stay alert for emotional trouble (Exeter had two suicide attempts Eddie's senior year), and dispense a modicum of home-away-from-home nurturing.*

"We really aren't very good at spotting trouble," one harried houseparent confessed. "It's not that kids aren't asking for help—in fact, they are asking for it all the time—they just don't do it directly. What they will do instead is come in and talk to you for forty-five minutes or an hour about everything under the sun and then they will say, 'Oh, by the way, my mother tried to commit suicide last night,' or 'My girlfriend is pregnant,' or 'I'm worried about drugs.' The trouble is, we don't have the time to sit back and listen until they come to the 'Oh, by the way' part. After eighteen hours a day with kids, you are sort of sick of them."

Nonetheless, it was the houseparents who were immediately on the line, the adults who, if only because of their proximity, ought to have known if Eddie was experiencing any difficulty. At McConnell, where there were thirty-six boys in residence, there were three such house-parents: Donald Dunbar, a bachelor mathematics instructor who had been at Exeter since 1955; and Aldo and Vicky Baggia, a recently married couple, both popular teachers in Exeter's department of foreign languages. Since Dunbar was the senior man in terms of service (the Baggias had been at McConnell only three years), I decided to try him first.

Over the phone, Dunbar was friendly though not particularly helpful, since, it turned out, he hadn't known Eddie well. What little of

---

*What nurturing Exeter students received varied from dorm to dorm and depended largely on the disposition of the faculty houseparents, whose performance was only casually checked. At some dorms the atmosphere was warm and familylike—in one instance, preps were given cookies and milk and tucked into bed at night. At other dorms, however, there was little contact between houseparents and their charges save over disciplinary matters. "It's sort of like living in a nice brownstone in a bad neighborhood," explained one member of the Exeter board of trustees. "You know there is trouble out there and you know how to deal with it: you just close the door."

One houseparent who did spend many off-hours counseling students attributed the relative lack of supervision to the kind of faculty members Exeter attracted. "In the old days," he said, "when the faculty was all male, it was a very hard, sink-or-swim kind of place. But the faculty played a very important role in the life of the kids. They enforced the discipline, they set standards, and they ensured that kids lived up to them. It was pretty iron stuff, but the kids got the impression that the faculty really cared about them. Now that isn't the case. The faculty people we are getting are much more professional in their attitude. They're Yuppies, and they're interested in getting ahead. They're terrific in their academic fields—the very best. But too often they come here without asking themselves whether they really like kids, and there are some faculty who plainly do not like kids. They think that if they do their job well, that is enough. Getting the job done is everything. People don't stop to ask themselves, Is this what I really ought to be doing?"

Eddie he did know, said Dunbar, did not suggest a boy who would
attempt to mug a police officer. "He was not a physical person, not a
kid you would find wrestling in the common room," as Dunbar put it.
"All the reports I got on him from Cilley were very favorable. Certainly he never caused any trouble here. Check-in time is ten in the
evening and he would come in on time and go straight to his room. The
other students liked and respected him. What can I tell you? He was a
very bright young man full of promise. He knew who he was and
where he was going."

The Baggias, I hoped, would tell me more, if only because they
were in a position to know more. Aldo Baggia, who spoke half a dozen
foreign languages fluently, had taught Eddie Spanish in his prep year;
while Vicky had been his academic adviser during his senior year.
Moreover, the Baggias' apartment was directly across the hall from
Eddie's room.

Any hope that the Baggias might have the answer, however, quickly
evaporated when they met me for brunch at the Exeter Inn, with their
six-month-old daughter, Jessica, in tow. "Those who say they know
what is really going on in the dorms are crazy," Aldo said frankly.
"They are living in a pipe dream. You hope you know. But that is all
you can do: hope."

"You know the capacity is there for trouble," Vicky agreed, spoon-
ing her daughter some applesauce. "But if they do what is asked, and
seem happy to do it, you don't have time to find out anything more."
She shrugged. "Who knows what they are capable of?"

Despite such disclaimers, it was the Baggias' impression that Mc-
Connell had greatly settled down during their tenure. There were no
overt drug problems, no noticeable drinking, no racism they had been
able to detect. The biggest problem in the dorm, said Aldo, "is
noise—it gets up to a tremendous volume."

As for Eddie, he seemed to have passed in and out of the Baggias'
lives leaving barely a trace. They remembered him as a good hitter on
the dorm softball team ("Hit a home run nearly every time he came
up," Aldo recalled), as someone who could occasionally seem gruff
("Eddie had the attitude that politeness was the white man's burden,"
said Vicky), and also as one of the few boys in the dorm who paid any
attention to either their baby or their cat ("he'd get right down on the

floor and start talking baby talk—you know, goo-gooing, and making cute faces,'' Aldo said. "The other kids wouldn't do that''). Beyond that, though, there was almost nothing. "He was not the sort of person who was used to intimate disclosures,'' said Vicky. "You use what time you have for the people who seem to respond. You don't go after the people who don't. People who need guidance and care don't come to this school. This school is for students who are very independent and self-motivated.''

Of one thing, however, the Baggias professed to be very certain, and that was that Eddie had neither caused nor experienced any note-worthy trouble. "He was fine,'' said Aldo. "Never any problem. We know pretty well who the kids are who are using alcohol and drugs and Eddie's name never came up. We never had any rumors or anything to that effect. The worst thing he did was checking in late sometimes. But when you talked to him, he straightened out. He would jump through a hoop if you asked him to. He was not the anti-rules type.'' He paused. "He seemed happy. He seemed to get along with everyone. But then, with kids it's hard to tell.''

Clearly the Baggias hadn't been able to tell, and neither had Donald Dunbar. None of them, in fact, seemed to have the slightest clue about Eddie or the distress that was so apparent to his friends. If they were so unaware of a boy who had lived, literally, under their noses, I won-dered how much stock I could put in the testimonials of more distant others. "A solid citizen,'' one dean had called him. "No trouble, no violence, no drugs,'' Exeter's principal, Steve Kurtz, had seconded. "We know who those characters are here, and Eddie was not one of them.''

With few exceptions, that's how the litany had gone since the night of June 12, not only at Exeter but in Harlem as well. It was heartwarm-ing to hear—but was it true?

The only other people who could tell me were Eddie's dormmates. I'd already tried Eddie's roommate, Malcolm Stephens, an ABC stu-dent from Bedford-Stuyvesant, but aside from venturing the opinion that "the ignorance of people bothered Eddie, and their racism both-ered him most of all,'' he'd not been very informative. But there were thirty-five other sources I had not yet interviewed.

Since it was summer, many of them were away on vacation; others were at home in places as distant as Japan and Saudi Arabia. But with the help of the Exeter "Face Book," a photographic compilation of every student at the Academy, I eventually succeeded in tracking most of them down.

My interviews with the first dozen McConnellites revealed that Eddie had been the subject of considerable opinion in the dorm, and that the bulk of it had been negative. His dormmates, all but two of whom were white or Asian, faulted Eddie on a number of counts. Some complained about his "arrogance"; others, his sarcastic tongue; still others, his supposed moodiness and selfishness. However differing their assessments, though, Eddie's dormmates were united on two counts: that Eddie had an extraordinary sensitivity concerning race—"He made such a huge point about being black," as one put it, "he was so proud of his race that he expected you to dislike him for it, to look down on him because of it"—and that it was altogether possible that he had, in fact, tried to mug a police officer. Typical were the comments of one senior, a boy who had spent a good deal of time with Eddie and claimed to know him quite well. Typical, too, was the fact that he did not want to be quoted by name.

> Eddie was interesting. His desire to succeed was very great. The problem was he wanted to succeed because it would be proof of something. He was always talking about how he was going to prove this and prove that, how he was going to succeed on his own, how he was going to prove that "his people," as he put it, could make it without any of our help. He was all the time coming on like this Black Panther militant, trying to make out like it was this racial battle and that all the whites were against him.
>
> I thought it was kind of silly. People are just people, you know, especially at Exeter. But you could never convince Eddie of that. For him, it was all competitive and relative. Everything he did was measured. He was never just himself.
>
> People tried to be his friend—a lot of us did at the beginning of the year—but he never reciprocated. He never gave back anything, not even his sociability. Instead, he treated us like things, like we were factors, two and two, to be put together in some grand scheme. Eddie was a user, and he used everything he could, like levers on a machine. He would use his color, he would

use his stature, and sometimes he would even use physical threats. Whatever it took for Eddie to get ahead, he would do it.

I wanted to give Eddie a chance. I really did. I remember once, I was doing this film, for an assignment, you know, and I asked Eddie if he wanted to be in it. The story was about a drug rip-off, where one side ambushes the other. And I wanted Eddie to be one of the ones who gets killed. He refused to do it. "I am immortal," he said. "I don't die. I never die." And he's saying it like he's serious, like I'm some sort of racist for suggesting he act in a school movie.

That kind of stuff went on all the time. It was always "black this" and "black that." I mean, who needs it? After a while, you don't care who he is or where he is from. You just say, "Fuck it." And that, more or less, is what happened. After the first semester, people just stopped connecting with him.

Though they were a decided minority, there were friendlier assessments of Eddie as well, including one from a midwestern sophomore who had watched television with Eddie the night of Ronald Reagan's reelection.

I'm pretty conservative, so as you can imagine, I was very pleased by how the election turned out. Eddie, of course, was not pleased at all. He was very upset, not only by the results but about how we all seemed to be enjoying them so much. I started talking to him about it, arguing with him, and finally he invited me back to his room. We wound up spending, I don't know, six hours together, talking about Harlem and how where he comes from is so different. I remember at one point he was talking about Reagan and the cutbacks in social programs. Eddie was saying we couldn't cut back anything, because a lot of people were dying. According to him, people couldn't get back on their feet because they had never been on their feet. He was very emotional about it. He was talking about something that was part of him, and a painful part of him. He certainly opened my eyes that night. I had no idea what it was like, that it was so horrible. Eddie said I should come home with him sometime to see what it was like.

I thought that would have been great, but we never got around

to it. Because in the second semester Eddie changed. I don't
know why, but for some reason he became fairly hostile to people—racially hostile. It was sad, because I really liked Eddie.
Coming from where he did, and being able to do the things he
had, I thought it was miraculous. He was going somewhere. He
deserved to go somewhere—but he was also living his own life. I
had never met anyone like him. He was different from anyone I
had experienced. He was no token black, that's for sure.

So it had gone with the first dozen interviews, and so, with one
exception, it went with the next dozen. The exception was the revelation, later confirmed elsewhere, that Eddie had been part of an inter-
racial Exeter ''sex club'' whose members supposedly passed initiation
by making love, blindfolded, to a stranger on a seminar table in one of
the Latin classrooms. Around McConnell, this gave Eddie the reputation of being a stereotypical black stud.

Aside from this sleazy bit of business, though, I was learning precious little else, and that was strange. For, unlike the Baggias and
Dunbar, who had told me nothing because they knew nothing, it was
clear, if only from the nervousness of their answers, that Eddie's dormmates did know something but were withholding it—possibly, I suspected, because whatever the something was, they had been involved
in it themselves.

Their reticence reminded me of the plot of *A Separate Peace*, the
classic novel of prep school life by John Knowles, a member of the
Exeter class of '44. In Knowles's book, the students at ''Devon Academy'' (a place of ''opulent sobriety,'' Knowles writes, ''as though
Versailles had been modified for the needs of a Sunday school'') out-
wit their would-be overseers at every turn until, as the result of a seemingly harmless prank, one of them dies. None of the students reveal the
circumstances of the accident because to do so would not only impli-
cate themselves but, worse, violate the student code. Perhaps, I
thought, something similar had happened at McConnell. Thus far,
however, I had been unable to unlock McConnell's secret. Then I
made another call, the twenty-fifth on my list.

The student—let's call him Simon—began by saying what nearly
all his dormmates had, namely, that Eddie had an inordinate preoccu-
pation with race.

Eddie was not a person who was comfortable with himself, especially at Exeter. He was a mystery to a lot of us. He had the ability
to charm people and the ability to alienate people, and he did a lot
of both. I never knew quite what to make of him. On the one
hand, I admired his politics and ideals, all the things he said he
wanted to do for black people, and on the other, I was always sort
of uneasy with him. Mostly, it was the race stuff. He would never
let go of it. Basically, anybody who didn't like him, or who didn't
appreciate black culture, Eddie called racists. The funny thing
was, if anyone was a racist it was Eddie. He didn't look at white
people the same way he looked at black people. Instead, he examined them. If you were white, he looked at you with a much more
skeptical eye.

Simon went on in that vein for another twenty minutes. Finally, he
said, "It's too bad what happened to Eddie, because he had the poten-
tial to be a really great person. I feel sorry for him in a way, and in a
way I don't. He had so many chances, and he threw them all away.
There was almost a wantonness to it."

I thanked Simon for his opinions and prepared to hang up. Then, out
of reflex, I asked him one more question, the throwaway I pose at the
end of every interview. "Is there anything I should have asked you that
I didn't? Anything more you want to tell me?"

Simon paused for a moment and then, very matter of factly, replied,
"You know, of course, that Eddie was a drug dealer."

15

I HADN'T KNOWN ANY SUCH THING, OF COURSE, BUT I WAS NOT about to tell Simon that. Instead, feigning knowledge and promising him anonymity, I encouraged him to talk more. Talk Simon did, and armed with what he told me, I was to get many others, both at Exeter and in Harlem, to talk as well. The story that emerged from these conversations was a detailed, depressing one, and by the time I had heard all of it, some of the mystery of what had happened to Eddie Perry had begun to fall away.

According to his friends, Eddie had begun using drugs, marijuana principally, at a relatively early age, though exactly when was impossible for me to determine. By his second year at Exeter, however, he was a regular marijuana smoker and was being supplied on a steady basis by a dealer friend in Harlem. The shipments came in the mail, tucked inside a secret pocket sewn into the lining of a favorite sky-blue shirt. Every visit home, Eddie would bring the shirt back to his dealer, who would subsequently mail it to Exeter when Eddie's stash ran out. According to the dealer, this occurred half a dozen or so times per year.

The dealer himself was a likable young man who had gone to junior high school with Eddie and hung out with him often on his visits home from Exeter. Eddie, he said, was not troubled by drugs—"Ain't too much wrong with it as long as you know how to use it," the dealer quoted him as saying—and claimed that his own drug use was minor compared with what his classmates were doing at Exeter. This the dealer found hard to believe—"Don't make no sense them boys doing this, smart as they are" is how he put it to me—until Eddie proved it to him one night by putting several of his obviously stoned classmates on the phone. The dealer was impressed. He was even more taken by the stories Eddie told of his own exploits, which included, according to the dealer, attacking two white football players with a baseball bat. As related by the dealer, Eddie was sitting in the Exeter dining hall when the football players approached and, for no apparent reason, began calling him racial names. Eddie, who was about to play baseball and thus had a bat with him, warned the boys that if they continued, he would use it on them. They did, and Eddie cracked them. This story the dealer had no trouble at all believing; as it happened, it was a complete fabrication.

The relationship between Eddie and the dealer continued to flourish, interrupted only by Eddie's school year abroad in Spain. While in Barcelona, Eddie bought his drugs on the well-stocked local market and was well known to his classmates as a frequent user, both of marijuana and hashish. His involvement with drugs, which included sending an occasional package of hash home to his dealer, did not attract much attention, however, partly because Eddie seemed to handle them well, and partly because some in the group were using far more powerful substances, notably LSD.

Eddie himself was said to have very negative views about LSD and flew into a rage after discovering that a classmate had employed it to spike the punch at a farewell party held at a local disco. Eddie did not drink the punch, but a number of his classmates, unaware of what it contained, did, and there were several bad trips. One of the worst was suffered by a white girl to whom Eddie was particularly close. "The girl was just torn to pieces," a student who was at the party recalled. "She was crying. She didn't know what was going on. It was a very scary and very frightening thing. Eddie was there, trying to help her, trying to keep her, basically, from losing her brains. He was so pissed off at the jerk who had done it. I hate to think what would have happened if he had gotten his hands on him."

The girl eventually recovered, and shortly thereafter Eddie returned home and renewed connections with his dealer. He smoked marijuana heavily that summer and continued smoking it during his senior year at Exeter.

In this activity he was hardly alone. Though never as prevalant as alcohol and not nearly as widespread as on many other prep school campuses, drugs were a persistent problem at Exeter, and had been since the middle 1960s. According to a survey conducted by the campus newspaper in the fall of Eddie's senior year, over 50 percent of the Exeter student body had tried drugs at least once, and 15 percent identified themselves as daily or weekly users. By common reckoning, these numbers escalated as the school year went on, as did the potency of the substances consumed. The most alarming trend was an increasing fondness for LSD, which, after a decade of justly horrendous publicity, was staging a major comeback. Just how much acid was being popped at Exeter was difficult to measure, but apparently it was a lot. I heard credible stories of one campus dealer unloading a thousand tabs of high-powered ''windowpane'' acid during the first semester, and of another dealer who, in a single month, managed to dispose of eight hundred tabs at three dollars per hit. Though there had been a number of bad trips (in one instance, a student was discovered, cowlike, munching the grass outside the library), none, fortunately, had resulted in permanent psychiatric damage. Still, the danger was real, and during Eddie's tenure at Exeter there had been several schoolwide counseling sessions about the hazards of drug abuse. The preaching did not do much good. ''We'll have these people from Freedom from Chemical Dependency in here to give some talks,'' a faculty member said, ''and for a week or so, you'll notice a real drop-off in the level of consumption. After a couple of weeks, though, it will begin to slowly climb back, and by the time a month has gone by, it'll be right back at the level it was at before.''

The faculty offered various reasons for this, from adolescent rebellion to the cultural climate to the nature of Exeter itself. ''This can be a cold, hard place,'' said one teacher with considerable experience in drug counseling. ''If you are fourteen or fifteen years old and you are having problems at home or are feeling kind of down or the course work is getting to you, or if you are plain feeling lonely, well, you don't have to think too hard to imagine how seductive drugs can be.'' Another teacher, equally experienced (according to several students, he smoked pot himself), ascribed the problem to ''kids with too much free time, too much money, too many smarts. That,'' he added, ''is a combination that breeds difficulty.'' Still another teacher, one with a reputation for being close to students, thought that a lust for danger might have something to do with it. ''The country's been at peace now for ten years,'' he mused. ''We've made everyone safe and comfortable. But in doing that, we've taken something out of the adolescent psyche and we haven't replaced it with something. These kids want not just excitement but a kind of jeopardy. Everything else comes so easily for them. They need drugs for the same reason everyone has the urge to look over a cliff. It's scary, it's exhilarating, it's fun.''

The druggies themselves tended to explain things more simply. ''You get high for a number of reasons,'' said one student who did so frequently. ''To have a social life, which there isn't a lot of at Exeter, to game on the faculty—I was high every time I talked to my faculty adviser and he never caught it, which was another high in itself—to get rid of all the tension. Basically, though, kids get high because they would rather be stoned than unstoned. Not as an escape, but as a permanent way of conducting life here.''

Nowhere was this attitude more in evidence than at McConnell, which by all accounts was the headquarters and center of the Exeter drug culture.

While it was clear that the majority of McConnell's students had nothing to do with drugs, those who did went at it with real abandon. For the hard core in McConnell, a tight group of half a dozen white upperclassmen, among them some of the most gifted students in the school, the daily regimen would begin with a toke or two before first-period class. There would be a few more tokes at mid-morning, still more at the noon hour, and then again at three-thirty, when most classes were dismissed for the day. The truly serious drug-taking, however, did not commence until eleven-thirty in the evening, after homework assignments were completed and the faculty was safely in bed. Then the druggies, augmented by students who had snuck in from neighboring dorms, would gather in an upper room and, in the words of one of them, ''party all night.''

It was into this atmosphere that Eddie Perry, fresh from the freedom of Spain, tried to settle. At first he fit in well. As one of the McConnell druggies put it: ''Eddie Perry had a lot of drugs, so Eddie Perry was cool.''

Eddie Perry did have drugs, and according to the testimony of numerous friends, he both sold and used them. By McConnell standards, his usage was not particularly high, no more, it was generally agreed, than a joint or two per day. His dealing, too, was comparatively limited. Where others on campus were swinging single transactions involving thousands of dollars, Eddie doled out his supply of unusually high-powered marijuana and "Thai stick" ("Buddha Thai," Eddie called it) an ounce at a time. However minor-league his activities may have been, however, they were enough to win him admittance to the McConnell Club.

He was a regular participant in the nightly drug parties, and, impressed by his knowledge of drug lore, which according to Eddie included a personal acquaintance with several major New York dealers, they made him part of all their activities. They also took him along on a picnic that fall at Fort Rock, a secluded wooded area a mile or so from the campus and a favored druggie hangout.

The day of the outing was picture-postcard New England perfect. The sun was shining, the leaves were turning, and the druggies, who had brought along steaks, LSD, and Grateful Dead tapes, were in a mellow mood. Eddie, however, couldn't relax. "For some reason, he was really uptight," one of the druggies remembered. "He kept pacing around, saying that the woods were 'boring' and 'stupid.' We said, 'Come on, chill out, have some food and get wasted.' But he kept going on about how much he hated it in the country. He said he liked being in the city. He was talking about walking down the streets, with people all around, getting into fights, and stuff like that. I remember he said he had hit a teacher of his in junior high school and that he had three friends who had been murdered in Central Park. It was weird, hearing all of this stuff on such a nice day, but Eddie wouldn't shut up about it. He kept talking about violence. He said it was 'cool' and 'fun.'"

In fact, all the events Eddie spoke of so knowingly were, like the tales he told his dealer friend in Harlem, pure invention. He had never struck a teacher at Wadleigh, never known anyone who had been murdered in Central Park, and hadn't been in any more fights than the average white boy in the suburbs. A few of his druggie friends guessed as much. "Sometimes," said one, "I thought he was making things up. I mean, you had to wonder: how could such a super street kid be at Exeter? He definitely tried to portray himself as a street kid, though. He used to say that we wouldn't last five minutes on the street. What he was sort of saying was 'I can last a hundred years on the street. I am super streetwise.' I had my doubts, but since I had never known anyone else from Harlem, I went along with it. Besides, they were great stories."

They were great stories, and nearly all who heard them believed them wholeheartedly. As a result, Eddie's stature continued to grow. Within McConnell it was said that Ed Perry—"this dangerous, seedy person," as one of the druggies called him—was capable of anything, including getting them PCP.

Until then, no one at McConnell had ever tried PCP, and for good reason: of all the mind-altering chemicals, phencyclidine hydro-chloride, otherwise known as "angel dust," was far and away the most dangerous. Developed in the 1950s as a surgical anesthetic, PCP produced such drastic side effects that its use was soon restricted to veterinarians, who found it an ideal substance for knocking out elephants. Eventually, however, PCP made its way to the streets. By the late 1960s it had gained an enthusiastic following among the San Francisco flower children, who dubbed it "the peace pill" and lauded its ability to create intense euphoric states. They soon discovered that PCP was prone to create other states as well, including extreme disorientation, schizophrenia, coma, and psychotic violence. In one widely reported instance, a PCP user tore his eyes out with his bare hands. In another, a person suffocated after burrowing his head into the earth, while in still another, a PCP user burned to death after setting his chair on fire. There were also numerous drownings, murders, and suicides—not to mention seven thousand emergency-room visits each year—and as a result, PCP quickly fell from favor.

A decade later, however, PCP was back, more widespread than ever, especially in places like Harlem, where "dust" was linked to 20 percent of all homicides. What accounted for PCP's resurgence, apart from the ease of its manufacture (a high school chemistry student would have no trouble brewing it up) and the huge profits from its sale (an investment in a hundred dollars' worth of chemicals could turn a profit of a hundred thousand dollars), was something of a mystery. "It's hard to understand why people are taking PCP," one government official was quoted as saying. "They don't take it to get high. They don't take it to make sex better. They take it to get themselves zonked out. In a way, it's a disguised death wish."

For the McConnell heads, the tales of PCP's terrors made for adventuresome reading, particularly when they were contained in *Rolling Stone,* which in McConnell served as the Bible of the hip culture. It was just such an article that circulated through the dorm early in the first semester. Poring over it, the McConnell heads were frightened but intrigued. Who, they wondered, could procure them this stuff? They settled on their ghetto friend, Eddie.

Initially, Eddie was reluctant. Friends of his had tried PCP, he warned his dormmates, and had "bugged out" on it. He wanted no part of helping the McConnellites bug out as well. The druggies, however, were insistent, and finally Eddie agreed. After the Thanksgiving break he returned to Exeter with a small clear-plastic bag, inside of which, as one druggie described it, "was this black, really foul-smelling chemical spread over what looked like oregano leaves." It was PCP.

The heads, Eddie excepted, dipped their joints and took some puffs. "I thought it was great," said one. "Like being really high and alert at the same time." "It really weirded me out," reported another. "I kept thinking of violence and suicide. You know, all the stuff you read about." The heads, however, were unanimous about one thing: they wanted more.

This time Eddie declined, and no amount of money—the druggies were offering to pay him twenty-five dollars per PCP joint—or badgering could get him to change his mind. "He thought we were crazy," one of the druggies recalled. "He said if we wanted to fuck ourselves up, that was up to us. But he didn't want any part of it."

Despite the turndown, the PCP incident further enhanced Eddie's reputation among the McConnell druggies, few of whom had ever had a black friend before, especially one from so exotic a locale as Harlem. "It was exciting just being around him," one of them said. "He was a real outlaw."

Beneath the friendly façade, however, there was growing tension. Some of it was cultural: the white druggies liked Grateful Dead music, which Eddie scorned for soul and rap. Some of it, too, had to do with Eddie's involvement with drugs: he was "greedy," using other people's drugs, according to the druggies, even while selling his own at what were deemed to be "outrageously inflated prices"—a violation of the code that said that Exonians merely covered their costs. The druggies complaind as well that Eddie missed the whole point of the drug experience. "When we take drugs," said one of them, "it's to let go and get fried. Eddie liked to take drugs, but he also liked to be in control. He would smoke with his teeth gritted. You could almost hear him saying, 'I'm in control.' That's the way it was with Eddie about everything. He was so rigid. He wouldn't go outside himself." But by far the biggest source of friction was the difference of race. "All of us are white, and when you come down to it, a lot of us are pretty racist," one of the druggies admitted. "There are a few black kids we really like, but those are the ones who don't make a big deal about their blackness. When you have someone like Eddie, who's so self-conscious about his blackness, it makes people uncomfortable. That was Eddie's whole M.O. at Exeter: making a big deal about race. People were getting tired of the racial rap."

After a series of irritating episodes, the tension boiled over one night, just before the semester break. As usual, the heads were gathered in an upstairs room, tripping and listening to music, when Eddie walked in, asking whether there was any dope. There was none, but one of his friends offered him a hit of acid. For a long moment Eddie hesitated. He had never tried LSD, a supposed "white drug" and one well known for loosening inhibitions. "If you're trying to keep the lid on about anything," said an Exeter drug counselor, "acid is not the drug for you. It'll blow it right off." Whatever was holding Eddie back finally passed. He took the tab and gulped it down.

As the hallucinogen began to take effect, Eddie struck up a conversation with one of the boys in the room. The talk—"a typical acid rap about the nature of the universe and the meaning of life," according to one witness—went smoothly at first. But, as the moments slipped by, Eddie seemed increasingly agitated. To the boy doing the talking, however, nothing appeared particularly amiss. "I was saying something to him about morality, how things in life were finite," he remembered.

Like, there was nothing absolutely right and nothing absolutely wrong. It just depended on how you looked at it. I didn't think I was saying anything special. At Exeter, you have those kinds of conversations all the time. Eddie seemed to be taking it all in, accepting it, you know, like he liked it. But something must have gotten him. Because all at once I see him flying through the air at me. That's what happened: he just jumped up and threw himself across the room. No warning at all. Anyhow, he lands at my feet, and all of the sudden, there is this fist coming at my throat. He hits me once, and it knocks me back and then he hits me again and again. It wasn't like a regular punch, just an arm and a fist coming through the air. The scary thing, though, was the way he hit me, the crazy look he had.   It was like he was hitting some thing that had flesh and bone and talked. Not a person, just a thing. And all the time he's doing it, he's yelling, "Stop! Stop! Stop!"

Too stunned by what was happening to do anything, the other boys in the room looked on speechless. Finally Eddie picked himself up and, without saying another word, walked out of the room.

Thereafter most of the students in McConnell gave Eddie a wide berth. The few times he appeared in the drug-partying room, his former friends greeted him in silence. "There were some pretty awkward scenes," one of the druggies recalled. "Nobody wanted to have anything to do with him. After the first semester, he was completely isolated."

Cut off from his former friends, Eddie spent virtually all of his free time with Kennet or with other blacks. The few dealings he had with his McConnell dormmates were tense and hostile, and more than once flashed into violence. On one occasion Eddie got into a pushing match with a white student for no apparent reason. On another he took a poke at a student for making a racial joke. Later in the semester he was also suspected of stealing a white student's stereo radio. Though Eddie was known to possess an inexplicable number of duplicate stereo components, there was no proof for the allegation, and none of his dormmates ever questioned him about it. By then they didn't dare to. "You had the feeling," said one of his former friends, "that if you so much as said hello to him, he might jump you. If you did say hello, he would make a comment to one of his black friends about how insincere it was."

Eddie's change in mood was noted in Harlem as well. At one point, during Easter vacation, while Eddie was walking up 114th Street with a friend, a boy from a nearby block began ragging him about going to Exeter and ended up calling him a punk. "That'd happen to Ed all the time," his friend recalled. "Rowdy guys on the block would tease him, tell him, 'You ain't that smart, you gonna get kicked out of that school' or some jive like that. And Ed'd always laugh about it, walk off and say, 'You, too' or 'I get my brother on you.' This time, though, Ed did something I'd never seen before. The guy pushed him and Edmund swung around and hit him in the face. Then the guy picked up a soda bottle. They were gonna fight, but I stopped it. Me and Ed walked down the block. I told him, 'You just watch your back around these jealous niggers.' Ed didn't say nothing. He never did tell me why he got so upset.''

At Exeter, where drug-taking was considered an exclusively white phenomenon, almost no one guessed that Eddie was mixed up with drugs, much less that his involvement had led to racial conflict and violence. Though he was moody and sullen, the disciplinary reports from McConnell were all good. The few who suspected anything to the contrary, who wondered, for instance, where Eddie had gotten the money to buy his new ten-speed, had nothing to support their suspicion and so let the matter drop. "I knew something was wrong," said one faculty member. "I thought it might have something to do with drugs, just from the way he was swaggering around campus. I was going to talk to him about it, but I never did." The teacher added: "I guess I was afraid that Eddie would think I was accusing him because he was black."

Eddie, for his part, never discussed his drug use with adults, or the problems it had caused him at McConnell. The closest he came to admitting anything was wrong was in a long talk he had with David Daniels, who had come up to Exeter from New York to conduct the Easter service. "Eddie and Malcolm came over to the house where I was staying," Daniels recalled.

Eddie was very talkative and very animated. He was just going on and on. He was also using a lot of profanity. In fact, it seemed like every third word was profane. I had never heard that from Eddie before, and when I asked him why he was talking that way, he said it was because he felt comfortable with me now. It was like I had crossed over, become a different sort of friend, because I was no longer Exeter.

We talked for a long time, maybe two hours, about what had

happened the last nine months. He was relating a lot of incidents, not putting them into any perspective, but into some sort of context. He told me about the speech he had given at assembly, and the flack he had taken for it from the kids. He didn't seem to have any regrets, however. He thought that giving that speech had clarified for him some things he had been feeling. "When you go through an experience without having the right words for it," he said, "it's a problem. When you have the right words, you can handle it. It doesn't change it. It just makes it easier to deal with."

He did express some regret for other things he had done. He wasn't specific, he only said he had made some mistakes, things that, if he hadn't done them, would have made the year easier. I knew what went on in McConnell, and I told him that I hoped he wouldn't do anything stupid that would get him kicked out. He told me not to worry, because he wasn't associating with anyone in McConnell. He wasn't running with that crowd, and they weren't having anything to do with him. When I asked him why, he switched the subject and started talking about the future, saying how much he looked forward to going to Stanford, how much better it would be for him than Exeter had been. He didn't explain why; he just stated it. He also mentioned that he wanted to go back to Spain, and that when he got out of college, he was going to get a job that was going to pay him a lot of money. He didn't say what kind of job, and I got the impression that whatever it was, wasn't as important as the fact that it pay him a lot of money. He seemed very set on that, making a lot of money.

The thing that struck me about that conversation was the difference in Eddie's mood. When I had seen him in September, he had seemed very laid back. But now there was a lot of agitation. I wouldn't use the word "troubled" to describe him, and I wouldn't use the word "depressed." But there was an anxiousness there. It was like he had had a hard year, like he had had to do a lot of fighting. He gave you the sense of being worn down. I remember he said that he wished that there had been someone he could have talked to. When he said that, he used the past tense, as if whatever had been bothering him was over. He didn't give you any clue that he had any problems to solve. All he wanted to do was get out.

On June 2, Eddie did get out. On his way to the graduation ceremonies, accompanied by his mother, father, and sister, all of them dressed in their Sunday best, he encountered Bill Bolden, a black admissions officer who had known him as a prep. "Bet you didn't think I was going to make it," Eddie joked. "You're wrong, Eddie," said Bolden. "I always knew you were going to make it." Eddie shook his head. "Nope," he said, suddenly serious. "No one thought I was going to make it."

Ten days later, on a muggy night in New York City, Edmund Evans Perry was dead.

16

I WOULD NEVER KNOW FULLY WHAT WENT THROUGH EDDIE PERRY'S mind that night on Morningside Drive, but I had come as close as I was going to get. What remained was making sense of what I had found.

As I thought over what I had learned the previous months, only one thing was completely clear: that was that Edmund Perry had indeed been killed while trying to assault an officer of the law. Why he had done so was less apparent to me. None of the theories I had heard— that the streets had "eaten him alive"; that criminality was the inevitable product of racism; that Eddie had foolishly tempted fate by trying to live in two different worlds—made complete sense. Other young people had grown up in Harlem and had not mugged anyone, just as other young people had experienced racism, gone to places like Exeter, and lived in two different worlds, and the overwhelming majority of them had survived, their lives and dignity intact. Despite all he had going for him, Eddie had not.

There was no one I could think of to blame for this, not Lee Van Houten, who seemed to me more scared than trigger-happy, not anyone in Harlem or at Exeter. With few exceptions, the people in both those places, so dissimilar yet so alike in demanding so much of children, seemed to have had, for Eddie, only the best intentions.

What I had found out about drugs and the events in McConnell Hall was appalling and went a long way toward explaining Eddie's behavior in his senior year. But drugs had not killed Eddie. If there had been PCP in his system at the time of his death, the violence of that evening would have been understandable. But the autopsy had found none, only a trace of marijuana from a joint that might have been smoked as long as a month before.

The only villain I had found was something amorphous, not a person or a thing, just a difference called race. It was race—not the fact of it, but the consequences flowing from it—that made Harlem the hellhole that it was, race that had destroyed the schools, race that had made criminality, violence, and idleness seem an altogether normal—and thus excusable—state of affairs. Ironically, it was also race—the billions New York City had spent trying to correct its inequities—that had helped create the New York fiscal crisis, which, in turn, had put a young officer like Lee Van Houten on the streets that night. It was ironic as well that race had given Eddie his chance for betterment, just as it was race that had prevented him from making full use of it. Every moment of his prep school career, race was reminding him he was different, every moment race was allowing and encouraging others, black and white, to treat him as different.

These were extraordinary pressures for a boy of seventeen, especially one with Eddie's impressionability. How those pressures had affected him, what role they had played in ending his life, was another thing I could only wonder about. But Eddie himself had left one clue.

It was an apparently autobiographical essay he had written in the second semester of his senior year. In it, Eddie described coming home from Exeter to a reunion with a friend with whom he had gone to school in Harlem. The friend has become a drug dealer and is making a handsome living at it. He has all the accoutrements of street status: a big car, a closetful of fine clothes, a foxy, fast-living woman. Eddie is both jealous of him and repelled by him. At the climax of the story, the dealer is being pursued by the police. He encounters Eddie on the street and asks him to help by hiding the bag containing his stash. For a long moment Eddie is torn, divided by what he has learned at Exeter and the ethics of the street. Finally, he takes the bag.

Before I drew any conclusions from this and the other things I had learned, there was one more person I had to talk to, a very particular friend. He was unusual in a number of ways—for his humor and insights, his taste and wit, his smarts and warmth—but the quality that made him special for me was that he was the only black friend I really had.

We had known each other, professionally and socially, for several years and had had a number of good times and talks together. The difference of race, however, had always shadowed our relationship. It was never a spoken thing, never anything that had caused overt discord. Still, it was there. We both just knew it.

We could talk about race—in fact, we seemed to talk about it every time we saw each other—but it was always at a safe remove. The hang-ups we joked about belonged to other people, the prejudices to some far-off system. Apart from some strained humor, we ourselves were immune, or so we liked to pretend. Occasionally, I could bring myself to believe that our fantasizing was true. Then I would wonder why I always felt vaguely uneasy when my friend was around.

The sensible thing, of course, would have been to bring what was bothering me out in the open, and on a few occasions I had been on the verge of doing so. But for one reason or another, I had always found a way to avoid it. Tiptoeing around what I imagined to be my friend's sensibilities might be wearying—and at times I thought damn silly— but it had always seemed preferable to an air-clearing conversation, the results of which I could not predict. The only consolation I could draw from my timidity was the knowledge that no one else I knew was talking honestly about racial feelings either. The subject had become so fraught with emotion, it was as if everyone, even us liberal veterans of the sixties, had made a collective decision it didn't exist.

Since the start of the Perry story, though, I had been giving my friend and the way we related to each other a lot of thought. Partly, it was because his background was in some respects, a lot like Eddie's. He too had grown up on the streets, he too was highly political, and he too had gone off to an elite school via the scholarship route. My friend, however, had survived and, in the ten years since his graduation from Yale, carved out a successful career in the white business world. Thinking of my friend, who possessed all of Eddie's racial sensitivity and a fair share of his prickliness, I could not help but wonder whether Eddie, had he been able to pass through adolescence, might not have ended up very much like him, able, as Jamie Snead had put it, to live in both worlds while being critical of each.

That was one of the questions I wanted to ask my friend, who was in a unique position to answer it. Because he wasn't just my friend. He had been Eddie's friend as well.

It was one of those improbable coincidences that sometimes simply happen, and I hadn't known about it until I was well along in my reporting. That I had found out about it at all was accidental, the result of a chance dinner-party conversation one weekend in the Hamptons. During a lull in some overly literary table talk, my friend had asked what I was up to, and I had told him about Eddie Perry, describing some of the things I had discovered. My friend listened to my facts and theorizing without comment, then finally offered, "You know, I knew him."

He had known him, in fact, extremely well, better perhaps than any other adult, but after describing the bare outlines of their relationship, which had begun just before Eddie enrolled at Exeter, my friend was reluctant to say much more. Apparently there were confidences he felt bound to keep. It was also apparent to me, however, that my friend was not entirely comfortable having a white reporter pry into Eddie's life, even if that reporter happened to be me. Nonetheless he did offer to guide me as my reporting went along, not by providing specific leads but by confirming whether or not what I came up with was correct.

It was not an entirely easy arrangement for either of us, and more than once I thought our friendship would unravel because of it. But we muddled our way through, and though my friend did not open up any new avenues of information, he kept me from straying down several blind alleys, and for that I was grateful. Now, however, I needed something more. I needed to know exactly what my friend knew.

Without revealing what was on my mind, I invited him to lunch at a quiet spot not far from his New York office. He was sitting at a rear table, nursing a Japanese beer, when I walked in, notebook in one hand, tape recorder in the other. Noting my paraphernalia, my friend smiled. "I see this is something more than a social occasion." I smiled back and without further prelude began to reveal everything I had learned about Eddie, concluding with my discovery of his drug involvement. Throughout my recitation my friend listened impassively, his only sign of surprise an occasional thin smile.

"So you know," he said when I finished.

"Not entirely," I replied. "I still haven't been able to get to you."

My friend reached over for one of my cigarettes, lit it, and drew in a deep drag. The smoke from his first inhale was still hanging in the air when he began to talk.

The first time I met Eddie was in the summer of 1981. I was having lunch at the McDonald's on 132nd Street and he was having lunch at the next table. For some reason we got to talking, and out of the blue, he mentioned that he was about to go away to Exeter. I guess he thought that would really blow me away, a kid like him going to a place like Exeter. The truth was, I was more surprised than I was impressed. I knew all about Exeter and the kind of kids who went there—there were a lot of them at Yale— and Eddie didn't strike me as one of those types. I mean, he was okay intellectually, but he wasn't that bright. All this talk since his death about his being Harlem's last, best hope—that's bull-shit, racial bullshit. There are a lot of bright kids in Harlem, some of them a lot brighter than Eddie Perry. But that was not some-thing you could have told Eddie—not that day. He was so high on himself. Just from the way he talked, you could tell he thought that he had really made it, that getting into Exeter was really *it*.

It was weird for me, hearing that arrogance, that sense of breakthrough. When I was going away to school, that's just the way I talked myself. There's a bizarre feeling that comes over you at a time like this. You start comparing yourself to masses of people. You start thinking you're the smartest person in your neighborhood—who knows, maybe the smartest nigger alive. That's what Eddie was like. He was filled with exhilaration. Just like that, he was leaping from a sense of absolute insecurity to this crazy sense of self-assurance.

Before we left, he asked me about some of my own experiences in school, how I handled being with whites and all that. I told him I thought the key was to develop a sense of aloofness, to chill out, so people would leave him alone. Stand off, I told him, so no one will know what to think, what to make of you. I also told him not to imagine himself what a black kid should be in that situation.

We saw each other half a dozen or so times a year after that. I liked him, and I guess he was kind of admiring of me because, in a way, I had made it. I could listen to him and try to give him advice. but I'm not sure how useful it was. The big problem was that I was so much older. I mean, he would express right-on soli-darity with me and all the rest, but deep down he saw my way of dealing with things as perhaps inappropriate to the times. To a certain degree he was astute in that perception. The times have changed radically. When I was going to school, I could take for granted a certain political context. There was talk in the air of black nationalism and black achievement. I was seeing white people march arm-in-arm with black people in the cause of civil rights. I could believe—I actually *did* believe—that a utopian society was possible, that blacks and whites would get along perfectly, and that there would be no prejudice. Now there isn't shit. The images black kids receive today are not of coexistence but of assimilation. The media is telling them that if you want America to love you, you have to be like Bill Cosby. If you're a kid like Eddie, you have a feeling of being out there by yourself.

Eddie knew he wasn't going to be like Bill Cosby. The trouble was, he didn't know what he was going to be. He hadn't figured out yet how he was going to make it in the world and not leave everything behind. He was always making it a choice: one or the other. It takes a real maturity, a real strength of character, to realize you don't have to make that choice, that you can be who you are and see what else is out there too. Some people get to that point, some don't. I was lucky, because I did, and I can remember the exact moment when it happened.

It was in my sophomore year at Yale, and I had done this paper on *Don Quixote* and gotten an A plus, the highest grade in the class. I was really excited about it and I brought it home to show my mother, thinking she would be excited too. Well, she couldn't have been less interested. It had nothing to do with her world. She didn't understand the paper or the point of it, and there was no reason for her to feel otherwise. I could have been ashamed, and I could have felt guilty. Instead, I thought to myself, "This is okay. So she doesn't understand. Why should she? I still love her." Really, it was one of the most important things that happened to me during my years at Yale.

Maybe, if he had lived to go off to college, Eddie would have had a moment like that. But in the time I knew him, it was always black or white for him, not both, not anything in between.

You can imagine, of course, how that attitude went down with the kids of Exeter. They weren't like the white kids I had gone to school with. They had never heard of a Martin Luther King or seen a Bull Conner with dogs and firehoses. There's no way for them to understand the justness of the struggle. As far as they're concerned, there's no reason for struggle. So when Eddie talked to them about racism, they thought he was crazy, and in fact, a lot of the stuff he talked about, like that assembly speech, *was* crazy.

But Eddie wasn't totally deluded. When he talked about politics, he picked his audience with care. You think he would have talked about Stokely Carmichael in Harlem? He wouldn't have lasted five minutes. They would have laughed him off the block. Politics was something he talked to white folks about, because up at Exeter they took this stuff seriously. They thought he was *political*. They thought he was *militant*. They thought he was expressing legitimate *black rage*. Legitimate, bullshit. The reality was that this was a human being who was having a very difficult time, who was living a fantasy life, who was looking for bogus solutions at every turn. He wasn't political—his political beliefs were so irrelevant, they were almost laughable—he was using politics as a psychological defense mechanism. All this posturing was his defense against hopelessness, a way of avoiding the acknowledgment that racial prejudice would never go away. Someone should have picked up on that. Someone should have gotten worried. But nobody ever did.

I don't want to lay it all off on Exeter. Eddie had problems that went beyond Exeter, especially about race. You know how a schizophrenic talks? Using contradictory conjunctions all the time, like "It's sunny outside and it's raining"? That's the way Eddie talked about race. One minute he'd give you this rap about white people being so evil, and the next he'd start talking about his best friend, who was white, and the girl he loved, who was also white. What can I tell you? He was a screwed-up kid.

But he was also a sensitive and tender and vulnerable kid, a lot more than he ever let on. All these Tarzan-and-the-jungle stories he told to the kids at Exeter, all these tales of how streetwise he was—they were all bullshit. But the white kids didn't know that. They ate them up, and the reason they ate them up is because that's what they wanted to believe. They were living vicariously through them. So was Eddie. He wanted to be that myth. He wanted to be the way he was defined and perceived. He wanted to come across to people as bad as bad can be. That was his ticket into the life of Exeter. They had their money and status, he had their image of him.

The drugs were just part of it. He told me about the drugs, not much, but enough for me to know he was really scared of them. Any black kid in that situation is going to be scared shitless about drugs. When you're black, and you're in a white prep school, control is the paramount thing in your life. You have to be in control—you can't give anything away, especially how you are really feeling. And the whole point of drugs is not being in control. So you are more scared of them than you would normally be. And you are absolutely terrified of something like LSD. You have the feeling that if you take it, it can all go away. You are going to be back on the corner.

I tried to talk to Eddie about drugs, but he never trusted me enough for me to get anywhere. And if he couldn't talk to me, who else was he going to talk to? His mother? Are you kidding? They were close and all that, but it wasn't as if she was his best friend. As far as what was going on at Exeter was concerned, she was totally out of it. Eddie felt like she didn't have the slightest glimmer of what Exeter was like. To me, they were always like two people looking out different windows in the same general direction. They were each getting a different picture of things.

Well, then, maybe he could have talked to Jonah. But how could he talk to Jonah when they were always at each other's throat? Besides, Eddie was the one who was better than Jonah, who was smarter, who was the special one. That's what Eddie had been told, that was the truth, and most important, that's what Eddie believed. He wanted to be the star of that family—in a way, he needed to be the star. He wanted people to envy him.

So that leaves the people on the street. And how in the hell is he supposed to talk to them? He wasn't a part of that block anymore. Shit, this kid couldn't even play basketball. They ridiculed him for that, they ridiculed him for going away to school, they ridiculed him for turning white. I know they did because he told me they did.

Were the kids wrong? Of course they were wrong, but Eddie brought a lot of it on himself. He could be unpleasantly arrogant when he got home, treat people with a slight sense of condescension, which in a way is a defense mechanism too. You have to understand, when you are black and you go away, you get a little paranoid. You are always thinking to yourself, "These people aren't going to like me. I have been given a special opportunity and they can't help but feel resentful"—whether or not they actually do. So, even before anything happens, your attitude becomes "Fuck them."

The bottom line is that Eddie didn't have anyone to talk to about his weaknesses or vulnerabilities. So he had to deal with things like drugs on his own. And the way he did it was to justify his amorality in terms of what whites had done to blacks over the course of hundreds of years. That became his excuse for everything. It's not uncommon. A lot of other black kids do the same thing. If you see the rules of the game as something that has been defined by white people, then breaking the rules becomes something virtuous. That's the confusion that kids like Eddie have to live with.

I wasn't surprised when he told me that he wanted to go away to California to college. The psychosis of the lies he was spinning about himself was getting him in deeper and deeper and deeper. He wanted to get away from Harlem, away from Exeter, away from everything, just as far as he could possibly get. He talked about "getting over" on people, about running a game on them, and in a way he was very successful in his pretensions. But the game was beginnning to catch up with him. He wanted to opt out of it. He wanted to go someplace where he could just have fun like anybody else. But he was never able to. Blacks and whites were always putting stereotypes on him. They wanted him to be more than the normal kid that he was. They wanted him to be a symbol. ABC wanted that, Exeter wanted that, the people in Harlem wanted that. He didn't have the freedom to be an individual. All his life he was a symbol, a slot-filler. And Eddie knew it.

The last time I talked to him, I guess it was a couple of months before his death, you could sense a real spiritual exhaustion in his voice. "It sure is rough, dealing with all those white people," he said. You could tell it was getting to him. He was worn out. He was getting tired of the whole thing. All this black/white stuff was really grinding him down, and he knew it wasn't going to go away. Yeah, he had gone to Exeter, and yeah, he was going to Stanford, but he was never going to be a member of the club. He was always going to be Eddie Perry, the smart black. Even if he wanted to be anything different, Harlem wasn't gonna let him. That boy was in a box, and he was going to have to deal with that box all the rest of his life.

The night he got shot, friends of mine called me from uptown. They told me all about it. I knew what happened. I mean, I knew *everything* that happened. And I wish I could say I was surprised. But I wasn't. I remember thinking to myself that night, Eddie didn't get killed. He committed suicide. That's what it was, you know. Suicide.

I switched off my tape recorder and put away my notebook. We both sat there a long moment, staring into our respective beers. "You know," I said at last, "there's something else we really should talk about sometime, something that doesn't have anything to do with Eddie." My friend smiled knowingly and copped another of my cigarettes. "Later," he said.

17

IN EARLY SEPTEMBER, I MADE THE LONG DRIVE UP TO PHILLIPS Exeter, where classes had begun two weeks earlier. A memorial service had been planned for Eddie in the campus chapel, and friends on the faculty had invited me to attend. I had been asked not to inform Mrs. Perry, who had not been invited to the service. "This is a community event," a teacher explained to me. "Not a platform for denouncing the police."

I arrived early Saturday, and a glorious New England morning it was. On discovering that my son, Sam, was still in class, I checked into the Exeter Inn and headed to an appointment I had scheduled with Steve Kurtz, the Academy principal. He was staring out the window of his ornate, antique-filled office when his secretary ushered me in. "Isn't it beautiful?" he said, gesturing out at the common. "Have you ever seen the campus looking lovelier? We're going to have a wonderful year. I just know it."

"There are some things you have to hear," I replied. "Perhaps we'd better sit down."

Kurtz flashed a fine, crinkled smile and motioned me to a chair in front of an empty fireplace. With his tweed sport coat and charcoal slacks, he looked, I thought, the way a prep school headmaster ought to look. He smiled again, warmly, expectantly.

"It's about Eddie," I began. "You have some problems."

As I proceeded to relate the things I had found, detailing the stories of racism, violence, and drugs, and how it had all gone on undetected, the smile vanished from Kurtz's face. His whole body seemed to sag and his face flushed. At one point, as I described some of the drug-dealing that had not involved Eddie, he put his hand up to his eyes, leaned forward, and shook his head. "Oh, God," he said. "Oh, God."

When I finished, Kurtz's eyes were glistening. He had the appearance of a man whose child has just been struck. "You know these things can happen," he said finally. "In your head, you know they happen everywhere. But still, you tell yourself, It can't happen here. We're better than that. We're Exeter. We're different. And now it has happened here." He shook his head again. "Oh, God," he repeated. "Oh, God."

I tried to reassure Kurtz, telling him that as far as I had been able to determine, the hard-core dealing had been confined to a relative handful of students, most of whom had graduated. "Besides," I added, "that's not the real problem. It's the racism. That's what got to Eddie." Kurtz did not appear to be listening. "I've got to address the faculty tomorrow," he said. "What am I going to tell them? How am I going to explain this?" Kurtz talked on, describing his own student days and how it had been for him to grow up poor. He recounted his time, years before, as dean at Hamilton College in the Ku Klux Klan country of southern Indiana, and the steps he had taken to make black students part of the institution. Then, disjointedly, he started talking of his early tenure at Exeter, and of the night he had held the hand of a boy who had just committed suicide. "You do what you can," he said. "You do what you think is right. But how do you reach kids today? They're so far off, so distant, so unapproachable. The black kids especially. They really don't approve of this honkey world of ours."

He gazed into the darkness of his empty fireplace. "I'll never forget Eddie's funeral," he went on. "I don't suppose I'll forget it as long as I live. The emotion, the passion, the sense of loss. And you know the thing that really sticks in my mind? The kids, the black kids of ours who were there. I went up to them afterward, you know, to offer my condolences. And none of them would shake my hand. Isn't that something? They wouldn't even shake my hand. How do you get to these kids? How do you let them know we're on their side?"

I had no answers for Stephen Kurtz, and a moment later I got up to go. At the door Kurtz thanked me—for what, I don't know—then looked back at his office window. "It really is a beautiful day," he said.

It was a beautiful day, and as I walked across the campus toward Phillips Church, I kept thinking what an extraordinary place Exeter was, especially on such a morning. The thought was still in my mind when I passed by McConnell Hall, with its broad concrete patio—

"McConnell beach" the kids called it. I imagined Eddie sitting on it, as I knew he had on so many sunny days with his friends, feet up, ghetto-blaster going, the cares of the world drifting by.

Outside the church Sam was waiting for me. His day, he reported, had been great; he was having no troubles at all. He seemed puzzled when I gave him a questioning look.

We went inside and took a pew. At first we were almost alone, and knowing Eddie's reputation, I worried about how many would join us. But as it got closer to noon the church began filling up, until virtually every place was taken. I recognized a number of Eddie's teachers, a dean or two, and a surprisingly large number of white students. I also recognized several of Eddie's black classmates, who came in last and seated themselves together in three of the front pews.

David McIlhiney, the Exeter chaplain, delivered the invocation, and then Jack Herney, the director of admissions who had recruited Eddie, read a passage from Scripture, an epistle from Saint Paul that included the lines "For your sake, we are being massacred daily, and reckoned as sheep for the slaughter. These are the trials through which we triumph, by the power of Him who loved us." Afterward, Tamara Horne, who had been the president of the Afro-Exonian Society in Eddie's senior year and was now a freshman at Brandeis, made some brief remarks. "Anyone who met Eddie thought he was a cool guy," she said. "But his last year, he seemed . . . like a bird who had gotten caught in a trap and needed to be let go. . . . He was not a black militant or a racist, but a young man who was not ashamed to say he was black. . . . He didn't want anyone to love him or to hate him, but to respect him. He was the kind of guy Exeter needs more of."

There were remarks from Eddie's senior English teacher, David Weber, who described Eddie as someone who tried to free the sinner from the sin—"from prejudice, from ignorance, from the emotional poverty of hatred and fear"—and then, after Dolores Kendrick read one of her poems—about hearing of the death of a black boy on the six o'clock news—and David Daniels said a prayer for the repose of Eddie's soul, Lamont O'Neil stood up to sing.

The song was an old Negro spiritual, from slavery times, a hymn that told of a people who worked and struggled and sinned, secure in the knowledge that one day, surely, God would carry them home.

As Lamont's haunting a cappella voice filled the church, people, black and white, began to weep and hold on to each other. Through my own tears I looked at my son, Sam, who is very tough about these things, and saw that he was weeping too.

When it was over I went up to Lamont, who smiled and, before I could say anything, told me, "I'm going to be all right, Mr. Anson. Everything's going to be fine."

Outside, the day was still gorgeous. As Sam and I walked up the path where so many famous feet had trod, I spotted a student tour group just ahead of us. A white upperclassman was showing a prospective student and his family around. The boy was very tiny and very black; his bright eyes were dancing. I drew my son in and held him close.

Epilogue

THE LAST UNFINISHED PIECE OF BUSINESS IN THE STORY OF EDMUND Perry was the trial of his brother, Jonah, on charges of assault and attempted robbery.

There were many in New York, myself among them, who had doubted that Jonah would come to trial, who believed that once passions had cooled, the matter would be quietly disposed of by a plea to a lesser offense, followed by a sentence of probation. "Nobody wants to hang this kid," said one of the investigating detectives. "His family has suffered, he's suffered. Let him get on with the rest of his life."

Jonah, his lawyer, and his mother had other ideas. However seemingly strong the evidence against him—and from the way the police and district attorney had been talking, the case was virtually open and shut—they were determined that he would have his day in court, even at the risk of a felony conviction. "This goes beyond Jonah," one of his friends explained. "It's the racist system we gotta put on trial."

After months of pretrial maneuvering, the case was finally heard in Manhattan Supreme Court in January 1986. Presiding was Judge Eve Preminger, a liberal Democrat with a reputation for being even-handed. Handling the prosecution was James Kindler, a mild-mannered Harvard Law graduate with ten years' experience in the D.A.'s office. The assignment of Kindler, a homicide specialist and one of Morgenthau's closest aides, was widely regarded as a sign of the importance the district attorney was attaching to the case. Though Morgenthau had had no trouble beating C. Vernon Mason in the Democratic primary, his office recently had suffered several public embarrassments, including bungling the case of "subway vigilante" Bernhard Goetz and failing to secure the conviction of six white transit police who had been charged with the beating death of a black subway graffiti artist. With the police on the defensive and the black community increasingly restive, convicting Jonah Perry of a crime that had attained symbolic importance was, for Morgenthau, politically and personally crucial.

The principal obstacle in his path was Jonah's lawyer, Alton Maddox, who, to the surprise of many, had been acquitted in December of charges of assaulting court officers. Maddox's trial had been argued on largely political grounds—an outspoken black lawyer persecuted by the white legal establishment—and it was expected that he would take the same racial tack in defending Jonah. "If you know Alton," said someone who did, well, "then you know how he's going to try this case: whitey did it."

In his opening statement, delivered to a jury of nine whites and three blacks, Maddox performed as predicted, charging an officially sanctioned cover-up and claiming that "the killing of blacks by white cops is condoned by the district attorney and the police. This," said Maddox, "is another instance of the police brutality that has rocked New York City. [The only difference is that] the victim this time was not just someone who had lived an unsavory life, but a young man who was trying to live out the American dream, [who] remained true to his ideals even though he came from a difficult background." Then Maddox made a startling accusation: Van Houten and his backup team, he claimed, had been "drinking and frolicking" for hours before the incident and were drunk at the time of the shooting. As Maddox put it: "Lee Van Houten was drunk and prowling around on his own. . . . [He] confronted two blacks. He pulled his revolver and blasted away. He didn't know what he was doing. He was in no condition to remember because he was drunk."

Neither then nor at any point subsequently did Maddox offer substantiation for his charge—nor did he have to. Under law, the burden of proving Van Houten's story lay with the prosecution, which called as its first witness a seventeen-year-old neighbor of the Perrys' named Ronald Smith.

On the stand, Smith, who had known Jonah and Eddie since childhood, testified that on the night of the shooting, he and several friends were playing cards on the stoop in front of one of the buildings on the Perrys' block when Jonah came up, out of breath and shaking. Jonah, according to Smith, said that he and his brother had "gone up on the Hill" (Morningside Park) and "run into some static." "He said he and Ed went out to rob somebody," Smith went on in a low, barely intelligible voice. "He said he grabbed the dude around the neck. He told me that he told Ed to go through his pockets. Jonah said he hit the man.

He said the man fell and reached for his gun. The man shot once and got Ed.'' As Jonah ran off, Smith continued, quoting Jonah, Eddie had called out to him, ''Jonah, don't leave me.'' Asked by Kindler why he was telling his story, Smith replied, ''I felt it was wrong for Ed to be dead and for Jonah to be outside.''

It was seemingly damning testimony, but on cross-examination, Maddox got Smith to admit that for the last two years he had been on probation, the result of an incident in which he had fired a shotgun at his mother's boyfriend. Under Maddox's probing Smith also conceded that he was unemployed, that he had had little education since the age of twelve, and that he had told his story to the police only after they had several times held him for questioning against his will. The look on the jurors' faces could not have been cheering to Kindler.

Several days later Kindler tried to make his case again, this time by summoning eighteen-year-old Alicia Arroyo, a high school senior who identified herself as ''one of Jonah's girlfriends.'' According to the police, Arroyo had been with Jonah in the Perry family apartment for nearly six hours the night of Eddie's death and had heard Jonah make incriminating admissions. Later she recorded these statements on a page of her diary, which she subsequently gave to the police. The police, however, had been unable to persuade Arroyo to make a signed statement, and thus the diary page was inadmissable as evidence. Nonetheless, Kindler was confident she would tell her story on the stand. It turned out to be a major miscalculation.

Under oath, Arroyo swore that Jonah had said nothing of the shooting during the time she had been with him. She further claimed that she had learned of Eddie's death only by reading about it in the newspapers. Incredulous, Kindler asked her if she understood the importance of testifying truthfully. Yes, Arroyo said, she did. ''Do you attend church? Do you believe in God?'' Kindler pressed. Indeed she did, Arroyo replied. ''And you still tell this court that Jonah Perry said nothing to you about the shooting of his brother?'' Kindler asked. ''Is that your sworn testimony?'' Yes, Alicia Arroyo answered firmly, it was. As she left the stand, Jonah, who until then had sat expressionless, permitted himself a small smile.

Kindler had better luck with two witnesses who had been patients at St. Luke's the night of the shooting. Both testified to having seen a scuffle from their hospital-room windows, and both said that three men—a white and two blacks—had been involved. Neither, however, was able to identify Jonah as one of them.

Then it was Lee Van Houten's turn.

In person, the young officer about whom so much had been alleged was calm and controlled and, in recalling the events of the night of June 12, extremely persuasive. He told of going on duty that evening and walking down Morningside Drive and, finally, of hearing footsteps behind him. "I turned to my left," Van Houten recounted.

> As soon as I turned, I got punched in the face. I was knocked back a couple of feet. I pulled my shield out and said, "Police." As soon as I did, I got hit again. There were two of them . . . tall black men . . . I couldn't see much. I could only tell they were bigger than I am. One of them said, "Give it up." He put his hand in my pocket. They kept punching me in the face, the mouth, the nose. I got knocked to the ground. I tried to get up. I was knocked down again. I was hurt . . . I was on the ground . . . on my hands and knees. I thought I was going out . . . that I was losing consciousness. I fired my weapon.

"Why did you fire your weapon?" Van Houten was asked.

In an even voice Van Houten replied, "I fired because if I didn't, I probably wouldn't be here now."

"Isn't it a fact," Maddox demanded, "that you confronted two black males who were at arm's length and fired without any struggle occurring between you and the two?"

"No," Van Houten answered, "it is not."

"Isn't it a fact," Maddox continued, "that after you fired, you went berserk and began to pound your head against the cars on Morningside Drive?"

No, Van Houten replied, it was not.

The sparring match continued that way another twenty minutes, Maddox accusing, Van Houten denying. Finally Maddox challenged, "It never struck a decent chord in your body that you should summon an ambulance?"

Before Van Houten could answer, Kindler rose to object. The objection was sustained.

Van Houten's testimony had been the most compelling in the trial thus far. It left little doubt that he had been attacked, that the attackers were strong and black, and that Van Houten had been in fear for his life. The only trouble, from the prosecution's standpoint, was that Van Houten had not been able to identify Jonah as one of those who had mugged him. Nor, for that matter, had any of the prosecution's eyewitnesses put Jonah at the scene. They had suggested, they had hinted; they had not been able to prove, and the result was that Kindler's entire case hung on the word of a reticent, barely educated young man with a criminal record. If Jonah was to be convicted, courtroom observers felt, the prosecution desperately needed something more, another witness who could substantiate Ronald Smith's tortured story. It got one, finally, the last day of the trial.

The courtroom that morning was packed, as it had been every day since the trial's beginning. As had also been the case from the beginning, nearly all of the seats were taken up by middle-class blacks, come to show their support of Jonah. "They gotta stop taking our young men," one well-dressed woman said to another. "That's right," her companion agreed. "If we don't stop it now, we ain't gonna have no leaders left."

Out of earshot, Jonah Perry sat at the defense table, clad in what had become his trial uniform: a red sleeveless sweater with the word "Cornell" stitched across the left breast. As his attorney gathered up papers, Jonah turned, smiled at several black classmates who had come down from Ithaca to be at his side, then pulled from his shirt pocket a small colored picture of Jesus. He stared at it intently, then began murmuring a prayer.

His mother, accompanied by Vivione Marshall, came in a few minutes later, her face wreathed in a broad, confident smile. Taking her seat, Veronica, who had recently been elected chairman of her community school board, began scanning the courtroom. In a rear row she spotted Ed Plummer, who had come to testify about Eddie's academic prowess. Their eyes met and both nodded. Veronica's head kept turning, looking for familiar faces. She seemed quite unworried.

The judge came in, order was commanded, and then, a little hesitantly, it seemed, Kindler rose to summon his twenty-third and final witness. "The People call Desiree Solomon."

There was a stirring in the courtroom, a low, whispering buzz; Ms.

Solomon, obviously, was not an unknown person. A minute passed, then another. Kindler, who had been suffering all that week from a cold and the flu, nervously began tapping his pencil. More minutes dragged by. Maddox began to smile. It appeared that Desiree Solomon was going to be a no-show. Then, just as Judge Preminger was beginning to clear her throat, a side door swung open and in sauntered a sullen-looking bespectacled black woman in her twenties, head downcast, hands thrust deep in the pockets of an oversized black coat. Putting her hand on the Bible, she swore to tell the truth and announced herself as Desiree Solomon, a resident of 234 West 114th Street.

The story she proceeded to tell confirmed everything Ronald Smith had said. She too had been sitting on the stoop that night, and she too had heard Jonah say that he and Edmund had "run into some static" near Morningside Park. According to Solomon, Jonah had told her that he had walked up behind a man, choked him, and started to beat him. Then, she quoted Jonah as saying, the man "reached into his sock, pulled out a pistol, and shot Eddie."

Did Jonah say who the man was? Kindler asked.

Yes, Desiree Solomon replied. "He was a DT"—a detective or undercover cop.

The questioning by Kindler took only fifteen minutes. Then Maddox pounced. "Where does your husband reside?" he asked.

"What's that got to do with it?" Solomon shot back, glaring at him.

Again Maddox asked the question, and again Solomon dodged. Finally, on instructions from the judge, she answered, "Sing Sing."

From there on Maddox was in complete command. He insinuated she was a drug addict—which she denied—that she was a prostitute—which she also denied—that the police had pulled her story out of her in exchange for granting favorable treatment to her husband—which she denied as well. She denied everything, including having any enmity toward Jonah. "I know he's a nice person," she said. "He's respected. He goes to school. He minds his own business and we grew up in the same neighborhood." A moment later, Desiree Solomon, who was neither a whore nor a drug addict but a department-store salesgirl—a fact Kindler had neglected to call to the attention of the jury—left the stand. As she walked from the courtroom, one of the black women spectators hissed at her, "Disgrace!"

For all practical purposes, the trial was over at that moment. Nonetheless Maddox called four witnesses, three of them teachers at Wadleigh, the fourth, the Perry family's minister, the Reverend Preston Washington. All attested to Eddie's talent and upstanding character. Jonah's qualities were barely mentioned. There were closing statements, Maddox once again accusing the police of brutality; a charge from the judge; and then the jury retired to consider its verdict. It took them slightly less than four hours to reach their decision: not guilty on all counts.

In the courtroom, there were cheers and applause when the foreman announced the verdict. Veronica Perry clasped her hand over her mouth as if stifling a gasp, closed her eyes tight, shook, and then shouted, "Oh, thank God! Praise Him!"

Outside the courtroom, she stood with her arm around her surviving son and addressed a mob of reporters. "I'm relieved and I'm thankful," she said. "God was on our side and we had twelve fair-minded jurors. They saw the injustice that was done to me and my family. They saw the frame-up and the cover-up and they came back with a just decision. It doesn't avenge Eddie's death, but it clears his name." Then, announcing that she would soon file a multimillion-dollar "wrongful death" suit against Van Houten, the police department, and the city, Mrs. Perry added, "They murdered my son. That officer shot Edmund down in cold blood, and for that someone must pay."

That night, at a block party called to celebrate Jonah's acquittal, there was more talk of punishing the police department and of the great victory over white racism that had been won. Jonah, who was packing his car for the drive back to Cornell, spoke of the "wickedness" of the police and said of Van Houten, "I hold him accountable for the murder of my brother."

"I miss him every day," Jonah went on, referring to Eddie. "I don't know what happened to him. I only know what didn't happen, that I did not help anyone beat up on anybody." He shook his head, as if trying to clear the memory. "I don't want to think about it anymore. I just wanna get back to school. I wanna get on with my life."

Jonah Perry did get on with his life, as did his mother, as, in fact, did nearly everyone who had been touched by the killing of Edmund Perry. The questions, however, remained.

According to the jurors who decided Jonah's fate, his innocence had not been proven, nor had it been theirs to decide. Rather, their charge had been to determine whether the People of the State of New York had established the case against him beyond a reasonable doubt, and on that score, the People had been found wanting. They had not believed Ronald Smith or Desiree Solomon, a number of jurors said afterward, nor had they believed Alton Maddox's charges of police brutality, cover-up, and murder. In the absence of overwhelming, convincing evidence, a single eyewitness identification, they had not known what to believe, and for them, that was reasonable doubt.

"We didn't know exactly what happened on June twelfth, and we probably never will," said Lisabeth Ballner, the jury foreman. "It didn't sit right that two boys with so much going for them, with so much ethical in their lives, would have done something like this. . . . [At the same time], I think there was general agreement among us that Jonah was there. That was my personal opinion and it was the opinion of a number of other jurors. . . . But that wasn't the issue for the jury. The proof—the precise proof—just wasn't there." "The Perrys can take the verdict any way they want to," another juror added. "That's our system. You're innocent until proven guilty—even if you did it."

Kindler was philosophical. "Juries are juries," he said. "We put on our best case. They just didn't believe it. That happens sometimes." Kindler shrugged. "There are thousands of crimes in New York every year, thousands of cases, thousands of verdicts. We lost this one. Life goes on."

One of those it went on for was Lee Van Houten, who went back to patrolling the streets, as he had before. The officers who worked with him said he was slowly returning to normal and predicted that in time the memories of what had happened would fade. They did not worry about the threats of the civil suit, which most thought would never be filed. "You got a civil suit, then you got the chance to get Jonah under oath, telling what really happened," said one of the investigating officers. "When they've had time to think it over, I don't think the Perrys are going to go for that."

Van Houten himself, however, was troubled, not so much by the prospect of a lawsuit, or even by what he had done that night, but by what the jury's verdict seemed to say about him.

"I was not out to kill somebody," he said in his first interview since the shooting. "I was the victim. I was doing my job the best way I can. I'm not a supercop. If I could have gone twenty years in this job playing ball with kids or walking a beat, I would have been very happy. They put the shooting on trial, not the facts. I don't think that it was fair. . . . The lies bother me. . . . This whole mess is affecting my family."

Van Houten paused. Despite everything that had happened to him, he still looked improbably young. "I know what happened," he continued. "I was there. The defense at the trial said it was racial. That's ridiculous. Black or white, a man is a man in this world and a person is a person. That's how I look at it."

He halted again. "The incident just happened like *that*," he said, snapping his fingers. "I was not out to kill somebody or to shoot somebody. I saw someone running away. I could have shot at him, but I didn't. . . . I could have said that he [Jonah] was the guy. But I couldn't do that. It would not have been right. All I know [is] I was beaten. The lights started to go out. That's when I yelled 'Police.' I thought it would stop. It didn't. They kept beating on me. It just didn't stop. It was very fast and very violent. When something like this happens, you do what you think is right. You don't sit there and think about it. Before this happened, when I heard about something like this, I would say to myself, 'I wouldn't want to be in that cop's shoes.' Now, all of a sudden, I'm there."

Van Houten's voice trailed off. "I was just trying to do my job," he repeated. "I wasn't trying to kill anybody. I was the victim."

Edmund Evans Perry, the boy Lee Van Houten shot to death, now lies in a loamy section of Fair Lawn cemetery in suburban New Jersey. Occasionally, flowers are put on his grave. Alexandra Wolf, his classmate in Spain and now a student at the Rhode Island School of Design, has begun soliciting funds in hopes of erecting a statue of him.

Wadleigh Junior High School was ordered closed for major renovations in the spring of 1986, just shy of the first anniversary of Eddie's death. The order came after a personal inspection tour by schools chancellor Nathan Quinones, who, through a spokesman, termed Wadleigh "one of the worst schools in the city" and himself "personally embarrassed" that it could exist.

At Phillips Exeter Academy, where another class has been graduated since the shooting, a number of changes have been made. Black
enrollment has been doubled, and the office of admissions has set out
to create a special scholarship fund, which, it is said, will make it
possible for any deserving student to attend Exeter, regardless of economic circumstance. The Academy has also toughened its disciplinary
procedures and instituted a new drug-counseling program. Houseparents have been informed that they are expected to provide closer
supervision of the boys and girls under their care, and to ensure they
do, deans now regularly patrol the dorms. Particular attention is being
paid to McConnell Hall, where in the year following Eddie's shooting
four students were expelled, two of them on drinking charges, two of
them for possession and use of drugs. Stephen Kurtz, the principal
who ordered these steps, announced in May 1986 that he was retiring
at the end of the next academic year. His decision, which caught most
Exonians by surprise, was accepted by the board of trustees with an
official expression of regret. As one of his last acts, Kurtz intensified
the search for qualified black faculty. He also approved the institution
of a special orientation program for incoming students like Eddie. It is
informally called "Help for People from Distant Places."

ABOUT THE AUTHOR

ROBERT SAM ANSON became a reporter for *Time* while still a student at the University of Notre Dame, where he was involved in antiwar and civil rights movements. In 1970, while on assignment in Cambodia, he was taken prisoner of war. Later an anchorman for public television and senior writer for *New Times* magazine, Anson now makes his career as a freelance magazine writer and author. *Best Intentions* is his fifth book. He is currently at work on a memoir of his Indochina experiences.